AFRICAN POLITICS IN SOUTH AFRICA

Consultations between the South African Prime Minister and Chief Ministers of the eight self-governing homelands, 6 March 1974. Left to right: Chief Ministers Gatsha Buthelezi (KwaZulu), Hudson Ntsanwisi (Gazankulu), Cedric Phatudi (Lebowa), Lucas Mangope (Bophuthatswana), Mr. Punt Janson (Deputy Minister of Bantu Administration and Development), Mr. M. C. Botha (Minister of Bantu Administration and Development), Mr Vorster (Prime Minister), Mr Braam Raubenheimer (Deputy Minister of Bantu Administration and Development), Chief Ministers Kaiser Matanzima (Transkei) Lennox Sebe (Ciskei) Patric Mphephu

D. A. KOTZÉ

University of South Africa, Pretoria

African Politics in South Africa

1964-1974

Parties and Issues

With a Foreword by
CHIEF M. GATSHA BUTHELEZI
Chief Executive Councillor, KwaZulu

ST. MARTIN'S PRESS · NEW YORK

CONTENTS

TABLES

MAP

FOREWORD

by Chief M. Gatsha Buthelezi
Chief Executive Councillor, KwaZulu

I have rather reluctantly agreed to write a foreword to a book after reading only a couple of chapters made available to me by the Author.

It is absolutely impossible to evaluate the whole book without going through it in its entirety. But there is no doubt about the fact that this book will satisfy a crying need in giving us an up-to-date analysis of our contemporary political history.

It is very difficult to see oneself as others see one. But I am rather fascinated to read of how Professor Kotzé sees Separate Development politics, and also politics outside the framework of Separate Development. His scholarship is in no doubt but I certainly do not share all his assessments of Black consciousness and on the attitude of Blacks towards party politics, particularly their motivation in adopting an anti-attitude towards party-politicking at this stage.

Among the so-called homeland leaders there are some like myself who believe in Black consciousness, and who believe they have done more in promoting the concept of Black consciousness than those who arrogantly dismiss them as "irrelevant". Although there is much talk today about Black consciousness as such, this concept was born long ago when Black people realised that their political salvation depended on their new socio-political concept of one African people, whose destiny could only be reached beyond the limits of ethnic grouping. As South Africa is a pigmentocracy, it follows that the plight of the voiceless is not just a class struggle but a colour battle. To "overthrow" the present pigmentocracy, it is clear that they must also rally themselves around their colour, just as White domination revolves around colour deification and colour prejudice. At the same time, as much as they cannot accept that they must be discriminated against for reasons of the colour of their skins, some of us do not believe that it is healthy for us to condemn all those who happen to be born with a White skin merely because Whites oppress us in South Africa. It is important to make it clear that one can believe in Black consciousness without including in one's nomenclature such derogatory terms as "White pigs" to describe Whites.

On party politics, I do not think that it tells the whole story merely to state that we are in favour of a non-party approach in decision-making. It must be remembered that even in the case of Britain, the home of the Mother of Parliaments, party politics developed after some time and was not prescribed but developed by trial and error. The party system was not built up overnight.

That does not necessarily mean that one does not appreciate that an Opposition party has an important role to play in keeping the ruling party on their toes. That fact should not be used to promote political parties artificially at the instance of Whites who in any case have dismally failed to be bearers of democracy in South Africa. It must also be stressed that even government departments of the Republican government have been implicated in inspiring the development of political parties in those cases where a head of a homeland government happens to be *persona non grata* as far as Pretoria is concerned. To be opposed to this kind of hypocrisy and fraud does not mean that one is only in favour of a non-party approach to decision-making. After all, Africans have Whites, who dominate them as "political enemies". So why should they dissipate their energies, sniping at each other to the great amusement of Whites, when so many forces of White domination are so heavily arrayed against them? Africans reach an agreement through a consensus. Look at some independent African countries and see how they have opted for a one-party system. It might be said that in the case of independent African countries there are no forces of White domination as a threat any more. Independent African countries find that they still have to contend with Neo-Colonialism in the form of economic colonialism. Their under-development and poverty are such fatal factors and such a threat to their newly acquired independence, that they can only wage a war against them only as one cohesive force, instead of two or more.

I think in looking at the contents of Professor D. A. Kotzé's book, there is one thing that is not in dispute at all, and that is that his book will be invaluable to all those who are battling to understand our present political scene in South Africa.

As in all things, it is not quite true in life that things are either black or white with nothing in between. It is in this sense not true that all of us working within Separate Development out of no choice whatsoever, are necessarily enemies of either SASO or the Black People's Convention. There is a lot of behind-the-scenes contact despite the differences in tactics. In principle, we believe in the same things and have the same goals which we are trying to accomplish in different ways.

Mahlabatini,
17 October 1974

M. GATSHA BUTHELEZI
Chief Executive Councillor
KwaZulu

ABBREVIATIONS

AAC	All-Africa Convention
AICA	African Independent Churches Association
ANC	African National Congress
Asseca	Association for the Educational and Cultural Advancement of the African People of South Africa
BDP	Bophuthatswana Democratic Party
BIC	Bantu Investment Corporation
BNCP	Bantu Nationalist Conservative Party
BNP	Bophuthatswana National Party
BPC	Black People's Convention
CNIP	Ciskei National Independence Party
CNP	Ciskei National Party
DP	Democratic Party (Transkei)
ICU	Industrial and Commercial Workers' Union
Idamasa	Inter-denominational African Ministers' Association of South Africa
LNP	Lebowa National Party
LPP	Lebowa People's Party
Mdali	Music, Drama, Arts and Literature Institute
MTLA	Member of Transkei Legislative Assembly
Nafcoc	National African Federated Chamber of Commerce
NEUM	Non-European Unity Movement
NIC	Natal Indian Congress
Nusas	National Union of South African Students
PAC	Pan-Africanist Congress
SABC	South African Broadcasting Corporation
Sabtu	South African Black Theatre Union
Sactu	South African Congress of Trade Unions
Saso	South African Students' Organisation
SP	Seoposengwe Party (Bophuthatswana)
TNIP	Transkei National Independence Party
TNP	Tswana National Party
TPDP	Transkei People's Democratic Party
TPFP	Transkei People's Freedom Party
Tuata	Transvaal United African Teachers' Association
UCM	University Christian Movement
UZNP	Umlazi Zulu National Party
VIP	Venda Independence People's Party
VNP	Venda National Party
XDC	Xhosa Development Corporation
ZNP	Zulu National Party

I

INTRODUCTION

Most of the political parties referred to in this book were established during and immediately prior to field research. The political parties in the Transkei, and the South African Students' Organisation, preceded the beginning of field research by some eight and three years respectively, and accordingly receive more attention in various respects, as well as providing bases for generalisation and important indicators for field research.

In the subsequent chapters the structure and functions of African political parties in South Africa are described in order to throw some light on African political participation in South Africa. The period covered by this book begins immediately after the suppression of certain African political organisations, and coincided with the establishment of the first homeland-based African political parties, namely in the Transkei in 1964. This ten-year period also saw the establishment of African political parties opposed to the homeland idea, and the rise of Black consciousness in South Africa.

An attempt will be made to describe the aspirations of the African population as expressed through political organisations. Attention will be devoted to certain situational factors, such as Black consciousness, organisational interrelationships, structure of and support for political organisations, and leadership questions. Descriptions will be offered on the participation of African political organisations in homeland elections, the formulation of policy by political organisations, and decisions and activities of these organisations. Finally the homeland leaders' reaction to separate development, and the prospects for African unity will be examined.

Field research was conducted in the period between October 1972 and February 1974. Permits from local authorities and the Department of Bantu Administration and Development to enter African residential areas and homelands were granted in a most helpful way. The leaders and office-bearers of the various political parties and voluntary associations encountered during research were also extremely helpful. Only four times have areas of research been closed: towards the middle of the project the Department of

Bantu Administration and Development refused consultation of files and granting of interviews with officials on the grounds that the time was not ripe for this particular research project; the Black People's Convention decided not to assist in any way; and the Secretary for the Department of the Chief Minister in Lebowa, as well as the Western Cape regional secretary of the Transkei's Democratic Party, refused to accept my credentials as bona fide researcher attached to the teaching staff of the University of South Africa.

A brief note on terminology is necessary. "Homelands" is used as a collective term to refer to the African areas reserved as such in terms of the Bantu Land Act, 1913, and the Bantu Trust and Land Act, 1936. "Africans" does not refer to Whites, Coloureds and Indians who mostly also regard themselves as Africans, but only to Black Africans of aboriginal extraction. "Blacks" is used as a collective term to refer to Black Africans, Coloureds and Indians, and, like "Bantu", is sometimes used in particular contexts, such as reference to words used by people or in documents.

Footnotes were kept to a minimum by omitting many references to interviews, newspaper reports, and texts of speeches by African leaders, and where the source of information is evident in the text.

I am indebted to colleagues at several South African universities and the Africa Institute in Pretoria, numerous members and officials of African parties and voluntary associations, government servants, and friends in many parts of South Africa for their assistance during research; to the University of South Africa for a prolonged period of study leave; and particularly to the South African Institute of Race Relations for reference material in Chapter 2, and to Mr. C. J. Coetzee of the University of Potchefstroom for a first draft of Chapter 3. I am thankful for their permission to use, amend, and add to their manuscripts to suit the purposes of this book.

2

AFRICAN POLITICS AND APARTHEID
1910–1963

The Conciliatory Approach

The first African national political organisation in South Africa,
the South African Native National Congress, established in 1912,
was the result of increasing political awareness and activity among
the country's African population. There were already in existence
several regional political organisations, such as the Free State Native
Congress under Thomas Mapikela, the Cape Native Congress under
Walter Rubusana, the Bantu Union of the Eastern Cape under
Meshach Pelem, and the Transvaal Native Organisation under Sam
Makgatho. Two main objectives of the Congress at its establishment were the achievement of African unity among various tribes,
organisations and élite groups; and the defence of African interests
in general. A guiding principle of Congress was the acceptance of a
multi-racial South Africa where increasing political participation
of Africans would be possible.

The establishment of the South African Native National Congress
was precipitated by two events. First, it was decided at the national
convention for the unification of South Africa in 1909 that Africans
would not be enfranchised in the two northern provinces. Prominent
men, including John Jabavu, the Rev. J. L. Dube, and the Rev.
W. B. Rubusana called a South African Native Convention which
met at Bloemfontein in March 1909, and at which it was decided to
send a delegation to London to urge that the draft South Africa Bill
should not be enacted.

For the African population the establishment of the Union of
South Africa in 1910 held little prospect of change in their system of
government. A central Department of Native Affairs was established,
replacing similar departments in the four constituent territories
(Cape Colony, Natal, Transvaal and Orange Free State). It was
also stipulated for the first time that members of parliament (house
of assembly and senate) should be Whites; and four senators had to
be nominated (by the Governor-General without necessarily con-

sulting the Blacks) on the grounds of their special knowledge of the needs of the "coloured races" of the Union.

The position in 1910, therefore, was that everybody could be registered on a common voters' roll, subject to the same conditions in the Cape Province; whereas in Natal Africans had to comply with additional strict conditions before they could register on the common roll. In both these provinces Blacks could be elected to the provincial councils, as in fact happened in the Cape Province. In Natal as well as the Cape Province tribal Africans were practically excluded from registering as voters. In the Cape Province a law of 1892 stipulated that land occupied in terms of communal, or traditional, land tenure could not be regarded as a qualification for the franchise; and in Natal the Law Disqualifying Certain Natives from Exercising Electoral Franchise, 1865, required exemption from traditional Native Law, as well as certain other conditions applying to Africans only, such as twelve years' residence in Natal, and a written recommendation by three White voters endorsed by a magistrate or a justice of the peace.

In the Transvaal and the Orange Free State Blacks were explicitly excluded from the franchise.

Immediately before Union the franchise was distributed as follows in the two colonies including Black voters:[1]

	Cape Colony (1909)	Natal (1907)
Whites	121,346	23,480
Coloureds (including Malays, Asians, Chinese, Hottentots)	14,388	200
Africans	6,633	6
Total	142,367	23,686

A second matter, which heightened resentment immediately after the Act of Union, was the introduction of the Natives Land Bill which allotted the numerically superior African population about 7.3 per cent of the land (roughly 35,000 square miles).

In 1912 Dr. Pixley Ka I. Seme, a Natal barrister, arranged a meeting in Bloemfontein of prominent African chiefs and commoners from many parts of the country. It was decided to found a South African Native National Congress (renamed the African National Congress in 1925) to work for African unity, for the extension to them of political rights, and for their economic and social advancement. The first president was the Rev. J. L. Dube. Solomon T. Plaatjie was elected corresponding secretary, and Dr. Seme one of the two treasurers. Four provincial congresses were established. For many years the ANC was a widely respected body among all population groups, a reputation which was highly treasured by the organisation itself.

A period of severe industrial unrest, among Whites as well as Blacks, followed the First World War. African dockworkers in Cape Town, mineworkers in the Transvaal, municipal workers in Port Elizabeth, and others were dissatisfied with wages and working conditions. The ANC relied on conciliatory methods of negotiation, such as sending petitions and deputations to the authorities in respect of a variety of matters, including political representation, freehold tenure outside African areas and civil rights. This approach was maintained almost until the end of the Second World War. Although beginning to despair of this approach soon after the First World War, the ANC failed to recognise the political opportunity of establishing a trade union under Congress protection. This lost opportunity was highlighted by the rapid growth of the Industrial and Commercial Workers' Union (ICU) during the 1920s.

Established in 1918 by Clements Kadalie, an African originally from Nyasaland, the ICU's membership, which included a minority of Coloureds, grew rapidly to about 80,000 by 1928. Possibly half of these were of poor financial standing, being migratory workers who could not pay regular subscriptions. By the end of the 1930s the ICU had almost disintegrated as a result of internal quarrels and organisational shortcomings. It had built up too elaborate a structure on a loosely knit foundation, and it ran into debt. During its years of existence, however, the ICU was a significant body in the political as well as economic field. Even after the demise of the ICU, the African National Congress (ANC) still failed to benefit from the example of the ICU, and at a time of much dissatisfaction over the economic colour bar, it insisted upon the encouragement of African entrepreneurship as a means to African advancement.

After the collapse of the ICU, a number of trade unions were organised on an industrial basis whereas the ICU had catered for workers in a variety of occupations. Some of these unions were organized and led by members of the Communist Party, which had been founded in South Africa in 1921. Others resisted communist influence. Various co-ordinating bodies were formed, but unity was never achieved.

The rapid increase in numbers of African voters caused them to hold the balance between opposing White political parties in about seven Eastern Cape constituencies. This caused some concern among Whites who realised that under the existing system the franchise could not be withheld indefinitely from the Africans in the remaining provinces; and that eventually the Whites would be a minority voters' group. Accordingly, the National Party and Labour Party coalition government under General J. B. M. Hertzog decided in the mid-1920s that a separation of franchise rights was necessary. Separate representation of all the Africans in the country by seven indirectly elected representatives was consequently proposed in 1926, as well as a countrywide native advisory council.

A two-thirds majority was necessary for the removal of the Africans from the Cape voters' roll (in terms of the constitution of 1910) and this was postponed until 1936 by bickering between the opposing White political parties. The required majority was achieved only after fusion in 1933 of the two main parties, viz. the National Party and the South African Party, forming the United Party under the leadership of Hertzog.* But by 1936 the original proposition was considerably watered down and the Natives Representation Act, 1936 (Act No. 12/1936), provided for a separate Cape African voters' roll for the direct election of three (of the 153) White members of the house of assembly, and the establishment of a countrywide Natives Representative Council. In addition the Cape African voters could elect two White members of the Cape Provincial Council; and four senators could be indirectly elected by the African population of the Union. For the purposes of the election of the three members of the House of Assembly, the Cape Province was divided into three electoral circles, viz. Eastern Cape, Western Cape, and Transkei. Voters had to comply with the old franchise conditions. One senator was elected for each of the following areas: Transvaal and Orange Free State, Natal, Cape Province excluding Transkei, and Transkei. The senators were elected by electoral colleges consisting of chiefs, local councils, urban advisory councils, and electoral committees.

Immediately after parliament had passed the law relating to African representation, a bill was introduced and passed for the expansion of the African areas by some 7¼ million morgen. A principle of *quid pro quo* can be discerned here: separation and re-

---

* Remnants of the National Party remained in opposition until 1939 when it was joined by Hertzog who was then involved in a split in the United Party over the declaration of war on Germany. In 1948 the Re-united National Party, under the leadership of Dr. D. F. Malan, with the assistance of the Afrikaner Party, won the general election, and has remained in power ever since.

striction of political representation in the South African Parliament called for increased *Lebensraum* in the African areas. The stage was now set for channelling African political participation and aspiration to the African areas. Influx control of Africans to White areas was considerably strengthened in 1937. The Native Representative Council consisted of 23 members with the Secretary of the Department of Native Affairs as chairman. Twelve African members were indirectly elected, and four were nominated by the Governor-General, while six chief native commissioners were ex-officio members.

The contents of these bills drew serious opposition from the African population. At this time the ANC's organisation, membership and activities had reached a low ebb. A prominent educationalist, Professor D. D. T. Jabavu, who had remained somewhat aloof from the ANC, grasped the initiative and invited representatives of a number of African and Coloured organisations to an All-African Convention, with the object of consolidating opposition to the measures. Petitions and deputations were arranged to urge that the bills be dropped. When these attempts failed, it was decided that the Convention should remain in being as a federal body, with the object of promoting non-white unity and presenting a common front against legislation that was considered discriminatory. The All-Africa Convention (AAC) elected to its first executive in 1935 several members of the ANC executive. In spite of this overlapping membership the ANC regarded the AAC as a rival in the struggle for African unity. In 1937, with the election of the first Natives' Representatives to the House of Assembly and Senate it became clear that a successful revival in the ANC was under way, whereas the AAC was losing ground as the only national African representative body. This trend was confirmed when Dr. A. B. Xuma, first Vice-president of the AAC, was elected President-General of the ANC in 1940 – an event which led to the organisational reconstruction of the ANC during the 1940s, as well as a steadily rising membership. The AAC remained on the scene and took the lead in establishing in 1943 the Non-European Unity Movement, which included Africans and Coloureds, and pursued a policy of non-collaboration with the authorities, following the example of its parent organisation. The AAC and NEUM remained fairly influential in the Transkei, especially among African teachers, many of whom belonged to the Cape African Teachers' Association which was affiliated to NEUM. By 1963, however, the Transkeian teachers had abandoned the non-collaboration stand, and supported the drive for the registration of voters for the first Transkeian general election.

The ANC considered the Native Representative Council a poor substitute for the common-roll franchise in the Cape, but decided to suspend judgement until this body had at least been given a trial. Some of the ANC leaders accepted membership of the Council. During the years that followed, the African members became increasingly dissatisfied with purely advisory powers. The Council's resolutions were, in general, ignored by the authorities – in particular, repeated demands for the abolition of the pass laws. In 1946 the Council adjourned *sine die*, in protest. Early in 1948 General J. C. Smuts, then Prime Minister, made an attempt to break the deadlock, but his proposals were unacceptable to the African leaders whom he consulted. The Council was abolished by the National Party government in 1951.

The changes brought about by the 1936 Act left the position in Natal, Orange Free State and Transvaal undisturbed, except for the provision regarding the election of senators by Africans.

The situation concerning the franchise at the time of the coming into power of the National Party in 1948 can be summarised as follows: all Whites above the age of 21 could register as voters. Blacks had to comply with certain requirements to qualify for registration as voters. In the Cape Province, Africans were on a separate roll and other Blacks on the common roll; all, however, were subject to the same property, income and other qualifications as before 1910. In Natal, Africans and other Blacks could be registered on the common roll subject to the same income, property and other special qualifications as before 1910. The Asiatic Land Tenure and Indian Representation Act, 1946, granted franchise to the Indians in Natal and Transvaal on the same basis on which it had been granted to the Africans in 1936. This Act was repealed in 1948 before it came into force. In the Transvaal and Orange Free State Blacks therefore remained without franchise.* Feelings of frustration mounted within the ANC. The pass laws, involving frequent police raids and imprisonment, were especially resented.

In 1943 a group of younger ANC members formed a Youth League within the Congress to act as a pressure group for the use of more militant (although not communist) techniques to secure the abolition of discriminatory laws: among the leaders were W. Nkomo, Oliver Tambo, Nelson Mandela, Govan Mbeki and Walter Sisulu. They were supported by members of the Congress Women's League. Another group, led by Paul R. Mosaka, broke away to form an

---

* The only surviving African voter in Natal died in 1946. Theoretically Africans in Natal could still be registered as voters until 1956 when this right was terminated by Act No. 9/1956.

African Democratic Party. They, too, repudiated communism but wanted more activism.

The Congress Youth League accepted the concept of African Nationalism as a point of reference, and believed in the employment of extra-constitutional methods such as strikes, boycotts and civil disobedience for the exercising of pressure against official policy. It succeeded in obtaining the endorsement of the 1939 annual conference of the ANC of a "Programme of Action", thus adopting a new, more militant approach. This new approach resulted directly in the Defiance Campaign which started in 1952, and also resulted in a phenomenal increase of paying members, which reached a peak of about 100,000 during the Defiance Campaign. Thus ended the period in which the ANC was prepared to work within the legal and constitutional framework only – to compromise, co-operate and consult with the government. The end of this period was heralded with renewed ANC activity following the 1936 African legislation.

A major historic contribution of the Youth League to African political orientations was its emphasis on the African cultural heritage and ability for progress through community efforts (which it contrasted with the White man's individualism). The instilling of African self-confidence and dignity was one of the objectives of the Programme of Action. This is held by Walshe to be the first manifestation of Black consciousness in South Africa.[2]

Defiance Campaign and Aftermath

Much of the early apartheid legislation adopted by the National Party government after coming into power in 1948 was opposed by African political leaders. Thus the new form of local self-government – created through the Bantu Authorities Act (1951) – which strengthened the powers of chiefs, was opposed on the grounds that it fragmented the people. The Native Labour (Settlement of Disputes) Act (1953) set up separate industrial conciliation machinery for Africans. The Bantu Education Act (1953) transferred control of education for Africans from the provinces and missions to the state, and a ministerial statement gave Africans cause to fear the type of education provided for them would be inferior. Particularly obnoxious to Africans was the extension of influx control to all urban areas and the application of the system to African women and to exempted Africans whose freedom of movement had not hitherto been controlled. One concession was made: Africans who were born in South Africa became entitled to visit an urban area for up to 72 hours without requiring a special permit. The Governor-

General was empowered to prohibit gatherings of ten or more Africans except for bona fide religious, social and certain other purposes. On the other hand, constructive steps were taken in the provision of housing for urban Africans, through the Native Building Workers' Act (1951) and the creation of the Native Services Levy Fund Act (1952). The former Act lifted the colour bar on construction work in the urban African townships; the latter required employers of Africans to pay a levy, the proceeds of which went to improve public services in urban African townships.

In order to control the activities of persons whom it considered were fomenting unrest, the government introduced the Suppression of Communism Act (1950), banning the South African Communist Party and enabling the authorities to ban other organisations deemed to be furthering the aims of communism (this term was very widely defined), and to impose various bans on persons, publications and gatherings considered to be promoting such aims. The banning of the Communist Party was preceded by an increasing rapprochement between members of the Party and of the Congress Youth League, resulting from a willingness on both sides to employ radical methods. Marxist terminology came to be used increasingly by members of the Youth League, and although in 1950 there was still mutual suspicion between the League and the Party, certain Youth League leaders began to adhere to Marxist doctrines.[3]

In November 1949 and during the following January there was serious rioting along the Witwatersrand. A commission of enquiry found, *inter alia*, a widespread feeling of hostility against the police; that a cause of much resentment was indiscriminate raiding for passes and liquor; and that adequate housing and social, educational and recreational facilities were lacking. There were further disturbances in May 1950.

During this period, for the first time, the political leaders of the African, Coloured, and Indian peoples met (on 29 July 1951) to plan action against laws that were considered discriminatory. Among the Africans were Oliver Tambo, Chief Albert J. Luthuli and Dr. J. S. Moroka. They held discussions with the (mainly Coloured) Franchise Action Council of the Cape, and the S.A. Indian Congress (dating from 1894), then led by Dr. G. M. Naicker and Dr. Y. M. Dadoo. At this time many Coloured people were embittered because of the official plan to remove them from the common voters' roll in the Cape. Indians were deeply resentful of controls placed on their tenure of land. In February 1951 the three organisations set up a Franchise Action Committee.

Towards the end of that year the ANC wrote to the Prime Minister stating that unless various discriminatory laws were abolished mass action would be taken, commencing with the defiance of selected laws and regulations. The Prime Minister replied that his government had no intention of repealing these laws, but added that it was only too willing to encourage Bantu initiative within the Bantu community. The ANC wrote again, saying that it had no alternative but to embark on a campaign of defiance of unjust laws, which would be conducted in a peaceful manner. The campaign was launched on 26 June 1952. Volunteers were asked to commit technical offences such as contraventions of pass laws, apartheid regulations at railway stations and post offices, and curfew regulations. Those arrested would go to gaol rather than pay fines. By the end of 1952 just over 8,000 volunteers had been arrested: increasingly heavy sentences were imposed. Some of the leaders, including Dr. J. S. Moroka and Dr. Y. M. Dadoo, were charged with offences under the Suppression of Communism Act (1950): in most cases they received suspended sentences. Heavier penalties acted as a deterrent and it looked as if the campaign would peter out.

Early in 1953 the government introduced the Public Safety Act, enabling it to declare a state of emergency and then to issue emergency regulations; and the Criminal Law Amendment Act (1953), which laid down severe penalties for persons convicted of offences committed by way of protest against any law. In the face of such stiff opposition the organisers of the Defiance Campaign then decided to bring it to an honourable end – that is, before it fizzled out. They also felt that it would be unwise to arrange further demonstrations at a time of tension, and unfair to expose volunteers to the severe new penalties. The ANC issued an appeal to the African people to remain calm and at all costs to prevent further outbreaks of violence.[4] During this period, namely in October and November 1952, there was serious rioting in Port Elizabeth, Johannesburg, Kimberley and East London, in each case being sparked off by minor events. Less grave disturbances occurred in other centres. Whites' attitudes hardened as atrocities committed by rioting Africans, in particular a case of cannibalism in East London, became known.

Further apartheid measures were announced during and immediately after the Defiance Campaign. The Secretary for Native Affairs declared that it was the government's intention ultimately to remove all Africans from the Western Cape, and meanwhile to apply strict influx control. A "Bantu Resettlement Board" was established in Johannesburg to resettle in new housing schemes more than 10,000 African families (including 350 Africans who held freehold titles) living in slum conditions in the Western Areas of Johannesburg. In 1953 the Bantu Education Act was adopted and implementation started. Africans, Coloureds and Indians began to experience the practical effects of the Group Areas Act which provided for residential segregation in urban areas, and the Industrial Conciliation Act which perpetuated job reservation and facilitated the division of trade unions along racial lines. The government assumed power to control the number of African labour tenants and squatters on farms of Whites, and no longer undertook to find alternative land for those who were in consequence displaced.

The ANC singled out during 1954 the Western Areas resettlement scheme and the Bantu Education Act as targets for its next attempt at mass mobilisation, and as focal points in its resistance to apartheid. Although the broad objectives of the two campaigns were published far and wide, the ANC apparently had no clear-cut tactical plans for achieving its objectives. People were merely told to resist, not how to resist. Furthermore, successful resistance depended on voluntary, sustained mass participation – which was not forthcoming. The failure of Congress in the Western Areas campaign also followed a misjudgement of the feelings of the people concerned. The greater majority were eager to leave the overcrowded slum areas. The resistance to Bantu Education was of greater importance, since it was to be a national protest, in the form of a boycott of government-controlled schools during 1955. The national executive decided, in the face of a government warning that children who boycotted school would not be re-admitted, to postpone the school boycott and rather boycott the school boards. At this stage the national executive lost control of the campaign and rebellious branches induced people again to proceed with the boycott of schools. The task was entrusted to the Youth League and the Women's League, but again no proper plans were available as to how the boycott should be carried out and sustained. Congress plans for alternative educational facilities did not materialise and the campaign collapsed, seriously damaging the prestige of the ANC. In 1957 and following years, Congress turned to strike action, but achieved only limited success.

In the meantime several new organisations had come into being. As a result of the constitutional struggle over the Coloured franchise, a Coloured People's Organisation (later known as Coloured People's Congress) had been established to campaign for full democratic rights for all adult men and women. A Federation of South African Women was created, primarily to campaign against the extension of the pass laws to African women. Its membership, mainly African, included a few people of other racial groups, and it was led by Mrs. Helen Joseph and Mrs. Lilian Ngoyi.

Trade unionists who feared that the Industrial Conciliation Bill would interfere with the collective bargaining system formed a new co-ordinating body called the Trade Union Council of South Africa. In an endeavour to obtain as much support as possible from established unions they decided to confine membership to registered unions, thus excluding African unions. Some unions that disagreed with this decision established the rival S.A. Congress of Trade Unions (Sactu). This had predominantly African members but was led by a White, Leon Levy.

The foundation for the formation of a "Congress Alliance" was laid in 1947 when Dr. A. B. Xuma and Dr. Y. M. Dadoo, respectively presidents of the ANC and the Transvaal Indian Congress, signed a pact declaring their common opposition to racial discrimination. At the invitation of the national executive of the ANC, the executives of the South African Indian Congress, the ANC, and the Franchise Action Council of the Cape (a Coloured organisation) met on 29 July 1951 in order to discuss increasing apartheid measures. The outcome of the meeting was a resolution to recommend to their respective organisations the commencement of a passive resistance campaign – which ultimately became known as the Defiance Campaign. Congress Alliance consisted of the ANC, the South African Indian Congress, the Coloured People's Congress, and the Congress of Democrats (which was formed during the Defiance Campaign by sympathetic Whites and controlled by the underground South African Communist Party). It met for the first time in 1953 and one of its first tasks was to call a Congress of the People (COP). The proposal came from the ANC, and was implemented by a co-ordinating committee of the Congress Alliance which in theory acted in an advisory capacity to the constituting Congresses. The main function of the COP was to ratify a Freedom Charter and to voice the demands of the people. Committees were to be established all over South Africa for the election of delegates to the COP and the formulation of demands. Afterwards these committees could be employed for organisational expansion of the ANC. These plans proved too grandiose and did not rise to expectations. Nevertheless, about 3,000 delegates attended the COP in June 1955 in Johannesburg and ratified the Freedom Charter, which then had to be ratified by the various Congress organisations. The COP also received the support of the Federation of South African Women, Sactu, and (initially) the Liberal Party. During 1956–60 the so-called pass laws were considerably tightened, and the government took power to serve banishment orders without prior notice on Africans in rural areas. The Minister of Bantu Administration and Development was empowered, subject to certain conditions, to control the presence of Africans at church services, schools, hospitals, clubs and places of entertainment in urban areas outside African townships. Apartheid was insisted upon in welfare organisations and some professional bodies.

The government began building separate university colleges for African, Coloured and Asian students. The rates of African taxation were raised; and for the first time African women whose incomes exceeded R360 a year became liable to taxation. The cost of living was rising more rapidly than African wages. New urban housing schemes were on an "economic" basis: the Africans had, over a period of years, to repay the capital costs and interest. Many new group areas proclamations were gazetted.

During December 1956 the police arrested 156 persons on charges of high treason, many of them leaders of organisations forming the Congress Alliance. At the end of a year-long preparatory examination 91 were committed for trial. Their trial opened in August 1958, but after lengthy legal argument the state withdrew the indictment. A new indictment was framed against 30 of the accused, its essence being an allegation of conspiracy to overthrow the state by violence and to substitute for it a communist state or some other form of state. The trial began in November 1960 and the accused were acquitted and discharged in March 1961, the case against the others being then withdrawn. The presiding judge said that the alleged policy of violence attributed to the ANC was the corner-stone of the case for the prosecution: if this case failed, it must fail against the other organisations of the Congress Alliance. The evidence showed that these organisations had been working to replace the existing form of state by one based on the demands set out in the Freedom Charter. It had, however, not been proved that such a form of state would be a communist one, nor that the ANC's policy was to overthrow the state by violence.

Numerous grave disturbances took place during the period 1956 to 1959. In towns and villages throughout the country, notably Kroonstad, Virginia, Paarl, Standerton, Nelspruit, Johannesburg, Pretoria, Durban and Pietermaritzburg there were demonstrations against passes for African women, and other irritants, some of which ended in violence. Serious unrest continued for about a year in the Bahurutshe Reserve in the Zeerust area, the initial cause being the issuing of reference books to women. Two bitterly antagonistic factions developed: supporters of chiefs who were helping to implement government policy, and their opponents. There were cases of arson and murder. Even worse troubles, leading for a time to a reign of terror, took place in the Sekhukhuneland Reserve.

These were sparked off by the introduction of the Bantu authorities and cattle-culling schemes.

Many hundreds of Africans were arrested and charged with offences ranging from murder, assault, and arson to participation in prohibited meetings. Some of those found guilty were sentenced to life imprisonment. A few anti-government chiefs and others were banished to remote farms.

For about four years dating from 1960, there was a grave state of unrest throughout the Transkei, appearing initially to stem from the introduction of Bantu authorities, cattle-culling and increased taxation. Chiefs who supported government policies were attacked and in a few cases murdered, huts were burned, fencing and other farming betterment works were destroyed, and about 25 Africans were murdered. Hundreds of arrests were made and 14 people were shot as the result of police action. Thirty men were sentenced to death (of whom nine lodged successful appeals) and at least 11 were banished from the Transkei.

During this period there was a steadily growing cohesion among members of the Congress Alliance. The ANC convened a National Workers' Conference in 1958, at which it was decided to campaign for a minimum wage of R2 a day and the abolition of the Group Areas Act and the pass laws. Two stay-at-home demonstrations were called for, the second on the eve of the 1958 South African general election. Ex-Chief Luthuli issued a message to White voters pointing out that, lacking the franchise, Africans could not seek to have their grievances remedied through direct parliamentary action. He emphasised that the ANC's aim was to achieve a common South African multi-racial society, based upon friendship, equality of rights, and mutual respect.

Earlier tensions within the ANC now came to a head. Mistrust of communists and fear of foreign manipulation of African aspirations had for a long time governed relations between the ANC and the South African Communist Party. The greater radicalism within Congress that went with the establishment of the Youth League in 1943 led to a gradual thawing in Congress attitudes towards the communists. A rift began to appear between the africanists who advocated majority African rule and who rejected the old Congress stand of multi-racialism, and those who strove for a non-racial, classless society. The africanists became increasingly suspicious of communist manipulation of the ANC through the Congress Alliance, and the matter was rapidly brought to a conclusion by the adoption of the Freedom Charter by the ANC in 1956, and the call by ANC leaders to support the stay-at-home strike in 1958. In both decisions the africanists saw the hand of outside organisations and accordingly opposed the 1958 strike on the grounds that it did not rest on ANC resolutions. The africanists were then expelled from the ANC – a step which directly contributed to the establishment of the Pan-Africanist Congress (PAC) in 1959 under the leadership of Robert Sobukwe, Josias Madzunya and Potlako Leballo, of whom the latter two were among the leaders of the 1958 rebels.

The PAC claimed that by early 1960 entire branches of the ANC, including their funds and office equipment, had joined the PAC. Sobukwe also stated that in March 1960 the PAC had 30,000 paying members, in spite of a relatively high entrance fee of 50c and a monthly due of 20c. Indians were excluded from membership because the PAC saw no possibility of co-operating with them until they had abandoned their reputedly anti-Black leaders. The Pan-Africanist Charter of March 1960 declared that the PAC was not against anybody; only against a particular system. Absolute non-violence was pledged, and Sobukwe claimed that he was leading his followers towards full citizenship in a non-racial South Africa, to African independence and a United States of Africa.[5]

After this breakaway, there was an upsurge of new confidence among remaining members of the ANC in their leaders, who included Albert Luthuli, Oliver Tambo, Duma Nokwe and Robert Resha. A plan was adopted for a major campaign against the pass laws. As a first step, on 31 March 1960 deputations would wait upon local authorities and government officials throughout the country, urging the abolition of these laws. Demonstrations would be arranged during the following month. The PAC anticipated these plans and instructed its members to present themselves at police stations without their passes on 21 March, passively inviting arrest, and going to gaol rather than paying fines.

In the atmosphere of extreme tension that existed on 21 March outbursts of emotionalism were inevitable, and these occurred throughout the country. Crowds of Africans assembled. In some cases they were dispersed by the police without incident, but in others, for example at Sharpeville, the police resorted to shooting. It was reported that, between 21 March and 19 April, 83 civilians and 3 policemen lost their lives (69 of the civilians at Sharpeville), while 365 civilians and 59 policemen were injured. Both the ANC and the PAC called for a day of mourning on 28 March, Africans being urged to stay away from work. This demonstration was particularly effective in Cape Town, Johannesburg and Port Elizabeth; the Africans of Cape Town remained at home for more than a week, disrupting many industries.

On 24 March the government banned public meetings of all

races in the large towns. This ban remained in force until 30 June. Four days later the Unlawful Organisations Bill was introduced, to enable the authorities to ban the ANC, the PAC and organisations deemed to be carrying on any of the activities of these bodies. Then, on 30 March, a state of emergency was proclaimed throughout most of the country. Emergency regulations were gazetted which provided, *inter alia*, for the arrest without warrant and detention of any person if this was considered desirable in the public interest. Hundreds of people were arrested before dawn on 30 March. This precipitated further disturbances in numerous towns, thousands of Africans marching in processions to demand the release of their leaders. Rioting occurred in some places, and considerable damage was done to property. The most impressive march was of some 30,000 Africans in Cape Town, led by Philip Kgosana of the PAC.

The defence force was called up to assist the police. The emergency regulations were gradually relaxed, but not repealed until 31 August. According to the Minister of Justice, 98 Whites, 36 Coloured persons, 90 Asians, and 11,279 Africans were detained and held *incommunicado*, 400 of them until the state of emergency ended. Many were charged and found guilty of offences such as incitement, participation in riots or the possession of dangerous weapons. Robert Sobukwe of the PAC was sentenced to three years' imprisonment. Immediately after the Unlawful Organisation Act was passed both the ANC and the PAC were declared unlawful. Most of the leaders were placed under orders severely restricting their movements and activities.

Militant Regrouping

During 1961 the late H. F. Verwoerd, then Prime Minister, elaborated on the policy of separate development, stating that the Bantu would be enabled to develop separate Bantu states, possibly even being granted full independence. Bantu in the White areas of South Africa, Verwoerd said, were to be regarded as temporary migrants, who must exercise their political rights in their respective homelands. Partial self-government was granted to the Transkei in 1963. Larger sums of money than in previous years were voted by the government for the development of the reserves, and plans were made for attracting White entrepreneurs to establish industrial concerns at selected points bordering on these areas. Schemes were pursued for the consolidation of scattered African areas, and the laws governing the influx of Africans to the towns were made yet more strict. Restrictions on the sale of liquor to non-whites were removed: this did away with one constant source of friction between Africans and the police. Wage levels rose; but average African incomes continued to lag considerably behind the poverty datum line.

In December 1960 about 40 Africans who were prominent in various fields of activity met to discuss ways of representing African opinion, which could no longer be done through the ANC or PAC. A committee was appointed under the chairmanship of Jordan K. Ngubane to plan an "All-in" Conference, to take place in Pietermaritzburg at the end of March 1961. Five days before this date thirteen of the original planners were arrested and accused of furthering the aims of the ANC. One of them fled the country while on bail, the rest each being sentenced to 12 months' imprisonment. However, their appeals against these sentences succeeded. The judge said that there were probably many organisations in the country with objects similar to some of the ANC's, including the All-in Conference. But this did not mean that it was assisting the ANC in the achievement of any of its objectives.

The conference was held in spite of the arrest of some of the organisers. It called for a national convention of elected representatives of adult men and women of all racial groups, to be held not later than 31 May 1961. If the government ignored this demand (as it did), the people would be called upon to organise mass demonstrations. The Indian and Coloured communities and "all democratic Whites" would be invited to join the Africans in opposition "to a regime which is bringing South Africa to disaster". A National Action Council was appointed. It was made known that Nelson Mandela was the honorary secretary; but otherwise the names of members were a closely guarded secret. Thousands of leaflets were distributed calling on non-whites to remain at home from 29 to 31 May 1961 (the time when South Africa was to become a republic), and to make the intervening period a time of active protest, demonstration, and organisation against a "Verwoerd republic".

The government promptly introduced a General Law Amendment Act providing, among other things, that the Attorney-General, if he considered it necessary in the interests of public safety or the maintenance of public order, might direct that a person who had been arrested should not be released on bail or otherwise for twelve days. This provision remained in force until 1965, when it was replaced by a law allowing for longer periods of detention. With certain exceptions (church services, entertainments, business meetings of statutory bodies, etc.) all gatherings were prohibited throughout the country unless they had been authorised by a magistrate. This prohibition was in force from 19 May to 6 June. Police leave was cancelled, and the defence force was brought to a state of "preparedness for service". Large-scale raids were conducted by the police on offices and private homes. In view of this government action and because ex-PAC members opposed the scheme, the demonstrations planned by the National Action Council were a relative failure. A warrant was issued for Mandela's arrest; but for sixteen months he succeeded in evading the police. He became popularly known as the "Black Pimpernel".

There were other pleas for a multi-racial national convention – by a Coloured Convention held in the Cape in July 1961, by a multi-racial Natal Convention, by the Methodist Church, the Liberal and Progressive Parties, the Civil Rights League, and various members of staff and students of the English-medium universities. But the Prime Minister rejected these requests. "If Whites in the Opposition", he said, "could not even stay together in connection with the question of colour policy, how on earth is one going to achieve anything with a convention in which all these conflicting groups are gathered together? . . . Such a convention . . . would be nothing but a breeding-ground for communistic conditioning."

After the banning of the ANC, some of its leaders were in gaol or (like ex-chief Luthuli) subject to restrictive orders; others had left the country. Still others were in hiding, operating underground. Many of them began to despair of a peaceful solution. Mandela[6] recalled that Africans had warned that they would employ violence and force and that the government itself had often used violence to crush opposition. Nevertheless the ANC, which by 1959 was under considerable communist pressure, maintained that change should be obtained through peaceful means. Only after its banning in 1960 did the ANC in a leaflet call for public support for violent resistance.

Once having decided upon a course of violence, the underground ANC established a military wing in 1961, called Umkhonto we Sizwe (Spear of the Nation), which would immediately start recruiting volunteers for training in sabotage. According to a former member of the South African Communist Party, Umkhonto we Sizwe was a military wing of the Communist Party as well. He maintains that at the 1962 (and last) national conference of the Communist Party it transpired that Umkhonto had been established, financed and controlled by the S.A. Communist Party. Finances were controlled by Abram Fischer, the Party's head, who received money from overseas. At the first meeting of the Central Committee after the 1962 conference Operation Mayibuye was considered:

this was a planned military onslaught on South Africa. For its
execution a secretariat was elected and Joe Slovo, a member of the
Central Committee, was appointed head of the High Command of
Umkhonto we Sizwe, which was to supervise the Operation. Regional and sub-regional committeess and cells were to operate under
the High Command. It also operated a spasmodic "Freedom Radio"
from Johannesburg and Cape Town. Slovo and J. B. Marks (former
president of the Transvaal ANC and a member of the Central Committee) went overseas to recruit support for the attack on South
Africa. They visited London and some African and Asian countries.[7]
Meanwhile, Umkhonto sent recruits to Algeria, Egypt, Ethiopia,
Moscow, Communist China, Cuba and other countries for training
in sabotage and guerilla fighting. Many of these recruits were under
the impression that they were going to take up educational scholarships. On discovering the nature of the training, they were afraid
to desert, lacked the money to return and faced penalties if they did
so, as they had left illegally without travel documents.

Other bodies with violent aims also sprang up. One was the
African Resistance Movement, composed of young professionals,
lecturers and students (men and women), mainly White. It started
towards the end of 1961 as an academically oriented, peaceful
discussion group under the auspices of the National Committee
for Liberation. But sabotage as a means of protest was soon contemplated and in 1963 it was finally committed. By this time the organisation was known as African Resistance Movement. After some success and several failures the Movement decided towards the end of
1963 to concentrate on its other main objective, namely the construction of a political intelligence unit which could collect and disseminate political information to persons and organisations opposing
apartheid. Operating mainly in the Western Cape the Movement
worked in isolation, but in 1964 its leaders were arrested, some flee-
ing the country.[8] Another was the Yu Chi Chan Club, consisting of a
small group of Coloured people, mainly in the Western Cape. The
African People's Democratic Union of South Africa (Apdusa)
apparently had similar aims; it had African, Coloured, and Indian
members.

Another organisation known as Poqo was formed by certain extremist members of the PAC in 1961. Mr. Sobukwe was then in
gaol, and Philip Kgosana had fled from South Africa. A struggle
for leadership ensued. Later, Potlako Leballo claimed to be leader
of the movement. After it became dangerous for him to remain
in South Africa he operated secretly from offices in Maseru. The
word *poqo* means "only" or "pure", implying that it was a purely
African movement. Mr. Justice Snyman, who subsequently con-

ducted an enquiry, found that the organisation was the PAC gone underground. Its ultimate aim, the judge reported, was to over-throw the government by revolutionary means and to create an africanist socialist democratic state in which only Africans would have any voice. It planned to abolish the tribal system because under it Poqo members, as men of little tribal status, had no hope of attaining leadership. Acts of violence were directed against Whites and chiefs. Chief Kaiser Matanzima, Chief Minister of the Transkei, was a particular target because he supported government policies.

The judge found that it was only among the thin upper crust of Poqo members that the full aims of the movement were clearly understood. It was organised into cells, local branches, regional divisions, and national headquarters. Some members joined the cells voluntarily: they were stated to be mainly men in the Western Cape who were highly resentful of the strict influx control measures in force there. Many others were terrorised into joining and, once having done so, then keeping silent about Poqo activities. The judge reported that several gruesome murders had been committed to frighten the unwilling and force them to co-operate. Officials who gave evidence at the enquiry said that some members of Poqo appeared to have been trained in the use of petrol bombs, but that most of them used pangas, axes, long knives or assegais. It was re-ported that witch-doctors gave some members medicine to protect them against bullets. Poqo was held to be responsible for acts of violence in Paarl, the Transkei, and various other places. Paarl at the time was a fertile breeding-ground for trouble: seven men were arrested there in connection with the murders of several Africans and three Coloured women, apparently committed as part of the Poqo terrorisation campaign. In an attempt by a mob of Africans to free the prisoners on the night of 21 November two White civilians were killed and three injured, as well as five Africans killed and four wounded.

From the end of 1962 members of Poqo from the Western Cape infiltrated into the Transkei with the object of taking reprisals against pro-government chiefs. Several attempts were made to kill Chief Kaiser Matanzima, and at least two headmen were murdered. In several places there was fighting between police and bands of Poqo members, with deaths on both sides. According to police evidence in court cases, early in 1963 Poqo members in several centres decided to murder local Whites. Then, on 2 February, five Whites (including a woman and two young girls) were mur-dered at a road camp near the Bashee River, in the Transkei.

The Prime Minister reported that Mr. Leballo had planned

Poqo attacks throughout the Republic for the week-end of 7–8 April 1963, but the police acted in time to prevent serious trouble. The aim had been to destroy installations and communications, steal weapons and murder Whites. Attempts to carry out these objectives were made at King William's Town, East London, Pretoria, Benoni, Johannesburg, Germiston, Cape Town, Lady Frere and Victoria West, resulting in many arrests. Many acts of sabotage and violence took place between 1961 and 1964. Only later did it transpire which organisations were responsible. Those described first were subsequently attributed to bodies connected with the National Committee for Liberation. Sporadic acts of sabotage occurred, mainly through the use of plastic or pipe bombs. The aim appeared to be to blow up offices of the Bantu Administration Department, police stations, post offices and goals; to destroy electric transformers, pylons carrying power lines, railway lines, signal boxes and cables, and telephone wires and booths. In some areas train, electricity, and telephone services were temporarily disrupted. There were a few casualties. The Minister of Justice reported that, up to 10 March 1964, there had been 203 serious cases of sabotage. Others took place later that year. The police were called out in strength to guard key installations, and were able to prevent some attempts at sabotage. The final act of sabotage was on 24 July 1964 when a time-bomb, left in a suitcase, exploded in the concourse of the main railway station in Johannesburg. A number of people, including children, were seriously injured and one later died. Following police action against members of banned organisations and subsequent convictions, many remaining activists fled the country. According to the Minister of Justice (on 10 May 1964 in the Senate), 562 people who would have been charged had fled the country. Estimates of those who left for military training varied from 900 to 5,000.

Conclusion

Early African political organisations culminated in a total confrontation with the South African government, resulting in their designation as unlawful organisations. None of these organisations accepted the government policy of separate development and therefore rejected the African homelands as bases for political action. The demise of the ANC and PAC and their underground successors and collaborators was simultaneous with the rise of new opportunities for political action as a result of a clearer definition of the political aspects of the policy of separate development. Africans in White areas were afforded new scope for participation in politics, albeit largely within the framework of organisations based in African homelands. This was made possible, although perhaps not quite realised at the time, by the trend which National Party government policy took in the late 1950s and early 1960s – especially as expressed in the Promotion of Bantu Self-government Act, 1959, and the Transkei Constitution Act, 1963. This policy encourages African political participation and self-determination, with the homelands as focal points, but does not acknowledge the permanent residence of about eight million Africans in White areas. In order to be consistent, government policy had to allow political organisation and mobilisation of Africans in White areas with a view to participation in homeland affairs. The large number of Africans in White areas and the economic integration of White and Black in South Africa, together with the possibilities raised by homeland politics, resulted in new South African political relationships—the outcome of which only time will prove, and the beginnings of which form the subject of this book.

REFERENCES

1. C. M. Tatz, *Shadow and Substance in South Africa*, Pietermaritzburg, University of Natal Press, 1962, pp. 3, 4.
2. Peter Walshe, *Black Nationalism in South Africa: a Short History*, Johannesburg, Spro-cas, 1973, p. 30; and *The Rise of African Nationalism in South Africa*, London, C. Hurst, 1970, pp. 354–5.
3. Walshe, *The Rise of African Nationalism . . .*, op. cit., pp. 358–60.
4. Also see Edward Feit, *African Opposition in South Africa*, Stanford, Hoover Institution, 1967.
5. Norman Phillips, *The Tragedy of Apartheid*, London, George Allen and Unwin, 1961, pp. 60–6.
6. Speech made in a court case, November 1962, subsequently quoted in House of Assembly by Mrs. H. Suzman, M.P., 23 January 1963, Hansard 1, Col. 109.
7. Gerard Ludi and Blaar Grobbelaar, *Die Verbasende Bram Fischer*, Cape Town, Nasionale Boekhandel, 1966, pp. 35–48.
8. Miles Brokensha and Robert Knowles, *The Fourth of July Raids*, Cape Town, Simondium, 1965.

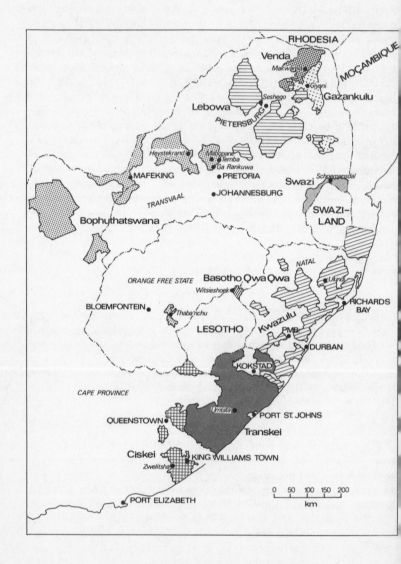

The African "Homelands" of South Africa

3

POLITICAL PLATFORMS

In this chapter the constitutional framework for contemporary African political action in South Africa is briefly described. Undoubtedly the political platforms created in the ethnic states of South Africa have brought a revival of African politics either through employment of the machinery of homeland governments, or by way of reaction against institutions created under the separate development policy. Reference is made to South African security laws, which do not prohibit anti-government African political parties, but which, in their implementation, affect some of them; they do not affect the homeland-based political parties.

Separate Territorial Representation

The statutory recognition accorded by the Natives Land Act, 1913 (Act No. 27/1913), to separate African areas was an important prerequisite for the establishment of separate governmental institutions for these areas. Local councils already existed in some African areas, notably in the Transkei where district councils and a general council were established in 1894, but several decades were to elapse before the African areas were considered capable of managing more than local governmental institutions.

The system of local councils was extended in 1920 to all African areas (in terms of the Native Affairs Act). Local councils could be established and provision was made for the division of local council areas into wards for the election of the councillors. General councils consisted of the Chief Native Commissioner of the region and the chairmen and two members from each of the constituent local councils. While these councils afforded the inhabitants an opportunity for participation in local government, they also provided a channel of communication between central government and the people.

When the National Party came to power in 1948 there were in existence the well-developed Transkeian council system, fourteen local councils in Transvaal, three in Natal, two in British Bechuanaland (no part of Bophuthatswana) and eight in the Ciskei. The only general council was that of the Transkei.

The National Party's declared policies of separation of the two racial groups in the country brought about a shift in emphasis in the nature and purpose of local government in the African areas. This was embodied in the Bantu Authorities Act of 1951. The Bantu authority system was intended to form a basis for the expansion of local government in the African areas, building upon the traditional governmental institutions to restore the traditional tribal democracy of the Africans – according to the Minister of Native Affairs, Dr. H. F. Verwoerd. The Act provided for a three-tiered system of local government. Only the first tier, consisting of the tribal authorities, resembled the traditional system. The second and third tiers, regional and territorial authorities, were traditionally unknown, and were established for progressively larger geographical areas. These Bantu authorities gradually replaced all previous local and general councils. Inmediate establishment was not compulsory. The establishment of territorial authorities implied the development of national governmental institutions for each ethnic group. The political separation of Whites and Africans, started by General Hertzog in 1926, was taken another step forward.

African opposition to the Bantu authorities was manifest. By this time (1951) the ANC was taking a more militant stand against measures designed to elaborate separate development. The Defiance Campaign was aimed at various new legislation, including the Bantu Authorities Act, Group Areas Act, Separate Representation of Voters Act, Suppression of Communism Act, pass laws, and stock limitation measures. It was also felt by educated Africans that the system of Bantu authorities would perpetuate the traditional rule of chiefs and tribal fragmentation.

The abolition of the Native Representative Council and the establishment of Bantu authorities in 1951 were the first steps towards African political representation in accordance with not only racial, but also ethnic differentiation. The Promotion of Bantu Self-government Act, 1959 (Act No. 46/1959), was a further legal elaboration of this principle. The White Paper accompanying the Act held out the prospect for the implementation of the following important points of policy (it became fashionable at the same time to refer to African "homelands"): (a) ethnic grouping with a view to constitutional development was set as a basic premise; (b) gradual withdrawal of the White government from the African areas was envisaged; (c) the White authority would continue to give advice during the period of withdrawal; (d) liaison between African population groups in the cities and those in the homelands

was envisaged; (e) African representation in the South African parliament and provincial councils was terminated; (f) social and economic development would go hand in hand with constitutional
development; (g) it was recognised that progress to self-governing
status also required the development of a judiciary and administrative institutions. Accordingly the powers and functions of territorial authorities were greatly increased preparatory to self-
government; urban representatives were appointed by territorial
authorities and chiefs; ethnic groups were delineated; and a
commissioner-general was appointed in respect of each ethnic
group as a representative of the South African government, and to
promote the constitutional, economic, and social development of
the African population.[1]

It is evident from the title of the Promotion of Bantu Self-government Act that it contained a promise to extend the Africans' right
of self-determination, albeit in the homelands only. Because the
Act deprived the African population of an existing right without
providing a suitable immediate alternative, its passing provoked
considerable controversy. Opponents of the measure felt that in
exchange for the Cape African franchise the promise of future development was not substantial enough. Soon after the passing of the
Act the ANC and PAC were banned, and as a result radical African
opposition to the measure was largely silenced.

. The proposals for homeland representation left urban Africans
in the cold. They were free, however, to seek political affiliation
with the governments that were to be established in the homelands.
Since 1961, local authorities could also establish elected urban
Bantu councils (now wholly elected) in respect of African urban
residential areas. These councils have remained entirely advisory,
although at the time of their establishment the prospect was held
out that certain decision-making and executive powers could be
conferred. The establishment of councils is not mandatory, and the
rate of establishment has been slow. A move by the Johannesburg
Urban Bantu Council to establish an association of councils on the
same basis as the defunct Urban Advisory Board Congress of the
1930s and 1940s was strongly and successfully resisted by the
government.

Self-governing African Areas

The United Transkeian Territories General Council (1894–1956)
continuously petitioned the government for greater powers, and in
1944 requested it to declare the Transkei "a Union Native Province
or state with Sovereign rights in the administration and govern-

ment of its affairs and people". This request, as well as one of 1946 that the Transkei become a fifth province of the Union, were fruitless.[2]

The subject of self-government was raised again only in 1961. A proposal was accepted by the Transkeian Territorial Authority that a recess committee be appointed "to go into the implications of the granting or otherwise of self-government to this Authority".[3] The proposal further charged the committee with considering (a) the financial implications of the granting of self-government and the different kinds of taxation paid by the Transkeian population; (b) that self-government should in no way tamper with the chieftainship system; (c) the relations between the South African government and the proposed state; (d) the possible date of granting self-government; and (e) the manner of approaching the South African government to effect self-government. The chairman of the Territorial Authority and of the recess committee, Chief K. D. Matanzima, issued a press statement on 7 May 1962 to the effect that independence had not been requested.

Hitherto the entire system of government in the African areas was based on traditional structures, or utilised such structures wherever possible. At one stage the South African authorities, particularly the Prime Minister Dr. H. F. Verwoerd, apparently had a short-lived change of heart on this score. Members of the Executive Committee of the Transkei Territorial Authority, accompanied by a number of chiefs and councillors, met Dr. Verwoerd in Pretoria in December 1961 and a discussion on the possibility of an elected majority in the Transkei Legislative Assembly reportedly took place. A member of the recess committee, Chief S. S. Majeke, later said that "Dr. Verwoerd was against the chiefs being in the majority in this Assembly". It was Chief Kaiser Matanzima, he said, who pressed "that the chiefs should come to this Assembly", and he proposed even less than the present 45 elected members. Majeke said that he himself, Paramount Chief Botha Sigcau, Chief D. D. P. Ndamase and Mr. P. Jozana had opposed Matanzima, and that Verwoerd also "said it would not be true democracy if . . . [the] chiefs should come to this Assembly".[4] In certain Transkeian political circles it is believed that Matanzima successfully contrasted the conservatism and stability of the chiefs against the Transkeian disturbances of 1960, and so won his argument in favour of a minority of elected members. Such a minority has since been accepted in all other homelands. When the Transkeian Territorial Authority finally discussed the draft constitution in December 1962, an amendment to increase the number of elected members to 64 – equal to the 64 ex-officio members – was narrowly defeated by 48 votes to 43.

Following the report of the recess committee, and approval thereof by the Transkeian Territorial Authority in 1962, the Transkei was granted self-government in terms of the Transkei Constitution Act, 1963 (Act No. 48/1963). Thus the pattern was set for the granting of self-government to the other African homelands by the South African government. Transkeian citizenship was created for all Africans born (or who had lived for more than five years) in any one of the Transkeian districts, all Xhosa-speaking Africans outside the Transkei and all Sotho-speaking Africans outside the Transkei who were members of tribes residing in the Transkei. For international purposes Transkeian citizens are regarded as South African citizens.

Legislation passed by the Transkeian government is subject to approval by the State President of South Africa. The system of rural local government was changed in 1965 when the Transkeian government reduced the powers and functions of tribal and regional authorities, and abolished district authorities. The latter type of authority was found only in the Transkei and was a heritage from the old district councils.

The legislative assembly consists of the 5 paramount chiefs of the Transkei, 60 chiefs elected by the chiefs on a district basis from among their own ranks; and 45 members elected by the voters of the Transkei. The number of chiefs and paramount chiefs may at no stage exceed 65 (the number was raised from 64 to 65 by an amendment of the Transkei Constitution Act, in 1971). The 26 districts constitute the electoral divisions for the election of the 45 elected members. The number of members per electoral division depends on the number of registered voters in that particular division. Voters are registered on the principle of universal suffrage. The executive power is vested in a cabinet consisting of the chief minister and six other ministers. The chief minister manages the Department of Finance. The other Departments are Justice, Education, the Interior, Agriculture and Forestry, and Roads and Works. The range of matters falling within the ambit of these departments was increased from time to time, while a new Department of Health with its own minister was added on 1 April 1973.

When drawing up their constitution, the Transkeian leaders and the South African government apparently proceeded on the assumption that there would be no political parties in the territory. Consequently it was stipulated that the members of the cabinet would be elected by the members of the legislative assembly. This ruling made it impossible for the Chief Minister to change members of his cabinet should the necessity arise; consequently the constitution was amended in 1971 (Act No. 31/1971 of the South

African Parliament) to enable the chief minister personally to make changes in his cabinet with the approval of the State President of South Africa. Another consequence of the initial non-party approach was that there was no provision until 1971 for a special allowance for the leader of the opposition.

The Transkei Legislative Assembly appointed a 27-member recess committee at its 1974 session to consider various implications of independence for the Transkei, and to draft a constitution for consideration of the Assembly. At the same time the South African government was requested to grant independence to the Transkei within five years. The recess committee's report was completed by the end of 1974 and negotiations with the South African government well under way.

The following table gives the composition of the respective legislative assemblies and cabinets in the homelands.

TABLE 3.I. COMPOSITION OF LEGISLATIVE ASSEMBLIES AND CABINETS
IN SELF-GOVERNING HOMELANDS

	Legislative Assembly			Cabinet	
Homeland	Elected	Nominated	Elected by L.A.[a]	Appointed by Chief Min.	Minimum no. of chiefs
Transkei	45	65[b]	1[d]	6	0
Ciskei	20	30	6	0	0
Bophuthatswana	24	48	1[d]	5	4[e]
Lebowa	40	60	6	0	4
Gazankulu	26	42	1[d]	5	2[f]
Venda	18	42	1[d]	5	4[c]

(a) The chief ministers of all homelands are elected by the respective legislative assemblies.
(b) Raised from 64 to 65 in 1970. Includes 5 paramount chiefs *ex-officio* and 60 chiefs elected from their own number.
(c) Including the chief minister.
(d) Chief minister only.
(e) Not more than four ministers shall be chiefs, including the chief minister who must be a chief.
(f) At least two and not more than three members of cabinet shall be chiefs.

By 1972, either territorial authorities or legislative assemblies had been established in all the homelands, except the Swazi homeland. In 1968 and 1969 limited executive powers were given to the territorial authorities of Bophuthatswana (Tswana), Basotho Qwaqwa (South Sotho), Ciskei, Lebowa (North Sotho), Venda and Gazankulu (Shangaan) homelands. All these territorial authorities were converted into non-self-governing legislative assemblies in terms of the Bantu Homelands Constitution Act, 1971 (Act No. 21/1971). A Zulu Territorial Authority was established for the first time only in 1970 and consequently non-self-governing legislative assemblies have been granted self-governing status between 1972 and 1973 in Bophuthatswana, Ciskei, Lebowa, Venda and Gazankulu.

A self-governing homeland is entitled to the symbols of its status, such as a flag and a national anthem. Citizens of all the homelands are issued with certificates of citizenship (in terms of the Bantu Homeland Citizenship Act, 1970), but they are also entitled to South African protection in terms of international law. The nature of matters under the jurisdiction of legislative assemblies is evident from the names of the portfolios entrusted to the cabinet: Authority Affairs (Chief Minister) and Finance, Education and Culture, Works, Community Affairs, Agriculture, and Justice. In Basotho Qwaqwa, which is very small, Agriculture and Works form one department and Justice and Community Affairs another, and there are only four portfolios.

The power to appeal or amend South African legislation operative in the homeland is received on the achievement of self-governing status. At the beginning of 1974 the only remaining non-self-governing homelands were KwaZulu, Basotho Qwaqwa and Swazi.

Certain matters are expressly excluded from legislation by homeland legislative assemblies: all matters of a military nature; manufacture of arms, ammunition and explosives; foreign affairs; the presence of a police force of the Republic of South Africa and all related matters; postal, telegraph, telephone, radio and television services; railways, harbours, national roads and civil aviation; the entry of persons other than citizens into the territory concerned; currency, public loans, banking, stock exchanges and financial institutions; customs and excise; and the Bantu Homelands Constitution Act, 1971 (and in the case of the Transkei, the amendment, repeal or substitution of the Transkei Constitution Act, 1963).

A higher court to replace any existing South African court in the homeland may be created by the State President; a Transkeian High Court was established in 1973, with right of appeal to the South African Appeal Court, but none had been created by mid-1974 in any other homeland.

The appointment, discharge, conditions of service, discipline and retirement of persons in the service of the homeland government are controlled by a government service commission in each homeland: it consists of three persons appointed by the cabinet, which retains final responsibility for the appointment and discharge of government servants.

The following table gives some particulars about the physical characteristics of the homelands.

TABLE 3.II. AFRICAN HOMELANDS IN SOUTH AFRCIA

(*Source: Afrika met 'n oogopslag 1973*, Africa Institute, Pretoria)

Homeland	Territory in Hectars (x1,000)	Blocks[a]	Population (de facto)[b] (x1,000) 1970	Population (de jure)[c] (x1,000) 1970	Tribal and Community Authorities	Regional Authorities
Transkei	3,671	2	1,726	2,997	138	9
Ciskei	927	19(4)	525	915	41	9
KwaZulu	3,143	29(10)	2,014	4,018	196	23
Lebowa	2,201	5(3)	1,084	2,097	122	11
Venda	604	3(2)	267	360	26	3
Gazankulu	668	4	265	650	31	3
Bophuthatswana	3,752	19(6)	865	1,680	76	12
Basotho Qwaqwa	46	1	24	1,357	2	2
Swazi Territory	208	2(1)	116	472	14	2

(a) The numbers in brackets refer to the number of territorial units of which each homeland will consist under the South African government's consolidation proposals. For example, it has been proposed that KwaZulu, comprising 29 separate units, be consolidated into 10 units. The final arrangements may of course differ from the proposals.

(b) In homeland only.

(c) Total for South Africa.

The way in which these constitutional enabling laws were put into practice can be briefly outlined through reference to the Lebowa and Bophuthatswana territories.

Chief T. Pilane, a former chairman of the Tswana Territorial Authority and presently leader of the opposition Seoposengwe Party in the Bophuthatswana Legislative Assembly, initiated the constitutional process in Bophuthatswana by tabling a motion with a request for self-government by 1973, at the 1970 session of the Tswana Territorial Authority. Anxious to maintain the initiative, the then Chairman of the Territorial Authority, Chief Lucas

Mangope (subsequently the first Chief Minister), proposed an amendment, which was accepted by Chief Pilane, that no target date should be mentioned and that the executive committee of the Territorial Authority with the aid of a few councillors should negotiate with the South African government and report back to the Territorial Authority. At the opening of the 1971 session of the Territorial Authority, Mangope announced that self-government would be granted. The Bantu Homelands Constitution Act, 1971, was then explained to the councillors, and it was moved by Mangope seconded by Pilane, that the Territorial Authority be converted into a Legislative Assembly, which could then draw up a new constitution preparatory to the granting of self-governing status.

The proposal was accepted and implemented by the South African government. At first, only designations changed; offices and their incumbents remained the same. The change was one involving status rather than organisation. This was made possible by a reorganisation of the Tswana Territorial Authority in 1968 whereby a Tswana government service was created while six embryo government departments were established, each headed by a member of the executive council of the Territorial Authority.

The constitutional committee appointed in 1971 tabled its proposals at the 1972 session (the first) of the Legislative Assembly. It was discussed clause by clause and adopted with minor alterations. Afterwards a unanimous motion called upon the State President to grant self-governing status to the territory on the basis of the new constitution. Self-governing status was conferred on 1 June, 1972 (Procl. No. R131 of 1972); the date of the first general election was set for 4 October 1972 and at the same time the first Legislative Assembly was dissolved (Procl. No. R163 of 1972). A Chief Minister and cabinet was elected shortly after the election. Self-governing status was achieved eleven years after the first Territorial Authority had been established in 1961 under the chairmanship of Chief Pilane.

Lebowa followed much the same path. The first Territorial Authority was established in 1962 with advisory powers only. It consisted of one-third of the members of the 11 regional authorities, and was reconstituted with limited legislative and executive powers in 1969. A government service and six government departments were also established. The next step was the creation of a Legislative Assembly with increased powers in 1971. Self-governing status was conferred on 2 October 1972; the first general election was held on 11 April, 1973, and the first Chief Minister for the new self-governing territory was elected shortly afterwards, on 9 May.

Elections in all homelands followed basically the same pattern, the main difference among them being the compilation of a voters' list for the Transkei only.

For the purposes of electing the 45 elected members of the Transkeian Legislative Assembly all Transkeian Africans over 21 years of age and all Transkeian African taxpayers over 18 became eligible to vote. Only a voter could be elected to the Legislative Assembly. A voters' list had been compiled by the South African Department of Bantu Administration and Development in preparation for the first election in November 1963, and has since then been maintained by the Transkeian Department of Internal Affairs. For the first election 880,425 voters were registered, i.e. about three-quarters of the possible total. About 250,000 voters were registered outside the Transkei, each of them in respect of a particular electoral division, determined on the basis of his descent. The Transkei was divided into nine electoral divisions – each of the nine regional authority areas forming an electoral division. As a result the number of voters in electoral divisions varied considerably, the smallest being Umzimkulu division with about 37,600 voters, and the largest Qaukeni division with about 170,000 voters. For the second general election, which took place in 1968, electoral divisions were established in respect of each of the 26 administrative districts of the Transkei. A much more even distribution of voters was obtained. Almost half (twelve) of the electoral divisions had between 30,000 and 40,000 voters; whereas the smallest division (Port St. John's) had 16,416 voters, and the largest division (Engcobo) 56,494 voters. The number of members to be elected per division is calculated as follows:

$$\frac{\text{Total number of registered voters}}{45} = X$$

(45 being the total number of elected members in the assembly)

$$\frac{\text{Registered voters in the division}}{X} = Y$$

(Y is then added, but fractions are discarded. If the total of Y is less than 45 the highest fractions are used to bring the total up to 45.)

In self-governing territories other than the Transkei, no voters' lists are compiled. In each the electoral divisions coincide with the administrative district boundaries. The number of elected members, as well as the number of chiefs (the totals being agreed during the preceding constitutional discussions), are determined for each electoral division in proportion to the population of the district as determined in the 1970 general census. No fixed formula is used in calculating these numbers. The number of possible voters staying outside the territory is not taken into account. In the case of Bophuthatswana it was decided to allow each of the twelve electoral divisions to return two elected members, irrespective of the size of its population.

People wishing to cast a vote could register as voters at any time until, and including, the day of the election. The franchise is open to all citizens of the particular territory who are over 18 years of age. Because the issuing of citizenship certificates in terms of the Bantu Homelands Citizenship Act, 1970, has lagged far behind schedule, registered voters therefore received a stamp in their reference books to the effect that they had been registered as such. Ciskeian voters had to register before a specified date in order that the number of elected members in each constituency might be calculated.

Urban Areas

In White urban areas African residents have, since 1923, elected native (later, Bantu) advisory boards to advise the White urban local authorities on matters relating to the African population (Native Urban Areas Act, 1923). The purely advisory duties in this case also led to frustration, and the further establishment of advisory boards was terminated in 1961 in favour of urban Bantu councils (Urban Bantu Councils Act, 1961). Members of these councils are elected by urban residents on an ethnic basis. The intention was that the councils should participate in urban local government, but only advisory duties have so far been allocated to them.

Where urban conditions develop in African homelands – such as at Mdantsane in the Ciskei and Ga-Rankuwa in Bophuthatswana – the townships are administered by the local magistrate or, in the case of larger townships, by a townships manager assisted by superintendents. In well-established towns town councils are elected. These councils may be allocated full local government powers, but so far they have received only advisory duties (Procl. No. 293/1962 as amended).

Although the Transkei received self-governing powers in 1963 the 26 towns – or district headquarters – fell outside the jurisdiction of the Transkei government, remaining White urban areas. Since 1965 almost all Transkeian towns have been declared Bantu areas, but still under republican jurisdiction. The larger towns of Umtata, Butterworth, Umzimkulu, Engcobo, and Idutywa have fairly large White populations and remained largely White area, whereas Matatiele and Port St. John's fell just outside the Transkei's territory. To provide for local government in the remaining 19

Transkeian towns (where White village management boards and town councils have been abolished) a Transkei Townships Board was established in 1970. The Board is responsible to the South African Minister for Bantu Administration and Development and is an all-White body. Its duties are performed through local committees appointed by the Board in every town. The majority of committees have African members only.

Outside the homelands the African population is subject to the rule of the South African government, without representation. The homeland governments make regular representations to the South African government on behalf of their citizens in White areas. Africans may also form interest groups and political organisations, which are not necessarily homeland-oriented, as long as the provisions of certain acts of Parliament are not contravened (see below).

Certain specified political organisations have been banned, as will be pointed out below. African trade unions may be formed but are not allowed to register as such and thus remain without official standing. The general embargo on strikes by Africans has been lifted by the Bantu Labour Relations Regulation Amendment Act, 1973 (Act No. 70/1973), which conceded a qualified right to strike in cases where all attempts through existing machinery, provided under the Act, have failed to produce a settlement. South African industrial legislation is applicable to the homelands, and the administering authority (i.e. either the homeland government or the South African government) has been determined under agreement between the South African and the homeland governments. Homeland governments administer the Apprenticeship Act, 1944 (Act No. 37/1944), and the Wage Act, 1957 (Act No. 5/1957), whereas the South African government through its Department of Labour administers the Industrial Conciliation Act (which prohibits the registration of African trade unions), and the Bantu Labour Relations Regulation Amendment Act, 1970. Agreements under the Industrial Conciliation Act pertaining to conditions of service and workers' benefits and the Wage Act were suspended on 20 March 1970 in respect of all African workers in the homelands. The suspension of these agreements, which were applicable to White and Black workers without discrimination, enabled homeland governments to initiate new conditions of service and wages.

In 1960 the mainly urban Pan Africanist Congress and the African National Congress were declared unlawful in terms of the Unlawful Organisations Act, 1960. Soon afterwards various new related legislative measures were introduced. The General Law Amendment Act of 1962 circumscribed the offence of sabotage, and provided for severe penalties. The system of house arrest was introduced, and the government's powers to control the activities of banned and listed persons were strengthened.

The General Law Amendment Act of 1963 enabled the authorities to declare Umkhonto we Sizwe, the Congress of Democrats, Yu Chi Chan Club and Poqo to be unlawful. Provision was made in the General Law Amendment Act of 1963, 1965 and 1966, and the Terrorism Act of 1967, for the arrest without warrant, and detention for interrogation of persons suspected of committing or having information about specified types of offences. It was rendered an offence to have undergone training or obtained information outside the Republic which could be of use in furthering the aims of communism or of an unlawful organisation. It also became unlawful to publish the utterances or writings of people under banning orders without the permission of the Minister of Justice. Security laws are also applicable to the homelands.

In African areas meetings of more than ten people require the consent of the Bantu Affairs Commissioner or magistrate. Domestic and sports meetings, meetings of local authorities, and gatherings for official administrative purposes, lawful instruction, and statutory bodies are not affected. These regulations (Procl. No. R268/1968) are not applicable to the Transkei, where a similar measure is in force, viz. Proclamation No. R400 of 1960, which also provides for detention without trial under certain circumstances.[5]

With the creation of a Coloured Persons' Representative Council (CRC) in 1970, the Coloureds' representation in the House of Assembly and the Cape Provincial Council was abolished. To prevent White political parties participating in the election of the 20 elected members of the CRC the Prohibition of Political Interference Act was adopted. The Act rendered racially mixed political parties illegal, and prevented people from one racial group to actively promote the candidature of a person of another race in any election.

Conclusion

By way of summary, the position of Africans in respect of representation on central and local government bodies is as follows: They have no representation whatsoever in the South African House of Assembly and Senate, or any of the provincial councils. With the exception of the Swazi ethnic group, legislative assemblies have been established in all the homelands, representing the members of the respective ethnic groups within and outside the homelands. In fact however, Africans outside homelands avail themselves only to a limited extent of these representative facilities.

In respect of local government in the homelands, rural local government bodies have been set up by the Bantu Authorities Act, 1951, and the Transkei Authorities Act, 1965. They are organised in two tiers, with tribal and community authorities on the lowest level, consisting mainly of chiefs, headmen, their counsellors and some elected members. The tribal and community authorities are represented on regional authorities, which have mainly advisory duties. Urban local government in the homelands is mostly in the hands of government officials, assisted by elected town councils with mainly advisory duties; whereas in the Transkei, urban local government falls under the Transkei Townships Board which is assisted locally by local committees.

Urban local government outside homelands is in the hands of elected White local authorities which co-operate (in respect of African affairs) with government-appointed urban Bantu affairs administration boards. These boards are advised by elected urban Bantu councils and advisory Bantu committees. Africans in White urban areas have no decision-making and executive functions. In White rural areas there is no provision for participation by Africans in local government, and there are also no advisory African bodies.

REFERENCES

1. Promotion of Bantu Self-government Act, 1959.
2. United Transkeian Territories General Council, *Proceedings and Reports*, 1944, p. 81, and 1946, p. 83.
3. Transkei Territorial Authority, *Proceedings and Reports*, 1961, p. 82.
4. Transkei Government, *Hansard*, 1966, pp. 230, 237. Also see Transkei Government, *Hansard*, 1964, pp. 249–50.
5. For a full description of security laws, see M. Horrell, *Action, Reaction and Counteraction*, Johannesburg, S.A. Institute of Race Relations, 1971.

4

AFRICAN POLITICAL REVIVAL

Since the banning of several African political organisations in the early 1960s new political parties have been established by Africans who wished to utilise the homeland governments as political platforms, and by those who wished to oppose all aspects of South African government policy. New non-political organisations came into being, while others continued to function after the cataclysmic years of the Defiance Campaign and its aftermath.

In this chapter we examine primarily the new political organisations, and secondarily voluntary associations. Because of its explicit political objectives the South African Students' Organisation (Saso) is treated as a political organisation.

Some Determinants

Whereas the majority of political organisations are homeland-based parties, the Black People's Convention (BPC) and Saso are national organisations in all respects. The main stimulus for their formation was a reaction against White minority rule of South Africa, which became so acute that it was transformed into an exclusivism which caused them to avoid all contact with Whites, White-controlled organisations, and even Blacks who were prepared to pursue a career in government employment or supported the homeland governments. They were formed without any hope of assisting in the recruitment of government leaders, and their exclusivist attitude debarred them from effective participation in policy formulation in South Africa and the African homelands.

Their formation was made possible by the increasing tide of Black consciousness among Blacks who saw no future for themselves in the homelands by virtue of the permanent necessity for them to earn a living in the White area. Their overriding objectives of Black unity and self-realisation in various fields led them to realise that they would only succeed if their activities permeated to all levels of Black society. They were accordingly the first political organisations in South African history consistently to employ voluntary associations to build a following and achieve their objectives. The secularisation of African life is thus an important requisite for their success. Little has resulted from their initial attempts to extend into rural tribal areas where traditional social structures remain fairly strong.

On the other hand, the homeland-based parties, although critical of South African government policy, employ the homeland constitutions as political platforms. With homeland citizens dispersed over the whole of South Africa, they are in fact also South African national organisations, but tend to have a rural and traditional orientation.

Ironically, when the first homeland constitution (for the Transkei) was drafted, it was assumed by South African and Transkei government leaders that there would be no political parties. The vague assumption that government would be by a traditionally related system of general consent was reflected in the stipulation that all cabinet members could be appointed and dismissed by a majority vote of the legislative assembly only. After parties had been established, this practice became obsolete. A new assumption – that the leader of the governing party enjoyed the confidence of the majority of the Legislative Assembly – was embodied in an amendment of the constitution in 1971 that ministers could be appointed and dismissed by the Chief Minister. This practice is now followed in most homelands.

Several factors contributed towards the formation of political parties in the homelands. The establishment of Legislative Assemblies and the resultant general elections provided the initial stimulus for a concentration of recruitment efforts by candidates. In Bophuthatswana, Venda and KwaZulu one or more political parties were formed before elections took place; in the Transkei, Ciskei, and Lebowa, political parties were established only after the first general elections. Pacts formed before the first elections in the latter three territories afterwards formed the nuclei of parties. The incumbent Venda government leaders formed an election pact without formal structure. Almost six months after the election, this pact led to the establishment of a political party. In all territories there was a correlation between the organisational rigour of these slates of candidates and their measure of success.

Conflicting aspirations for leadership were an important factor in the crystallisation of opposing groups – and ultimately of parties. In Bophuthatswana, Lebowa and the Ciskei, conflicts of personality were the most important causes of political opposition, and overshadowed ideological and policy matters. In KwaZulu and Gazankulu no serious opposition exists for the incumbent governments (respectively under the leadership of Buthelezi and Ntsanwisi). Opposing parties were established in KwaZulu in the face of a non-party approach by the government leaders. Increasing opposition and the necessities accompanying a general election campaign could bring to fruition plans to establish a party supporting the government of KwaZulu. The first general election of Gazankulu passed (October 1973) without political parties or election pacts being formed amid great satisfaction over the incumbent government of Ntsanwisi and unanimity in respect of his re-election as Chief Minister.

In the Transkei in 1963 two able candidates contested the election for Chief Minister after a long period of co-operation within the Transkei Territorial Authority. Their different attitudes towards separate development played a decisive role. Policy differences also led to the establishment of the Transkei People's Freedom Party under S. M. Sinaba in 1968. In other homelands ideological and serious policy differences were of less importance, although in Venda the Venda Independence People's Party is less amenable to compromising with separate development than the Venda National Party, and does not regard the Venda as a separate nation but as a part of the African nation; the division here between traditionalists and modernists, more than anything else, led to the establishment of different parties. In Lebowa, Collins Ramusi, one of the cabinet ministers, in his pre-election manifesto declared his support for racial integration, illustrating the extent to which homeland leaders are prepared to compromise within the framework of separate development. Ramusi's raising of multi-racialism as an issue drew no response from the later leader of the opposition in Lebowa, Chief M. M. Matlala, unlike the Transkei leaders who made this the main bone of contention.

Incentives which originated outside the African community, combined with stimuli initiated by and inside the African community promoted the establishment of new political organisations since the beginning of the 1960s. External incentives were provided under the auspices of separate development in the form of homeland governments and related institutions which were free from police interference. Secondly, there were inernal stimuli, such as the urgent political need within the African community for self-expression, and the sense of imminent crisis in respect of Black identity and unity which were considered in some quarters to be threatened by the South African "system".

There is a wide gulf between political organisations based on internal stimuli only (BPC and Saso), and those based on internal and external stimuli (the homeland parties). This is clear from the homeland parties' willingness to work within the framework of separate development (although with certain misgivings), their emphasis on African unity, the latent africanism in their ranks, and the relative esteem in which they hold banned ANC and PAC leaders. Whereas they differ in respect of each of these matters with BPC and Saso their greatly similar social and economic objectives makes future rapprochement a possibility.

Whereas the decade following 1963 was characterised by the proliferation of African political organisations, it is more than possible that the African political configuration will return in the next decade to the former pattern of one or two major national political organisations, a new feature being the greater involvement of voluntary associations in the achievement of political objectives.

Transkei

To all appearances Paramount Chief Kaiser Matanzima, leader of the Transkei National Independence Party, and Paramount Chief Victor Poto, first leader of the Democratic Party, co-operated closely before the granting of self-government to the Transkei. At that time Matanzima was chairman of the Transkei Territorial Authority and Poto a member of the executive committee and perhaps the most respected member of the Territorial Authority. Both were members of the Authority's recess committee appointed in 1961 to investigate the possibility of self-government for the Transkei. Cordial relations between them continued until the last session of the Territorial Authority in May 1963. Both supported the draft constitution through all stages of consultation with the Territorial Authority. After the recommendations of the recess committee had been finalised and approved by the Authority, a bill containing the proposals was drafted and submitted to the Territorial Authority in December 1962. Its speedy approval was due mainly to Poto's exhortations, made at a social function for members at the end of the first day of the session at which he received the deferential support of Matanzima.

At the last session of the Transkei Territorial Authority on 17 May 1963, a motion of appreciation to Poto as "the senior traditional leader" in the Transkei was tabled by George Matanzima (later Justice Minister) to thank him for the "manner in which he has preserved the dignity of chieftainship . . . as a result of which the Government resuscitated the institution. . . ." The motion was supported by Kaiser Matanzima, who said he hoped that Poto would have "a very important position in the Government of the Transkei". They also expressed respect and appreciation towards

Poto in response to the motion by the Transkei Chief Magistrate one of whose remarks was: "It is my sincere wish and the wish of the Government that he has many long years ahead of him to guide his people in the Transkei."[1]

When it was rumoured that Poto and some supporters had met that afternoon (17 May) to discuss an approach to the coming general election, the Chief Magistrate's words earlier in the day were then seen as implying support from the South African government for Poto as future Transkei Chief Minister, and that an early attempt would be made to promote his candidature. This date marks the open political parting of ways between Matanzima and Poto, although their respective parties were established almost a year later. Their activities as members of the constitutional recess committee laid bare earlier political differences. At the time this was not publicly known and Poto supported the recess committee's report.

Significantly, the motion which had led to the establishment of the recess committee and the ultimate granting of self-government was introduced in the Territorial Authority by L. Maninjwa, a counsellor of Poto and later his deputy in the legislative assembly. During its deliberations the committee members were handed a draft constitution drawn up by Matanzima. S. S. Majeke, supported by Poto, questioned whether the draft would be acceptable to the people, as well as its undertones of support for separate development. However, Matanzima had grasped the initiative and maintained it ever since. Majeke, who later became a leading member of Poto's Democratic Party, and Matanzima also differed over the procedure for the finalising of the recess committee report. According to Majeke, Matanzima proposed even less than the present 45 elected members of the legislative assembly, and was even opposed on this issue by the Prime Minister, H. F. Verwoerd, when he met the committee in Pretoria, as well as by Paramount Chief Botha Sigcau, Chief D. D. P. Ndamase, Mr. P. Jozana, Chief S. S. Majeke and other members of the committee. There is some difference of opinion as to what actually happened, and the Transkei Minister of Agriculture, Madikizela, thought that Verwoerd did not advocate a majority of elected members[2]— which, at least, can be assumed as correct, although it seems possible that Verwoerd was in favour of an equal number of elected and *ex-officio* members. Matanzima won his point for a majority of chiefs with the argument that during the 1960 unrest in Eastern Pondoland the chiefs had provided stability and continuity, but he had to settle for 45 elected members as well.

—Transkei National Independence Party

The election campaign which started with nomination of candidates on 2 October, and culminated in the first Transkei general election on 20 November 1963, provided the platform for the first overt political divisions in the Transkei which formed the bases of the subsequent political parties. The manifestos of most candidates did not reflect their adherence to the Poto-faction or the Matanzima faction. On the whole basic educational and economic needs were stressed, and a few candidates expressed their support either for multi-racialism or separate development, thus implying support either for Poto or for Matanzima. By this time Poto had come out firmly in favour of a multi-racial South Africa and rejected a separate Transkei state. In spite of the relatively uncommitted attitude of many candidates, it was clear early in the election campaign that voters would be required to select candidates on the basis of their support for either Poto or Matanzima.

Matanzima and Poto travelled extensively in the Transkei and the most populous White areas, seeking support among candidates and voters. In the beginning of October Matanzima challenged Poto to agree that the loser in the election for Chief Minister should not make himself available for another cabinet post (all of which at that time were elective). Acceptance of Matanzima's proposal would have implied a step nearer to a conventional party system, but Poto refused, saying that the assembly could alter the constitution if it wished. Thus Matanzima tried to intimidate Poto and his followers with a winner-takes-all attitude, while Poto wanted to hold out the possibility of recalcitrant cabinet ministers. Ten days later, towards the end of October, Matanzima added that no emigrant Tembu would accept a cabinet post under Poto. Matanzima's fortunes received an important stimulus when Paramount Chief Botha Sigcau of Eastern Pondoland declared himself in favour of separate development on 11 November. Hitherto he had refused to allow Poto and Matanzima in his area for canvassing on the grounds that their electors would make up their minds on election day. There was an earlier possibility that Sigcau might support Poto in return for the latter's support for Sigcau's accession to the Eastern Pondo paramountcy in the early 1940s. The Paramount Chief of the Tembu (second largest group after the Eastern Pondo), Sabata Dalindyebo, expressed his preference for Poto at an early stage and asked his people to support candidates favouring Poto. In Eastern Pondoland, however, the election produced several successful candidates who previously opposed the paramountcy of Sigcau, and who subsequently supported Poto and the Democratic Party. Slates of candidates supporting Poto and Matanzima were formed and were particularly successful in the constituencies of Emigrant Tembuland (which went to Matanzima), and Dalidyebo and Fingo (which went to Poto).

About two-thirds of the elected members supported Poto, and Matanzima had to rely on the chiefs for his main support. The day before the election of the Chief Minister and cabinet, on 5 December 1963, Matanzima and his known followers held a meeting with a view to establishing a political party. The Poto faction held a similar meeting on 9 December. Matanzima and the Eastern Pondo chiefs spent the night of 5 December at the official guest-house of the Commissioner-General for the Xhosa National Unit, and most other chiefs paid them a visit during the evening. The next day, the chiefs' support ensured Matanzima's election as Chief Minister. A factor which was strongly in Matanzima's favour was the belief among many chiefs that only his policy would be tolerated by the South African government.

The results of the election on 6 December show that Matanzima could still not be sure of the exact extent of his support. He received 54 votes (against Poto's 49), while four of the cabinet members proposed by him received 56 votes, and one 55 votes. Three members were absent: one had died, one had been injured, one was absent from the Transkei; two ballots were rejected; and one member refrained from voting. In an assembly of 109 members, Matanzima declared that neither he nor Poto knew who their supporters exactly were. He accordingly invited possible supporters to attend a meeting in support of his policy. At the meeting on 14 February, a committee was appointed to establish a governing party. On 11 March, the party's name was made known and a draft programme of principles was released. On 23 April the Transkei National Independence Party's first and inaugural congress was held at Umtata.

—The Democratic Party

As pointed out above, the Poto faction started planning for the 1963 election campaign six months before the election, namely in May 1963. During the election campaign certain candidates expressed their preference for Poto and his policy of multi-racialism, especially in the constituencies of Nyanda (where he is the Paramount Chief) and Dalindyebo. He also received substantial support from candidates in Eastern Pondoland (Qaukeni), where the chiefs tended to support Matanzima. Four candidates in Matanzima's home constituency, Emigrant Tembuland, also supported multi-racialism, but were not elected.

As the elder paramount chief in the Transkei, and personally widely respected by White and Black, Poto was indeed the strongest possible opponent for Matanzima. His long exprience since 1918 as member of Transkei local governing bodies and of the Native Representative Council from 1937 until 1945 made him a particularly suitable candidate. His support for various government measures such as Bantu authorities, modern agricultural practices and the new constitution at first gave the impression that he was in favour of separate development. His emergence as a proponent of multi-racialism generated much suspicion; it was felt in particular that he was acting on behalf of White economic interests in the Transkei. Had he been less definite about multi-racialism he would probably have been elected Chief Minister, and the party political dispensation in the Transkei would have been very different.

In his election manifesto of 1963 he declared himself in favour of political parties "which have the interests of our people at heart". His was the first party to be formally established – one week before the TNIP, (on 7 February 1964. The establishment of the Democratic Party resulted from the work of an action committee under the chairmanship of K. M. N. Guzana (Poto's successor as leader), which was appointed on 4 January 1964. The first DP congress was held at Umtata on 6 April 1964.

—Eastern Pondoland Peoples' Party

According to G. M. Carter, the African National Congress decided at a meeting in Botswana not to participate in the Transkei general election of 1963, but it possibly helped to establish the Eastern Pondoland Peoples' Party in August 1963. The secretary, M. S. Mdingi, and seven other members were nominated as candidates in the Qaukeni constituency. Mdingi was, however, taken into custody by the South African police shortly after nomination and was held for the duration of the election campaign.[3] This apparently spelled the end for a party which was regarded by some Transkei politicians as a subterfuge used by communists.[4]

—The Transkei People's Freedom Party

The Transkei Peoples' Freedom Party was established by S. M. Sinaba, first vice-chairman of the TNIP and its chief whip in the legislative assembly. Sinaba, who was a member of the assembly for Maluti, called a regional conference of the TNIP in January 1966 in the Maluti region. Sinaba said that the conference would be attended by the cabinet ministers George Matanzima and Jeremiah Moshesh (the latter also from Maluti), but in the end neither did so. At this conference a motion was adopted asking immediate independence for the Transkei. Sinaba's claim that he had a mandate from his voters to ask for independence was rejected by the TNIP. After this rejection, Sinaba felt compelled to resign from the TNIP and as chief whip in the assembly.

In Umtata on 21 May 1966, the TPFP called a national convention to mark its launching, which was attended by about 300 people, and because those people were mostly labourers, there was speculation that the TPFP would be converted into a labour party for the Transkei. Although Sinaba claimed the secret support of several members of the Legislative Assembly, his motion calling for independence only received the support of another member for Maluti, who belonged to the DP, namely the Rev. B. S. Rajuili, and the party never gained significant support; in 1968 it was joined by an elected DP member for Qaukeni, C. Diko. Its condidates were all defeated in the 1968 general election and the Flagstaff by-election of 1969, and the fact that the TPFP leaders disappeared from the political scene (except for Kobo, who soon afterwards became a prominent DP supporter, and Diko, who joined the TNIP) finally ended speculation that the TPFP had been a political flyer of the TNIP in order to determine the political climate in respect of the independence issue.

—*Transkei Peoples' Democratic Party*

The TPDP was established in February 1967 by T. M. Vanqa, a refuse truck driver in East London. Its founding members were all former DP supporters who regarded the DP as no longer representative of the African population, and objected to the leadership of Guzana. The party was in favour of a universal franchise and an upper house for chiefs in the TLA. It never participated in an election, but supported an independent candidate in the by-election of 1967 in Dalindyebo.

Following discussions between Vanqa and Sinaba the TPDP was dissolved on 28 April 1968, and members were asked to join the TPFP. The latter did not apparently benefit from this, as the TPDP did not operate outside East London's Duncan Village. The main objective of the merger was to oppose and "break" the DP.[5]

Bophuthatswana

No great policy differences existed between the Bophuthatswana National Party (BNP) and the Seoposengwe Party (SP), which were respectively under the leadership of Chief Minister Lucas Mangope and Chief Tidimane Pilane. Both leaders acknowledged that personality differences were at the root of their political differences and that they agreed on basic policy issues, except to some extent over the proposed federation for African homelands. The most serious differences were due to the priority which the BNP gave to the establishment of a university, and which was not shared by the SP, and the BNP's insistence that all people in Bophuthatswana should assume Tswana identity, whereas the SP would not enforce ethnic integration.

The first serious division between Pilane and Mangope was in 1966 when Pilane, then chairman of the Tswana Territorial Authority, was in favour of requesting self-government, whereas Mangope, the vice-chairman, maintained that his people were "not trained".[6] Mangope's volte-face on the self-government issue, when he succeeded Pilane as chairman in 1968, was deeply resented, and Pilane and his followers refused nomination for any offices in the Territorial Authority and so constituted an informal and very loose opposition. Never openly attacking each other, both continuously strove to maintain the lead and initiative over important issues, e.g. education, self-government, and land. Differences in approach and personality between the soft-spoken and apparently conciliatory Mangope, and the more outspoken but less articulate Pilane were obvious, and their establishment of opposing political parties came as no great surprise.

—Bophuthatswana National Party

The governing Bophuthatswana National Party had not yet been established at the time of the nomination (on 2 August 1972) of candidates for the first general election scheduled for 4 October 1972. The appointment of ex-officio members of the Legislative Assembly by the various regional authorities and certain tribal authorities had been completed (on 14 July) before the party was established.

Mangope had committed himself immediately before the nomination against the establishment of political parties, and so lost initiative. It was known that the Pilane faction had considered forming a party, but it was thought that "they would not have the guts" actually to do so, and that a stand by Mangope against parties would effectively detain them. The establishment of the SP thus caught the Mangope faction off guard. Some candidates supporting Mangope were even allowed to oppose one another in several constituencies.

The Mangope faction was forced to follow the SP's lead, and to canvass and select candidates. It established the BNP only eight days after the SP, and it appears that some preparations had been made for an emergency of this nature. Even before the SP's establishment, Mangope had warned that if an opposition party was established, it would have to bear the consequences: it would be treated as an opposition. The meaning of this warning was not entirely clear, except that it heralded the end of the non-party approach, and of attempts to accommodate Pilane supporters in the government hierarchy. A notable attempt in this direction was the offer to S. J. Lesolang, a leading member of the Pilane faction, in May 1970 of membership of the Bophuthatswana Public Service Commission. Lesolang refused and later became deputy leader of the SP.

The BNP was established on 6 August 1972 at the initiative of Mangope, who had called a meeting for this purpose. He said that for him there was "no alternative but to form another party on the condition, though, that its basis is an attempt to unify the Tswana (Bophuthatswana)".[7] Immediately after the BNP's establishment the new party executive, 41 of the appointed members of the Legislative Assembly, and all candidates supporting the party met at Mafeking to select the official BNP candidates. It was decided to return the deposits of those candidates who were not selected. Some of them resented these measures and decided to stand as independents to oppose the official candidates.

—Bophuthatswana Democratic Party

A split developed in the ranks of the BNP, the two factions headed by Chief Minister Mangope and Chief H. Maseloane, the Minister of Internal Affairs. After unsuccessfully trying to dismiss Maseloane from the cabinet (with the State President refusing to accede to Mangope's request, presumably on the grounds that it was not well enough motivated), Mangope was faced with a motion of no confidence in the Legislative Assembly, introduced by two leading members of the BNP. It appeared that the motion had the support of cabinet members Maseloane and Toto. Before it was brought to a vote it was withdrawn. Thereupon Mangope dismissed Maseloane and Toto from the BNP, but they were reinstated by order of the Supreme Court in September 1974. Mangope then decided to resign from the BNP and established the Bophuthatswana Democratic Party. He was joined by the majority of BNP members and in a special session of the Legislative Assembly in December 1974 obtained a motion of confidence with 35 votes against 23. Maseloane remained in charge of the BNP.

—Seoposengwe Party

With the establishment of the first Legislative Assembly and the conferring of limited self-government in 1971, the Pilane faction for the first time considered the establishment of an opposition party. These thoughts did not crystallise until 3 June 1972 when a private meeting of Pilane supporters was held at Ga-Rankuwa, near Pretoria, where Pilane was asked to form an opposition party. This meeting was preceded by a meeting at Mafeking during the 1972 session of the Legislative Assembly where the final decision in favour of a party was taken. The leading persons in the Pilane faction at this time besides Pilane himself were Messrs. S. J. Lesolang, Moliti, Mohatshe and Motlhabani, all prominent supporters of the present Seoposengwe Party. From 3 June onwards the SP gradually took shape. The formal establishment took place on 29 July 1972 at Saulspoort, the home of Chief Pilane. The meeting was attended by supporters from various districts of Bophuthatswana, and White urban areas.

—Tswana National Party and Progressive Party

M. N. Tsoke, who on nomination day supported the Mangope faction and was later excluded from the BNP list of candidates, later identified himself as a candidate for the Progressive Party in the Odi constituency. The party existed in name only and after the election disappeared from the scene.

The Tswana National Party was established by Lloyd Ndaba, a Zulu inhabitant of Soweto, Johannesburg, whose house is the headquarters of a number of ethnic political parties, e.g. the Zulu National Party, the Lebowa National Party and the Tswana National Party. Most of these parties appear to be a one-man effort by Ndaba, who professes to support separate development. In the Bophuthatswana general election Mrs. M. R. Modise was at first the only candidate of the Tswana National Party, later to be jointed by Mrs. Tswai. Ndaba assisted with advice and the distribution of pamphlets.

Ciskei

Although two parties were established in 1968 and 1972 respectively they remained insignificant for all practical purposes. The governing Ciskei National Independence Party (CNIP) and the opposition Ciskei National Party (CNP) crystallised towards the election of a new Chief Minister in May 1973 – three months after the first Ciskei general election of February 1973. Two opposing groups were already discernible immediately before the election, respectively under the leadership of L. L. Sebe and J. Mabandla. Neither group was clearly defined, although it became evident after the election that both groups (especially the Sebe group) had made considerable preparations to ensure the solidarity of its supporting candidates.

Candidates for the election were generally not overtly in favour of the one or the other person for the post of Chief Minister, with the exception of those previously included in the Sebe group. Even policy statements by the two candidates and their supporters showed almost no differences. The main differences were in personality and image. Chief Mabandla's image was that of a timid leader who was anxious to co-operate with the South African Government, while Sebe was the man who had achieved considerable professional status as inspector of schools and cabinet minister through hard work and a dynamic approach. It was also believed that he would more readily oppose the South African government if the need arose.

Tribal divisions formed the basis of political allegiance from the early stages of the election campaign. The Rarabe, Tembu and Fingo tribes each had an almost equal number of voters. The Fingos had a slight majority of about 4 per cent over the Rarabes, and the Rarabes even less than that over the Tembus. A local estimate which accounted for most Ciskeian voters, put the number of Fingo voters at 124,000, Rarabe at 116,000, Tembu at 113,000, and Basotho at 18,000.[8] The political allegiance of the Tembus and Basotho was not clearly crystallised but in the event it appeared that the Tembus tended to support the Sebe group, while the Basotho were divided between the Mabandla group and Sebe group.

Ciskei National Independence Party

The first task of L. L. Sebe in his ascent to the chief ministership was to consolidate his position within the Rarabe tribe. His task was difficult because the Rarabe Paramount Chief, Mxolisi Sandile, supported Mabandla for the post of Chief Minister, and Sandile's adviser, Sangotsha, who was also secretary of the tribe, was an equally staunch supporter. When Sangotsha's service as tribal secretary was terminated – reportedly due to Sebe's influence – the position of Sebe within the Rarabe tribe was considerably strengthened, and it was taken for granted that he would be a contender for the chief ministership. After the general election, Sangotsha acknowledged that they had lost, but pointed out the importance of the position as counsellor he held at the Paramount Chief's Great Place.[9]

The first indication that Sebe would contest the chief ministership came in October 1972. His "demotion" by Mabandla in November 1971 from the Ministry of Education to that of Agriculture caused some dissatisfaction among Rarabes, and when he returned

from a visit to the U.S.A. in October 1972, the praise-singer*
at the reception, Mr. Burns-Ncamashe (later Minister of Education)
proclaimed that Sebe would be the next Chief Minister. Mabandla
did not attend the reception.[10]

An election pact was carefully planned before nomination day
by 17 candidates in 7 of the 9 consituencies under the leadership
of Sebe. This step gave the Sebe group an organisational advantage
and contributed to its success; it was forerunner of the CNIP.
When the election result was made known, Sebe could claim a victory of 13 out of 20 members. Intensive canvassing of the 50 legislative assembly members (20 elected and 30 *ex-officio* chiefs) followed
preparatory to the election of a Chief Minister.

The first indication that his group would form a party was given
by Sebe in the middle of March 1973. He envisaged a party based
on the broad principles of separate devolopment, to be formed
after the election of the cabinet on 21 May. On 22 May the new
party was established, with Sebe as its leader.

—Ciskei National Party

The CNP was launched before the CNIP, and before the election of
a new Chief Minister. On April 24 it was announced that Chief
J. Mabandla would lead the new party, and that an interim committee had been appointed. It was declared that it had become necessary to form the party during the election campaign, as a result of
the enhanced constitutional status of the Ciskei, and the necessity
to owe allegiance to a body of principles. The party also hoped to
reconcile the aspirations and interests of traditional leaders and
"professional politicians".

The CNP was established after the proposed establishment of the
CNIP had been announced; this was apparently an attempt by the
Mabandla group to invigorate its canvassing campaign over the
election of a Chief Minister. However, the strength which the Sebe
group acquired during the election campaign successfully carried
it through the rigorous canvassing of votes for Sebe as Chief Minister.

—Bantu Nationalist Conservative Party

Established on 15 December 1968, the BNCP was the first political
party in the Ciskei. Its leader was, and remains,† Mr S. T. Bokwe,

---

* In traditional societies the retinue of dignitaries (chiefs and paramount
chiefs) included a praise-singer who had to extoll the virtues of his master
in self-composed songs, usually delivered at large gatherings. Nowadays
this honour is often extended to non-traditional dignitaries, and praise-
singing is seldom a specialised occupation.

† At the time of going to press.

a trader of Zwelitsha and Alice. An immediate objective was to block any attempt to amalgamate the Transkei and Ciskei, although the party was not against federal ties. In pursuit of its objective of a federation of African states in South Africa, the party attempted to establish itself in various other homelands, but in this it has had no success.

Mr. Bokwe and Mr. J. Mfaxa, the BNCP's only candidates in the Ciskei general election of 1973 (in the Victoria East and Herschel constituencies respectively), were unsuccessful.

—Labour Party and other Groups

Shortly before the Ciskei general election in February 1973, three candidates in the Glen Grey constituency announced that they had formed a Labour Party. They were Messrs. J. H. Saliwa, M. E. Dumezweni and W. O. Mhlom. Of the three only Saliwa was elected, and nothing further was heard of the Labour Party; indeed Saliwa was shortly afterwards taken on to the interim committee of the Ciskei National Party.

The only candidate in the election of 1973 who explicitly rejected separate development, Mr. L. D. Guzana (brother of the leader of the Transkei opposition Democratic Party, Mr. K. M. N. Guzana), announced before the election that he would form an opposition party after the election of a Chief Minister, based on the model of the Transkei's Democratic Party. Guzana was not elected and nothing further was heard of his party; towards the end of 1973 he joined the CNIP.

A group called the Black Movers appeared shortly after the election of the Chief Minister. Little is publicly known about it, and its only action was to force the car of the Ciskei Minister of Justice off the road and threaten him with assault in July 1973.

KwaZulu
—Zulu National Party (ZNP)

The ZNP was established in 1968 by Lloyd Ndaba, a former information officer in the Department of Bantu Administration and Development, who also spent ten years in Central and West Africa. The ZNP has remained inactive since its inception, despite Ndaba's personal propaganda efforts on its behalf. As owner-editor of a magazine *Africa South* (discontinued in 1970), Ndaba publicised the ZNP and other parties which he had established for the benefit of the various African ethnic groups in South Africa. After the Chief Executive Officer of KwaZulu, Chief Gatsha Buthelezi, had refused to join the ZNP, Ndaba attacked him and the KwaZulu government in *Africa South*.[11] The ZNP claimed that it had the support of members of the Zulu Royal Family as well as prominent Zulus in Durban and Johannesburg; however, it could not substantiate these claims, as the people mentioned by Ndaba all denied that they supported the ZNP. These included E. B. Tshabalala, a Johannesburg businessman; Paul Zulu, a civil servant in Durban, Prince* Clement Zulu, and A. W. G. Champion, deputy leader of the ICU during the 1920s. The ZNP's alternative Chief Executive Councillor to Buthelezi was Prince Clement Zulu, former chairman of the Zulu Territorial Authority. In spite of making no progress in KwaZulu, the ZNP was firmly resolved to participate in the first general elections.

An offshoot of the ZNP was the Umlazi Zulu National Party (UZNP) which was established by Prince Layton Zulu in November 1970 in order to participate in the Umlazi township council elections in April 1972. Umlazi is an African township within the KwaZulu territory, but on the outskirts of Durban. Officially there was no connection between the UZNP and the ZNP, but a relationship was popularly accepted. The party supported separate development, and one of its main objectives was separate representation of Umlazi in the KwaZulu Legislative Assembly, membership of the UZNP was restricted to Umlazi township. In the township elections of April 1972 the party put up candidates in all wards, but some candidates later withdrew their support. After the election the leader claimed victory for the UZNP in seven out of eleven wards, but it ultimately transpired that his party had the support of only himself and Prince David Zulu in the Umlazi council. Only 10,821 out of about 54,000 voters cast votes in the election. The party's defeat was put down to the general belief that its candidates were uneducated and its leader had dictatorial tendencies. After the UZNP's defeat most of its members left and some tore up their membership cards in public. It was reported that the leader, Prince Layton, gave his support to Buthelezi, and the party for all practical purposes ceased to function.

—Umkhonto KaShaka

Umkhonto KaShaka, a political party established on 24 October 1973 under the leadership of Chief Charles Hlengwa, the Chairman of the KwaZulu Legislative Assembly, took the place of the ZNP whose leader, Lloyd Ndaba, became its deputy leader and secretary-general; members of the UZNP also joined.

* Title used by inner circle of Zulu royal family.

The establishment of Umkhonto KaShaka met with bitter criticism from Chief Gatsha Buthelezi, who declared that it was a sacrilege to call a political party after the founder of the Zulu Nation. He also claimed that the South African security police assisted Hlengwa in the party's formation, and informed the South African Prime Minister of this a week before its formal establishment.[12] An emissary of Hlengwa visited the Zulu King on 28 October to notify him officially of the new party's existence but the King refused to receive him, objecting to the use of the name of Shaka.

Umkhonto KaShaka pledged to accelerate the rate of constitutional and economic development of KwaZulu and to stop the deterioration of Zulu traditions and culture. Unlike the Buthelezi government – although not explicitly stated – it fully accepted the official policy of separate development. An obvious discrepancy, which remained unexplained, was its desire that the King should "remain neutral in Zulu Party Politics", while at the same time being the government leader.

—Royal Intrigues

After the KwaZulu government had succeeded in securing for the King a position as constitutional monarch – against the wishes of some White officials – there was some speculation about the possibility of a serious rift between Buthelezi and King Zwelithini. A certain coolness in their personal relations and a dispute about the arrangements for the Shaka Day celebrations in 1972 strengthened these rumours, as well as the appointment of known opponents of Buthelezi and his executive council to the Zulu Royal Council.

This Council was appointed for the first time in July 1971 as an advisory council to the King. In December 1972 the King dismissed the entire council on the grounds of incompetence and immediately appointed a new one. Prince Clement Zulu and Prince Layton Zulu (who since April 1972 reportedly gave his support to Buthelezi) were omitted from the new council, and the former chairman and Zulu Regent, Prince Israel, was removed from the chairmanship and became an ordinary member. The chairman of the new council was Prince Sithela Zulu, a former chairman of Kwa-Mashu township council, while Prince Patric Zulu (secretary of the ZNP in Umlazi) became the new secretary. Another member was Prince David Zulu, elected to the Umlazi township council as UZNP candidate.[13]

The dismissal of Prince Clement from the council came as a surprise; he resigned as secretary and treasurer of the Buthelezi tribal authority in the Mahlabatini district in January 1972 immediately before the Zulu Territorial Authority met to discuss the KwaZulu Constitution and the position of the King. In the period preceding his resignation, Clement was an important spokesman for the King and led the deputation that requested the South African government to give the King executive powers. He also played an important role at the installation of King Zwelithini in December 1971. When Clement resigned from the Buthelezi Tribal Authority, Prince Israel called a meeting of the Zulu Royal Council which was interpreted as an attempt by the Zulu royalists to achieve unity for the coming constitutional debate in the Territorial Authority. Various princes declared that they wanted nothing to do with the meeting and that they were supporting Buthelezi. While these intrigues were being carried on by Zulu royalists, King Zwelithini himself remained in the background. After the terms of the Kwa-Zulu Constitution had been agreed upon, with the King in the position of constitutional monarch, Zwelithini said in a newspaper interview that he had no political ambitions and that he supported Buthelezi as political leader of the Zulus.[14]

The dispute between Buthelezi and the royalists started soon after the death of King Cyprian in 1968. Buthelezi, who had been Cyprian's chief counsellor for about sixteen years criticised the way in which the Zulu Regent, Prince Israel, had been handling certain affairs, and an open rift developed between the royal household and Buthelezi. The matter was resolved and this was announced by Prince Israel in the Zulu Territorial Authority in January 1971. The first Royal Council, with Prince Israel as chairman, was appointed only a few months later. Starting with the omission of Buthelezi from official participation in the installation ceremony of the King in December 1971 there was an ever-present possibility of the Royal Council developing into an opposition to the KwaZulu government.

After it had been discovered that the secretary of the Royal Council had been involved in the writing of a petition calling for the removal of Buthelezi, with the aid of a junior member of the South African Department of Information in Durban, the relationship between the council and the KwaZulu government deteriorated sharply. Its supporters maintained that the petition had been signed by the King, but he denied it. At the same time (towards the end of 1972) the King tried to intervene in disputes between Zulu labourers and White employers at the Coronation Brickworks near Durban – without success. Shortly afterwards, he stated his intention of making an opening address at a special session of the LegislativeAssembly to be held in January 1973, to discuss the South African proposals for land consolidation in KwaZulu. The KwaZulu government strongly reacted to the widening rift between themselves and the King by accusing the Royal Council of subversive activities and placing the full responsibility for the deteriorating situation on the shoulders of some of its members. The executive council expressed its concern that the Royal Council was acting like a political party while pretending not to be one and that it was a "front for certain manipulations". At the same time the executive council declared "unswerwing loyalty" to the monarchy as an institution, but declared its "disquiet and unhappiness at the possible degradation of the King's Office" if he should persist in actions such as he had taken at the Coronation Brickworks strike. Thus the King's actions had soon cost him considerable political support.

The end of the matter was not in sight yet, however, and in April 1973 the Royal Council, in a press statement, accused the KwaZulu government of "creating chaos in former King Mpande's family". Buthelezi retaliated by sayin gthat the Royal Council should tell the people what contribution it was prepared to make to the nations' progress.[15] Shortly afterwards, the King and the KwaZulu government came to an understanding whereby an additional allowance should be paid to the King, that Prince Israel should be employed by the KwaZulu government as special adviser to the King, and that the entire Royal Council should be dismissed. In this way, the possibly divisive influence of the Royal Council was eliminated for the time being.

Following his installation in December 1971, the King enjoyed his subjects' loyalty and considerable political support. The Royal Council's internal intrigues, its inclination to work behind the scene its inability to demonstrate any positive contribution towards resolving labour, economic developmental, and educational problems, the unsuccessful intervention of the King in labour disputes, left Buthelezi with undisputed political supremacy.

The KwaZulu executive councillors were in a better position to generate diffuse support than the Royal Councillors whose socioeconomic bases of support and influence were restricted to their ascriptive status positions. The altercations between the Royal Council and executive council are manifestations of the resentment by many traditional leaders against secular governmental authority, which was also in evidence elsewhere in Africa. Among the South African homelands, the relationship between traditional leaders and government was less structured in KwaZulu than elsewhere. The reason is that Bantu authorities (tribal, regional and territorial authorities), which had this structuring function, have been established comparatively recently in KwaZulu. Chiefs and headmen were consequently less sure of their position in the hierarchy, while

the status of the "princes" was not commensurate with their actual
duties and power.

—Alternative Organisations

Members of the KwaZulu government felt the need for an apparatus
which could assist in the formulation of policy and determination of
needs and preferences. It was proposed by the Executive Councillor
for Community Affairs, Barney Dladla, that advisory councils be
established for each tribal authority area. These should consist of
representatives of various interest groups, such as farmers, teachers,
chiefs and members of professions, so that they would be more
widely representative of the local population than the tribal authorities. Regional councils would then be established for each of the
twenty-six KwaZulu districts; these would be represented on a
national council, which in turn would be divided into six committees
corresponding with the six government departments. In this way
local people would be able to participate more effectively in development. However, the Director of Dladla's department refused to
make official cars available for such councils. Being in the first phase
of self-government, KwaZulu has no power to overrule such a decision. Yet three informal advisory councils were established early in
1973 in Estcourt district, Dladla's home district.

In 1973 the Zulu National Congress was revived. Established in
1928, its original objectives had been to unite the Zulu nation;
to "keep alive the Nation's fine traditions and its sense of the obligations imposed upon it by those traditions toward the other races of
the Union of South Africa . . .''; and to promote educational and
general economic development, as well as purchase additional
land.[16] The Zulu National Congress is commonly known as "Inkatha ka Zulu", a name which symbolises Zulu unity. At the May
1973 session of the legislative assembly Buthelezi handed out copies
of its constitution with the request that proposals be made for adaptation and improvement.

At this stage it was thought that a revived ZNC could stimulate
grass-roots development, and activate people to participate. This
objective has, however, not been achieved and it is presently employed as a rallying organisation for Zulus in urban areas on occasions of visits by the Zulu King and cabinet members. In the meanwhile it is building a grass-roots organisation which could be adapted
for political purposes. Formal membership is not contemplated
during this stage of the ZNC's existence. With its traditional symbo-
lism and latent developmental objectives, the ZNC could, if also
associated with Black consciousness, develop into a powerful political
movement.

Lebowa

First rumours of political organisations aimed at participating in the politics of Lebowa came from the Transvaal White urban areas. The Lebowa Maphotha Dichaba Party was established in Soweto in 1971. Its main objectives were to obtain links between urban and homeland citizens of Lebowa as well as representation in the Lebowa Legislative Assembly for those in White urban areas, and to take care of the educational, housing, and transport needs of Lebowa citizens. Before the first Lebowa general election of 1973 this party had disappeared from the scene.

No parties or national election pacts were formed in Lebowa immediately before the first general election of 11 April 1973, and the candidates' individual policy declarations showed no significant differences. However, speculation based on the personal differences between the Minister of Education, C. N. Phatudi, and the then Chief Minister, Chief M. M. Matlala, correctly foresaw that these two might oppose each other for the chief ministership. Phatudi's image as a more dynamic and educated person who favoured more rapid change also led people to believe that a change in the chief ministership might be desirable. These differences were not well articulated before the election.

Slate-forming by candidates occurred in all constituencies, but none of these slates was overtly connected with a central co-ordinating agency or person. With the results of the election known, more rapid movement towards the formation of parties took place. Soon after the election on 11 May 1973 of Phatudi as the new Chief Minister, the formal establishment of parties was announced and it can be assumed that their respective canvassing among the elected and *ex-officio* members (chiefs) had been completed before the election of the Chief Minister.

By 12 June 1973 government and opposition parties had been established. Phatudi became the leader of the Lebowa People's Party, with 53 of the 99 members of the legislative assembly in its ranks, and Matlala became the leader of the Lebowa National Party, with 42 members. The LNP never had a constitution, and remained quiet on all fronts during its entire existence. In March 1974 it decided to dissolve and join the LPP – a move preceded by pressure on Matlala by party members in the legislative assembly to join the LPP, and by dissatisfaction among Matlala's followers outside the assembly who thought that he had divided the people of Lebowa by establishing an opposition party.

A Lebowa National Party was formed in 1958 in Soweto, Johannesburg, concerned mainly with the election of Urban Bantu Councillors in Soweto; it was not, however, one of the ethnic parties created by Ndaba, nor had it any connection with the LNP established by Matlala in 1973. The LNP in Soweto was propagated by Lloyd Ndaba's magazine *Africa South*, which stated that it worked for Pedi "political independence".[17] It has since ceased to exist.

Venda and Gazankulu

Shortly before the Venda general elections of August 1973, the Venda Independence People's Party (VIP) was established by Baldwin Mudau, a former representative of the Venda Territorial Authority in urban areas of the Witwatersrand, to oppose the candidates supporting the incumbent government, headed by Chief Patric Mphephu, at the polls. Mudau clashed with his superiors over several policy aspects – such as the question whether Venda children should seek entrance to urban schools, and the granting of business licences – and was sacked along with his advisory boards. Members of these boards formed the core of the VIP at its establishment and did most of the initial campaigning.

The Venda government formed no party in the belief that parties were foreign institutions to the Venda, and would destroy Venda unity. An election pact had been formed by the Chief Minister, Patric Mphephu, and candidates were nominated in all vacancies of the three constituencies. The Mphephu faction was soundly defeated in the election, and gained only 5 seats against the 13 or the VIP. Mphephu was re-elected as Chief Minister with the aid of nominated members. After the election he threatened to ban the VIP – something which fell outside the power of his government. About six months after the general election, Chief Mphephu announced in January 1974 that he had launched a new party, the Venda National Party, which was in favour of the maintenance of the powers of chiefs, independence and land consolidation.

The first general election in Gazankulu of October 1973 passed off without parties or opposing factions. A non-party approach was maintained throughout, and Chief Minister H. W. E. Ntsanwisi was unanimously re-elected as Chief Minister. The Machangana Urban National Movement, established some years earlier, played no role in the election.

Swazi

The Swazi homeland has not proceeded beyond the establishment of two regional authorities. The main reason for its constitutional standstill is the unresolved problem of the future of the twenty-three Swazi chiefs and their followers living in White areas.

The general interests of these Swazis are in the care of the Swazi National Council, a body established during the 1950s and reorganised in 1968. Issues such as land, self-government and the prosecution of squatters have been discussed with the South African government. In 1971 the Swazi National Council and the two Swazi regional authorities, Nkomazi and Nsikazi, formed the Swazi Interim Committee in order to promote the granting of self-government.[18]

Progress has also been immobilised by dissension between Swazi lineages, which the ever-present possibility of joining independent Swaziland has intensified. There is great resentment in the Swazi National Council over the political prominence of the Dlamini clan, particularly in Swaziland, where the Swaziland King, Prime Minister and a majority of the cabinet ministers are from its ranks. Equality of all clans is propagated. On the other hand, the predominance of the Dlaminis is challenged through the presence in South Africa of the Amancamane, who have the overt support of five of the twenty-three Swazi chiefs in the White areas, and maintain that their leaders are the rightful heirs to the monarchy in Swaziland. Their claim dates back to the 1840s when Sidinga I of the Amancamane was routed by the Dlaminis. Sidinga II now lives in Lesotho in self-imposed exile.

Failure to agree with the South African government over land consolidation and questions of Swazi leadership have retarded the constitutional issue, and there is no immediate prospect of self-government along the lines followed by the other homelands.

Black People's Convention

Unlike the political parties in the homelands, the BPC is anti-collaborationist as regards South African government policy, and has no intention of availing itself of any opportunity for political expression through the structures of separate development. Black unity and solidarity under the banner of Black consciousness is its prime objective. The expression of political aspirations is considered to be the right of all communities, and the BPC was availing itself of this right at a time when its founding members considered that there was a political vacuum in South Africa.

The BPC considers that it arose from a need for a national political movement which would concentrate on self-help development efforts, rather than power-oriented action. In BPC terminology the Blacks are referred to as a "community" and never a "society": thus emphasis is on the subjugation of the interests of the individual to those of his fellow-Blacks, and on mutual assistance and obligations. The BPC also arose from a conviction among leading members, who were former members of Nusas and the University Christian Movement, that it was impossible to "liberate" their people when co-operating with those who were the "oppressors". From its inception the BPC has had an exclusive Black character; however, its political orientation was not clear at the preliminary stages and immediately before its formal establishment. The meeting that led to its establishment was held in April 1971 at Bloemfontein and was attended by delegates of various national organisations. They discussed possible mutual co-ordination. Only seven organisations were present at this meeting and these included Asseca, Saso, Idamasa and Aica. A bigger conference was arranged by an *ad hoc* committee of this conference, and took place in August 1971 in Pietermaritzburg, attended by more than 100 delegates from twenty-six organisations in the field of education, welfare, religion, sport and youth affairs. The main decisions at the August 1971 conference were: the formation of a confederate organisation of African organisations, which would co-operate with other Black groups in order to realise Black aspirations; there would be no co-operation with South African government policy and institutions but contact should be maintained with well-oriented Blacks inside the system; and the objectives of the organisation would be the representation of African political opinion and the promotion of community development programmes in the field of education, economic and cultural development.

A further *ad hoc* committee was appointed to compile a draft constitution and arrange a further national meeting for the establishment thereof. This committee assumed the name of National Organisations Conference, and it arranged the third national conference for December 1971 in Soweto. Chairman of the committee was *The World*'s editor, M. T. Moerane, who gave the conference a build-up in his newspaper, without indicating, however, that a political party was to be born. On 16 December, when the Whites were celebrating the Day of the Covenant (relating to the victory over the Zulus on 16 December 1838), 400 Africans attended a prayer meeting in Soweto, while the actual conference followed on 17, 18 and 19 December. More than forty organisations were present this time.

Two points of view regarding the future of the organisation were discussed. Some wanted a political organisation, while others preferred a federal cultural organisation. After behind-the-scenes preparatory work by Saso, supported by some older delegates, the former view prevailed, and a proposal to this effect was adopted by 40 votes to nil, with three abstentions. Thus a political party was established and a clear attempt was made to utilise the ready-made

machinery of more than forty cultural, sports, youth, educational
and religious organisations as the basis for the party's organisational
framework.

After the decision to establish a political party still another *ad hoc*
committee was appointed under the chairmanship of Drake Koka,
a trade unionist and member of the defunct Liberal Party, with the
task of investigating ways and means of launching the BPC, calling
a convention for this purpose and submitting a draft constitution.
The name of the BPC was accepted before this conference was held.
Some objectives of the BPC were already stated by this *ad hoc*
committee in a press statement on 14 January 1972, in which it was
declared that the committee was working towards the formation of a
political movement whose primary aim was to unite the Black
people with a view to their psychological and physical liberation.

The *ad hoc* committee organised symposia on the Witwatersrand
and in Durban, consulted Indian and Coloured leaders of the Natal
Indian Congress and (Coloured) Labour Party, and appointed
commissions on general planning and organisation, urban and
rural politics, economic development, Black education, community
work programme, financial and legal affairs, and Black communalism. A conference was held in July 1972 at Pietermaritzburg, at
which it was decided that a proper conference could only be held
after an intensive membership drive; hence the first proper national
conference was held on 16 and 17 December 1972 at Hammanskraal.
An interim executive was elected, however, in July 1972, consisting
of A. Mayatula (president), M. Shezi (vice-president), D. K. Koka
(secretary-general), S. Cooper (public relations officer), and A.
Dlamini (national organiser). More than 200 delegates attended the
December 1972 conference. There were fiery speeches, and Mrs.
Winnifred Kgware was elected national president.

Discussions at this conference were reported to be brief and to the
point, with much internal criticism, but with too much "bickering
over unimportant matters". The conference was permeated with the
idea of "liberation", but this also drew criticism: it was pointed out
by an African journalist that delegates were arrogant in believing
that they alone would "liberate" all Blacks in South Africa – even
those who held different viewpoints, such as the homeland government leaders whose objectives were often the same as those of the
BPC over education, land distribution and political rights.[19]

South African Students' Organisation

Saso arose from a belief among Black students that it was futile to
co-operate with White students within a single organisation. Dissatisfaction with the predominantly White National Union of South

African Students (Nusas) gave rise to the establishment of separate Black students' organisations, such as the Durban Students' Union and the Cape Peninsula Students' Union, which later merged into the Progressive National Students' Organisation. This Organisation adopted the slogan "non-cooperation with the collaborators". In Nusas they saw imperialistic aspirations and a desire to control the Blacks.

In 1961 and 1962 two rival African students' organisations were formed, the African Students' Association (ASA), and the African Students' Union of South Africa (ASUSA). Continuing differences between them, as well as the strength of Nusas, led to the collapse of the two African organisations. Nusas then adopted the role as spokesman for students at Black universities which were established in 1960, although Nusas was not allowed on the campuses by the university authorities. The formation, at the initiative of the Anglican Archbishop of Cape Town, of the University Christian Movement (UCM) as a multi-racial inter-denominational organisation in 1967 provided African students an opportunity for joining a students' organisation. The Black members of UCM almost immediately attempted to achieve Black solidarity. They were dissatisfied with the White domination of the UCM (with 70 per cent Black members) and Nusas. At the 1968 conference of UCM a Black caucus was formed by about forty Black students from the Universities of Fort Hare, Zululand, Western Cape, the North, University of Natal (Black Section) (UNB) and theological seminaries. This White-Black polarisation revolved around political and social issues and Black theology, with separate projects for White and Black members on literacy, Black theology, women's liberation, and White consciousness. This polarisation, as well as the withdrawal of support by the Methodist and Presbyterian Churches, led to the dissolution of the UCM in 1972.

Out of the Black caucus of the UCM, especially at the instigation of the UNB representatives, it was decided to form Saso. This decision was taken at a conference in December 1968 at Mariannhill, and Saso was inaugurated in July 1969 at a conference at Turfloop. Apart from the stimulus of Black consciousness, the banning of Nusas at Black campuses clearly acted as a stimulant for the formation of a Black students' organisation.

At first Saso's approach was cautious. It was afraid that a too radical standpoint would reduce its effectiveness, and so it merely maintained critical relations with Nusas. But by 1970 it had the support of its members to withdraw completely from Nusas. Subsequently Saso was banned at the campuses of the Universities of Durban Westville (for Indians), Western Cape (for Coloureds), and the North (Africans). University authorities alleged that Saso was responsible for boycotts of lectures and intimidation of students.[20]

The activities of Saso led to the establishment of several other organisations (see Chapter 5). Saso also became a member of the Southern Africa Students' Union, which is one of the four provincial bodies of the All-Africa Students' Union formed in Kumasi, Ghana, in 1971. At a meeting of the Southern Africa Students' Union at Roma, Lesotho, in June 1973, Saso opposed the presence of Nusas, being unwilling to share the same platform with a White South African organisation; accordingly the meeting decided to sever all ties with Nusas and expelled it from the inaugural conference.[21]

Parochial Urban Parties

In Soweto, Johannesburg, there are several self-styled political parties. Their two main functions are to put up and support candidates for election to the Urban Bantu Council of Soweto which is an advisory body to the West Rand Bantu Affairs Administration Board, and to make direct representations on civic matters to the proper authorities. The oldest of these parties is the Sofasonke Party which was established in 1935 by James Sofasonke Mpanza; others are the Masingafi Party, established in 1957, which consists mainly of Nguni members; the Lebowa National Party for Pedi-speaking people; the Chiawelo Residents' Protection Party, established in 1969 and consisting mainly of Venda and Tsonga members; the Imbumba Yama Xhosa, the Makgotla Party, the Independent Party and the Soweto Progressive Party. The ethnic base of these parties is promoted by the grouping of Soweto residents into ethnic neighbourhoods. The Sofasonke Party recruits supporters from various ethnic groups, however – especially after the death of its founder in 1970. For a considerable time it enjoyed a majority in the urban Bantu council, but was beaten by the Soweto Progressive Party in the 1974 urban Bantu council election.[22] None of these parties operates outside Soweto or concerns itself with national policy matters.

Purporting to be homeland-oriented are several political parties established and maintained mostly by the sole effort of Lloyd Ndaba at his home in Soweto. Of these, only the Zulu and Tswana National Parties have operated on a limited scale outside Soweto; whereas the Swazi, Venda, Sotho and Ndebele National Parties exist in name only. The Zulu National Party was succeeded in 1973 by the Umkhonto kaShaka, and the Tswana National Party suffered a severe defeat in the Bophuthatswana elections of October 1972.

Voluntary Associations

The pattern of voluntary associations is illustrative of the diversity of social and economic interests, and the differential levels of acculturation in African society in South Africa. Most of these associations operate totally or partly outside the homelands, a fact which is responsible for the lack of contact between them and the homeland-based parties. Within the homelands, contact with associations is made by homeland governments, rather than by the political parties, and it is always the associations which seek contact – except for certain local social welfare associations which are initiated and supported by government departments for purposes of social welfare. Associations are not used by parties to politicise existing grievances or needs and to recruit supporters. The associations therefore play no direct role in the achievement of national integration, but at best contribute to increasing awareness of public affairs. In this sense they help prepare an increasing number of people for more meaningful political participation. Only one association was encountered whose main purpose was to render advice to a homeland government, viz. the KwaZulu government. The association, Uboko, consists of approximately fifteen members, recruited from the new Zulu élite. Its deliberations are usually in the form of analytical discussions of economic problems and a member of the KwaZulu government is regularly invited.

Only two cases where homeland party branches in White urban areas rendered social services were encountered. The Sharpeville branch of the TNIP extends financial assistance to relatives of deceased members through special collections for this purpose. The second instance concerns the Women's League branch of the TNIP in Bloemfontein who assisted in the improvement of educational facilities for Xhosa children, and promoted a boys' club and other local self-help projects aimed at environmental improvement.

Few African associations can rightfully claim to represent interests on a national scale. Among these are the National African Federated Chamber of Commerce (Nafcoc), the African Independent Churches Association (Aica), the Inter-denominational African Ministers' Association of South Africa (Idamasa), Saso, the African Library Association of South Africa (Alasa), and several sports organisations. The names of others imply national membership and activities but are in fact limited to certain areas, such as the League of the African Youth, the Association for the Educational and Cultural Advancement of the African People of South Africa (Asseca), and the Women's Association of the African Independent Churches.

Several associations accept Black consciousness and unity – at various levels of articulation. They include Saso, the Transvaal United African Teachers' Association (Tuata), Asseca, Nafcoc, the League of the African Youth, the Swazi National Council, Idamasa, and the Black Community Programmes. A common characteristic among these organisations is their striving for African advancement through self-help efforts in their respective fields of activity. There are, however, vast differences among these organisations as to whether an accommodationist attitude should be adopted or not towards the South African government and the institutions created under separate development.

A covert africanism is expressed in the objectives of most organisations, including parties, especially in their emphasis on education for and by Africans, self-help efforts in social and economic fields, the bias towards African culture and development found in the Black consciousness movement, the willingness even to work within the separatistic framework of separate development in the homelands, and the desire for an African or Black theology.

Fragmentation characterises the configuration of African voluntary associations in South Africa. The traditionally oriented people tend to concentrate in multi-purpose ethnic organisations which in White areas perform some of the social integrative functions of the tribal structure. On the other hand, voluntary associations proliferated among the westernised, educated Africans. These include professional organisations (e.g. Black Travellers' Association, Transkei Teachers' Association, Tuata, Idamasa, African Teachers' Association of South Africa), specialised interest organisations (e.g. Aica, Alasa, Nafcoc, various regional and local chambers of commerce which are affiliated to Nafcoc and exist in homelands and White areas alike, and youth hostels associations), service organisations (e.g. Women's Association of the African Independent Churches, Black Community Programmes, Organisation for Tswana Development, Asseca), youth organisations (Saso, League of the African Youth), cultural organisations (the South African Black Theatre Union, the Music, Drama, Arts and Literature Institute, and local associations such as the Krakatoa Kultural Klub and the Jazz Appreciation Society of Soweto), residents' organisations (e.g. Masingafi Party, Motlana Community Association, Chiawelo Residents' Protection Party – all in Soweto), ethnic organisations (Swazi National Council, Reinland Junior Burial Society), and numerous sports organisations on a local, regional and national level. It will be noted that voluntary associations operating exclusively in any one homeland are relatively few.

Overlapping membership between the various political parties and the voluntary associations is common, but there is no indication of a penetration of voluntary associations by any one of the homeland parties. On the other hand, Saso and BPC actively penetrate existing organisations and sponsor the establishment of new ones.

Voluntary associations as a rule establish good working relationships with local authorities and the South African and homeland governments. Their activities are geared towards the promotion of the interests of their members, and contacts with the authorities are aimed at gaining special privileges (e.g. by residents' and teachers' associations), changing policy in favour of a particular interest (e.g. Nafcoc on the question of Africans as shareholders in the Bantu Investment Corporation), solving problems (e.g. teachers' associations in respect of promotions and disciplinary matters), improving public or government service (e.g. efforts by Asseca for the improvement of educational facilities for Africans) and rendering service (e.g. the provision of library services by Alasa and the training of ministers of religion by Aica).

Interrelationships

Working relationships and spiritual understanding exist between several organisations oriented towards Black consciousness, for example between Asseca and Saso, and Asseca and Idamasa, Idamasa and Nafcoc, BPC and Saso, BPC and various youth organisations, and between Saso and the many Black oriented youth and drama and arts associations. Overlapping membership between these organisations often exists and Saso leaders were especially active in youth, drama and arts associations. Asseca shared an office with Idamasa in Johannesburg when it had been unable to secure suitable accommodation; it assisted Saso members who were expelled from African universities during 1972 to further their studies elsewhere; and it granted a small loan to Saso in 1971.

Strained relations between Saso and Asseca developed when the former objected to an invitation from Asseca to the Secretary of Bantu Education to address the Asseca conference of 1972. Tuata objected to Saso's policy of confrontation, and warned it not to cause strife, misunderstanding and division among Africans.[23] Alienation between Saso and the Natal Indian Congress followed a resolution by the NIC in 1972 to reject Black consciousness and all policies of racial exclusiveness.

An interrelated network of voluntary associations is clearly developing in South Africa. A pioneer in this respect is Saso, whose rashness wrecked some promising relationships, but which tries to increase political and social consciousness and mobility through its concern with community development. The growing Black awareness and the growing material wealth of commercial and professional groups contribute to the newly developing relationships by providing common interests for otherwise diverging organisations.

The homeland political parties make no provision for corporate membership or affiliation of other organisations. None of them has made any attempt to establish relationships with voluntary associations. Mangope's exhortation of his followers during his 1972 election campaign to co-operate with the Organisation for Tswana Development was as far as any one of the party leaders went. Relations between homeland leaders and Saso are generally bad.

While there is some consensus among homeland-based parties in respect of their role in the political system, they disagree completely with BPC and Saso in respect of the style of political action and the recruitment of leaders through separate development structures. This is the most serious political division among the Africans of South Africa, which continue in spite of common attitudes on Black unity and material needs.

A resolution of Saso's 3rd General Students' Council (annual conference) in 1972 asked homeland leaders to withdraw from separate development and resign their posts. The call was rejected, and ignored in some cases, by homeland leaders. The attitude of the former Chief Minister of the Ciskei, Chief J. M. Mabandla, is representative of his colleagues in this respect. He maintained that Saso "say they hate dictatorship and yet they are dictating to us telling us what to do instead of discussing matters with us".[24] In July, Temba Sono was dismissed as president of Saso for propagating co-operation with homeland leaders and other critics of Saso. He said that people must not be made subject to an ideology; freedom must be practised as well as preached; and those who differ with Saso must be convinced. Sono's successor, Jerry Modisane, also warned – unsuccessfully – against harshness and a too arrogant and ready rejection of those who differed with Saso.

The relationship between Transkei political parties has been characterised by occasional severe antagonism and mistrust. The TNIP made various attempts to associate the DP with anti-government violence, and said it was "a revolutionary opposition" when it called for the release of political prisoners.[25] A circular of the TNIP, sent in 1965, tried to throw suspicion on the DP's policy of multi-racialism, by calling it illegitimate. A pamphlet obtained from the TNIP office, undated (probably issued in 1967) and unsigned, tried to associate the DP with communism by quoting from a document, "Draft Discussion Document", written by the former head of the Communist Party in South Africa, Bram Fischer, in which he praised, *inter alia*, the DP. In 1968 another TNIP pamphlet called the DP and the TPFP vultures and traitors, harbouring Whites who were "like lice in one's blanket, sticking there to suck one's blood". Afterwards the party leader apologised to the Whites, dissociated the TNIP from the remark, but said nothing about the reflection on the two opposing parties. Further attempts at casting doubt on the legitimacy of the DP and associating it with communism were made by the secretary-general of the TNIP in a speech in Orlando-East, Johannesburg, on 7 March 1968.

Thus the TNIP has contributed to a fairly widespread belief that the DP is an illegal party. The DP's situation was aggravated by a steadfast refusal of the Transkei government to support attempts by the DP to have it recognised as an official opposition. The struggle against these misconceptions is one of the DP's several problems in building up support. After the decisive defeat of the DP in 1968, the bitterness of attacks on the DP and attempts to bring it under suspicion by the TNIP disappeared almost completely. There is no doubt, however, that the DP leader, Guzana, is held in high regard by the TNIP-leadership.[26]

In other homelands relationships between parties deviated little from the Transkei pattern, and were characterised by disrespect and contempt. In Lebowa, however, the division between the Lebowa People's Party and the Lebowa National Party never crystallised into firm opposition, and after about six months of tenuous opposition the LNP decided in March 1974 to join the ruling LPP.

In the Ciskei the opposition Ciskei National Party did not accept its defeat in the 1973 election as a true reflection of voters' preferences and maintained that gross irregularities were responsible. The smallness of the majority of the Ciskei National Independence Party tended to aggravate the intensity of animosity across the floor, and angry interjections sometimes characterised debates in the legislative assembly in the first sessions after the election.

In Venda the relationship between the Venda Independence People's Party and the Mphephu faction was equally poor. The VIP accused the Mphephu faction of receiving help from White officials, of using ministerial transport to fight the election, and that its candidates were of poor quality. Candidates of the VIP were reportedly called "traitors, sewer-flies, wolves, jackals" in the 1973 election campaign.[27] The VIP was regarded as a city and businessman's party which did not represent the people living in Venda; and its constitution was regarded as foreign and dangerous to the Venda: it would destroy "the soul of the Venda people", undermine the traditional institutions of the Venda, and destroy the unity of the Venda nation.[28]

In KwaZulu the relationship between the KwaZulu government and its main former opponent, the Zulu National Party, was rather obscure because it was not at all clear on which points of policy the ZNP opposed the KwaZulu government, and its successor, the Umkhonto kaShaka, has not yet openly confronted the KwaZulu government. The ZNP's tactics consisted of launching attacks on the KwaZulu government through circular letters, pamphlets and press statements by its leader, Lloyd Ndaba. On two occasions Buthelezi challenged Ndaba to appear with him on the same platform in Soweto. On both occasions (February and August 1972) Ndaba refused. Buthelezi expressed his contempt of this party by calling it "the stooges of the oppressors",[29] and after the establishment of Umkhonto kaShaka, the latter was also rejected by Buthelezi as a creation of the South African government.

In several homelands, such as KwaZulu, Transkei and Bophuthatswana, there is difference of opinion in respect of the position of traditional leaders in the legislature. In the Lebowa legislative assembly unanimity was reached to create an upper chamber of chiefs and a lower chamber of elected members.

Whereas the future role of chiefs in politics remains obscure, little attention has been given by Africans to the question whether homeland leaders can be regarded as representatives of urban Africans as well. Their legitimacy in this respect has been put under doubt by the low voter participation in urban areas in homeland elections. The success of the integrative function of homeland governments and parties in relation to the urban Africans is also doubtful. It is more likely that the large urban African population is an integrating force which retards the fragmentation of South Africa among homelands, maintaining these governments' relevance to and integration within the greater South African political system.

In spite of serious differences among parties there are large areas where they are able to agree and co-operate. In ten years of opposition across the floor of the Transkei legislative assembly the pattern of co-operation between government and opposition is relatively clear. The Transkei parties often co-operate in respect of matters on which they hold similar views. In respect of certain motions before the legislative assembly the party leaders consult each other in order to obtain unanimous support and to save time. Such motions were, for instance, those by the TNIP in 1966 in respect of the increase in the number of constituencies from nine to twenty-six, and the appointment of the sixty-four chiefs as members of the assembly before the nomination of election candidates; and a motion by the DP in 1967 that Transkei citizens who live in Ciskei towns should not forfeit their Transkei citizenship.

Several motions concerning labour problems received the unanimous support of all members of the legislative assembly over a number of years. They included DP motions in favour of the abolition of influx control and reference books or passes (1969 and 1970), revision of the contract labour system which is the backbone of the migrant labour system (1972), and allowing relatives and dependants of Transkeians working in White areas to visit them at any time (1972); and TNIP-motions in favour of establishment of factories in the Transkei (1970), better treatment at the hands of South African police in connection with pass offences (1972), and higher wages for Africans (1973). Both parties also supported military training for Blacks during a debate in the assembly in 1973, because the "security of the state knew no colour bar".

DP motions seeking a rise in the emoluments and stipendia of chiefs and headmen posed a dilemma for the TNIP, who wanted to take the credit for rises actually given by the Transkei government, and who therefore could not oppose motions to this effect tabled by the DP. The TNIP's most effective reply was to amend DP motions (e.g. in 1970) to read that the government should be congratulated on the improvements made in this respect and that it could be relied upon to review the position from time to time.

Outside the assembly there is very little consultation between the parties, and only one instance of consultation on an important policy issue is known. In preparation for his talks with the South African Prime Minister in 1972, the Transkei Chief Minister called a meeting of about fifty members of the Legislative Assembly from both parties in an attempt to obtain a mandate to request additional land for the Transkei. However, the DP refused to co-operate because they were against the Bantustan concept in principle, and a request for more land would in their view be a strengthening of this concept.

The DP supported the TNIP's demand in 1973 that the Commissioner-General for the Xhosa National Unit should be replaced. These officers were appointed in respect of each of the African ethnic groups in 1959 when African parliamentary representation was abolished. Their duties are to promote the various ethnic groups in several fields. If the DP wanted to be true to its opposition to the Bantustan concept, it should have regarded the request for the Commissioner-General's replacement as irrelevant. The issue demonstrated the DP's dilemma. On the one hand it is compelled to accept the institutional trappings of separate development if it wishes to participate in the political process of the Transkei, and on the other hand it is compelled by its policy to stand aloof from separate development.

In other homelands co-operation on vital issues was also achieved between opposing parties. In Bophuthatswana, members of the BNP and the SP are members of the Land Commission which investigated Bophuthatswana's land claims. In Lebowa the LPP and the LNP were both represented on a similar commission for Lebowa.

Co-operation among parties remained superficial, except in Lebowa where no deep-rooted differences existed between the LPP and LNP. After general elections in all homelands individual members tended to change party loyalties; sometimes in favour of the governing party, and sometimes not (see Chapter 9). Splinter parties tended to disintegrate, rather than join one of the major parties, and individual members of such parties tended to support one of the (and sometimes different) major parties.

The Transkei's Democratic Party at one stage seriously considered a formal approach to the ruling TNIP for discussions on possible common policy aspects. When Matanzima declared in August 1972 that he would allow Whites who are occupying certain tracts of land, and who are agreeable, to become citizens of the Transkei if the South African government transferred those lands to the Transkei, many people were reminded of the 1963 election manifesto of Poto, the first DP leader, in which he declared that Non-Africans "who are prepared to serve under an African Government will always be welcome in the Transkei". In 1972 Matanzima also propagated a Black federation in South Africa, and when the idea was further elaborated by his brother George (also a cabinet member), it appeared that White South Africa would be invited to join the federation. Again, the DP policy in favour of provincial status for the Transkei seemed relevant.

The DP tried to exploit the situation to its own advantage, but also had to prevent some of its members from joining the TNIP in the belief that the TNIP's policy had become similar to their own. At its September 1972 conference the division within the DP was apparent in motions submitted by the secretary (T. H. Bubu) and the deputy leader (O. O. Mpondo). Bubu's proposal was "that the Democratic Party should approach Chief K. D. Matanzima regarding his changed stand", and Mpondo's counter-motion was: "That Chief K. D. Matanzima should come to the Democratic Party if he has changed his outlook." Mpondo's motion was carried by 37 votes to 4. Another motion concerning the DP's relationship with the TNIP was proposed by Guzana and was also accepted: "That the Democratic Party reaffirms its policy of multi-racialism and rejects a claim for Independence and short-sighted land claims which are implicit in the policy of separate development." While Guzana thought that the "political ball" was before the TNIP's feet, Bubu continued to express his views that Matanzima has created an opportunity for unity which should be utilised by both parties.[30] These overtures by Bubu were considered by the TNIP to be feelers from the DP, and its only reaction was that DP supporters were free to join the TNIP. A year later Bubu resigned from the DP and contested (and lost) the Lusikisiki constituency as an independent.

Conclusion

The relationship among voluntary associations, and political parties provides some insight into the latter's support bases. The almost total lack of contact between homeland-based parties and voluntary associations could be the result of the problem of these parties in relating their activities to Africans outside the homelands – where most voluntary associations are found. The recruitment policy of the homeland parties is deliberately directed, in the first place, at traditional communities in the homelands, and secondly at élite groups in the homelands, with homeland citizens in White areas relatively poorly attended to.

In contrast to the homeland-based parties, Saso and BPC purposely relate their activities to as many voluntary associations as possible, and initiate new ones where necessary. As a result they have supportive contact with diverse professional and interest groups which leaves an impression of much wider socio-economic bases of support than those of the homeland-based parties. In actual fact, however, Saso and BPC cannot claim active support of the many individual members of these associations, as contact is mostly restricted to the executive level. These contacts, however, provide Saso and BPC with a national geographical dispersal of diffuse support, which the homeland parties are striving for by extending their grass-roots organisation to all parts of South Africa.

The comparative lack of external contact of homeland parties strengthens their homeland orientation. This tendency to ethnic fragmentation is offset, however, by the frequent contact among the homeland leaders. This homeland orientation is largely responsible for the often vitriolic nature of opposition among homeland parties. Opposition to Whites is not a consolidating factor in the homelands, and it is in connection with purely domestic affairs, often very petty, that the parties differ fiercely. There is greater unity, however, among homeland parties in their relationship with the South African government regarding matters outside the powers of homeland governments. Very little ideological differences exist among homeland parties as almost all accept separate development as an unwanted but unavoidable fact of South African politics. Homeland unity is a relative concept, especially if the large measure of withdrawal from homeland politics by urban Africans is considered. The insecure position of the urban Africans in White areas also gives rise to the most unifying policy aspects among homeland parties.

The greater social mobility in urban areas renders it easier for urban Africans to enter new, secular organisational relationships, and although homeland parties could use their urban supporters to penetrate this field, they have so far failed to do so; a failure due to the fact that the parties are embedded in a more traditional social environment in the homelands where secular organisations are of lesser importance. It also reveals an ambivalence in homeland parties: concern over the urban Africans, but failure to appreciate their social organisation for political purposes.

REFERENCES

1. Transkei Territorial Authority, *Proceedings and Reports*, 1963, pp. 33–4.
2. Transkei, *Hansard*, 1964, pp. 249–50 and 261; and *Hansard*, 1966, pp. 230 and 237.
3. G. M. Carter *et al.*, *South Africa's Transkei*, Heinemann, London, 1967, p. 129.
4. Transkei, *Hansard*, 1965, p. 277.
5. *Daily Dispatch*, 27 and 29.4.1968.
6. Tswana Territorial Authority, *Minutes of Proceedings*, 1966, pp. 63–5.
7. Notes made by Mangope for his speech at the meeting.
8. W. Le Roux, "Ciskeise verkiesing: Partypolitiek of stamnasionalisme?" *Bulletin*, Africa Institute, Pretoria, XIII, 3, pp. 122–3.
9. *Daily Dispatch*, 19.4.1973.
10. *Daily Dispatch*, 23.10.1972.
11. *Drum*, March 1972, pp. 14–17; *The World*, 28.1.1972.
12. *Weekend World*, 28.10.1973 and 4.11.1973.
13. *Daily News*, 14.12.1972.
14. *Sunday Tribune*, 2.7.1972.
15. *Weekend World*, 8.4.1973.
16. Preamble to "Deed of Trust and Constitution" and section 2 of Constitution.
17. *Africa South*, January 1971, p. 4.
18. D. Lukhele, "Political development amongst the Republican Swazis vs. relations with Swaziland", roneoed, n.d. Lukhele is national organiser of the Swazi National Council. This and subsequent information on the Swazi also obtained from Dr. W. Breytenbach of the Africa Institute, Pretoria.
19. S. Motjuwadi, in *Drum*, 8.2.1973, p. 43.
20. *Die Transvaler*, 18.7.1972.
21. *Rand Daily Mail*, 22 and 28.6.1973.

22. *The World*, 5.10.1970; H. J. Swanepoel, "Die aandeel van die Bantoe aan stedelike Bantoe-administrasie in Johannesburg . . .", M.A. dissertation, University of South Africa, 1974, Chapter 5; *Rand Daily Mail*, 9.10.1974.
23. Editorial in *Tuata*, August 1972, pp. 2–3.
24. *Daily Dispatch*, 24.11.1972.
25. Transkei, *Hansard*, 1965, p. 272.
26. Transkei, *Hansard*, 1971, p. 19.
27. Statement by J. P. Mutsila on "Venda Politics Today", 1973, roneoed
28. Statement by Mphephu faction, "Whither does the Venda Party–V.I.P. want to lead the Venda People? . . .", 1973.
29. Speech by Buthelezi to (Coloured) Labour Party Conference, Durban, 20.4.1973.
30. *Daily Dispatch*, 11.9.1972 and 16.11.1972.

5

BLACK CONSCIOUNESS

Introduction

Black consciousness in South Africa is still in its formative stages. It tends to be a politically divisive element: the dividing line runs between pragmatists, who are prepared to come to terms with the realities of separate development, and ideologists who are not. The pragmatists are led mainly by homeland-based politicians and middle-class moderates, and the ideologists by Black university students and urban middle-class radicals.

At the beginning of the 1970s neither of the two groups had succeeded in obtaining firm support on a mass scale among the urban Black population. Here the ideologists are at an advantage, and their emotional appeal and promises of ultimate well-being through self-help overshadow the pragmatists' attempts to compromise with separate development. The strong africanist orientation in the South African Black consciousness movement tends to strengthen its appeal particularly among the African population, and it remains largely an African movement with comparatively small support from Indians and Coloureds.

Black consciousness is a common factor unifying radical opponents of separate development. It supplies the base for the building of a political movement for those people who do not support homeland-based parties. Essentially an élitist movement, it brings together students and graduates of Black universities, and recruits supporters mainly among the professional and educated élite, theologians, separatist African churches and leaders of Black voluntary associations. It spreads its influence, where possible, through the creation and then the penetration of voluntary associations.

Realising the political appeal of Black consciousness, the homeland-based leaders were increasingly outspoken in favour of Black unity in South Africa. They referred increasingly to Black dignity and pride and to Black advance through self-help efforts; and they became amenable to manifestations of African culture in dress, art, literature and history. This new emphasis on their common Blackness undoubtedly helped to bring homeland-based leaders

77

nearer to a common approach to their problems, as expressed in their policies. However, this did not close the gap between them and the ideologists – or Black consciousness leaders.

Despite its partial penetration of the middle-class and the favourable attitudes of homeland-based leaders, Black consciousness did not succeed in its first five years of activity in South Africa – from 1969 onwards – in achieving a major impact on the political scene, mainly as a result of its failure to relate its philosophy to a common Black political cause, and its excessive concern with ideology. Its insistence on a common Blackness, common problems, a common destiny and a common enemy did not take account of differential levels of educational, social and economic development in South Africa's rural and urban areas, and cultural differences among the constituent population groups.

In this chapter we shall examine the concept of Black consciousness in South Africa, together with some of its significant manifestations, and the support it received from outside the movement. We shall often refer to the Black consciousness "movement" – meaning no particular organisation, but the many organisations and individuals who share a common set of beliefs on the interpretation of the present position of Africans, Coloureds and Indians in South Africa, on their future role in South Africa and the world, and on the way in which this role could be fulfilled.

Black consciousness was first forced on the attention of South African Whites early in 1970 when the withdrawal of Blacks from White institutions was remarked upon by the South African Institute of Race Relations and by the journal *Reality*, a mouthpiece of former Liberal Party members. Later in 1970 the Christian Institute, which was organised on a non-racial basis, observed that Blacks and Black institutions were withdrawing from its ranks. From 1970 onwards Black consciousness has been actively propagated.

Moerane, editor of *The World*, pointed out that Black solidarity was "not a new and sudden freakish happening, but an evolutionary development over the years . . . germane to the soil and nurtured in the climate of this country".[1] He traced the history of the movement back to the protests by Africans at African legislation in 1911 and particularly to the actions of the All-Africa Convention of 1935 and the thoughts of Anton Lembede of the ANC Youth League in 1940, who stated for the first time that the Africans had been trying in vain to be like the Whites instead of fostering their own abilities. By claiming a relationship between Black consciousness and the Africanism manifested in South Africa during the 1930s and 1940s, the universality of Blackness is denied, the movement becomes Africa-bound, and the status of Coloured and Indian supporters becomes doubtful. However, such a relationship is not officially and widely claimed, and (pan-) africanism should be regarded as only one of the ideologies which has fed the Black consciousness movement. Though seldom referred to, the Black consciousness movement in the U.S.A. is clearly regarded as some sort of forerunner and example for the South African Blacks. Solidarity with Black Americans has been demonstrated and recognition given to their senior position in the movement by the invitations to Black American civil rights leaders to open Saso's annual congresses.

There is no doubt that the Black consciousness movement in South Africa has received its greatest support and recruited most of its leaders from among the Africans. African nationalism, fed by the ever-present opposition to South African laws affecting Africans, is probably the greatest single sustaining force behind the movement. Ironically, the South African official emphasis on colour distinction has undoubtedly encouraged the development of a colour exclusivism, which is a fertile breeding-ground for nationalism. Government-created institutions for Africans, Coloureds and Indians – for example, the African homeland governments, the Coloured Representative Council and the South African Indian Council – provided opportunities for political mobilisation and expression at a time when the banning of the PAC and ANC had caused a vacuum. Although now rejected by the Black consciousness movement, these institutions helped to keep political awareness alive.

If pan-africanism is the nearest relative to Black consciousness, it is by no means the only one. The vagueness and contradictions present in the expositions of Black consciousness make it difficult to draw a genealogical tree. Philip Frankel rightly points out that "since the notion Black Consciousness tends to be highly eclectic from an ideological point of view . . . it is extremely difficult even for its most intellectually advanced exponents to easily and precisely identify the philosophical undertones of the doctrine itself". He observes that its terminology was drawn from Marxism-Leninism, pan-africanism, African socialism and welfare capitalism. Another reason for this inarticulacy is a powerful anti-intellectual trend: there is, says Frankel, an "emphasis on the 'primacy of experience' which seems to make concrete rationalisation and expression not only unnecessary but positively untoward".[2] However its rather shaky philosophical and ideological basis has not deterred the movement in South Africa from concrete action aimed at achieving Black solidarity and promoting Black consciousness. This will now receive some attention.

The South African Concept

Definitions of Black consciousness in South Africa tend to emphasise what it is not, and remain vague and even contradictory on the philosophical bases and objectives of the movement. The place of traditional African culture, and the relationship between the culture of Africans, Coloureds and Indians (who regard themselves as Black) is not made clear. Black theology is defined in terms of its political objectives rather than its theological content; Black power, except for isolated mention, remains undefined; and key concepts such as liberation, emancipation, alienation, self-reliance and identity are to be understood more by their contextual usage than through explicit elucidation. The existential nature of Black consciousness is a dominant feature, and what cohesion the movement has can be attributed to the common experience of its adherents in White-ruled South Africa, and not to a common agreement on the nature and function of "Black culture", on the compatibility or not of communalism and economic development, and on social norms and values – to mention some prominent issues. One of the clearest definitions of Black consciousness is given by N. C. Manganyi, a clinical psychologist: "Black consciousness should be understood to mean that there is mutuality of knowledge with respect to the 'totality' of impressions, thoughts and feelings of all black people." The Blacks are conscious of "mutual suffering", of their "cultural heritage", and Black consciousness is expressive of a new creative responsibility and self-improvement in numerous fields – not only the political.[3]

Describing Black consciousness as a way of life, a Saso paper[4] gives no particulars on the rules and norms to be followed, or the characteristics of this way of life, and it was probably a reference to the Blacks' endurance of discriminatory legislation. In the Saso policy manifesto, being Black is called a mental attitude committing Blacks to oppose all forms of oppression.

Sometimes the reaction against "oppression" seems to be directed solely against South African legislation – e.g. in Saso's emphasis on the existential nature of the movement. Other exponents are opposed to the entire Western way of life: thus M. T. Moerane, president of Asseca, wrote that the Black man had discovered that the "oppressive life he suffers is inherent in the whole system evolved by Western institutionalised life and ways".[5] Generally, the reaction seems to be directed at Western social values, materialism and institutions, and against South African White-created systems and institutions in particular.

Black consciousness is also seen[6] as something through which the Blacks can look at themselves with new eyes and not by reference

to the values of White society. This could be achieved through
studying the theory of Black power; the encouragement of voluntary associations such as social, educational, economic and religious
societies; and the teaching of the advantages of group action,
even if the people have to make use of government-created institutions to demonstrate the power of unity. Black consciousness
needs to be on its guard against three dangers: the first is the mistake
of adopting White attitudes which are hostile to the sharing of possessions, a concept characteristic of African culture. A Black middle
class with only skin-deep Blackness must not come into being.
The second danger is the teaching of hatred towards Whites, a
negative step which would not penetrate to the core of the issue.
The third danger is to discriminate among Whites; they are all
alike and should be viewed with equal suspicion. Sympathetic
Whites should be encouraged but kept at a distance. The exclusion
of Whites would activate the Black people to take the lead in their
own struggle.

Rejection of White/Western values is universal among the
exponents of Black consciousness. White values are responsible for
instilling inferiority complexes among Blacks, and for their alienation.[7] Adam Small, a leading Coloured exponent, illustrates the
reaction against White society. According to him, Black consciousness is no exclusivist apartheid philosophy; it rejects a negative
definition of people – such as "non-Whites". It rejects the idea
that Black people exist through the mercy of the Whites; it rejects White patronising; and it rehabilitates the spirit of the Blacks.[8]
Unlike other exponents, Small contends that understanding is one
of the objectives of the Black consciousness movement: while
White and Black fight each other they will have to learn to understand each other.[9] Small's qualified acceptance of Whites is shared
by M. T. Moerane (a moderate but forthright spokesman for
African civil rights), who welcomed White assistance for Blacks
without paternalism.[10] However, Moerane wrote in his newspaper, *The World*, that the Black consciousness movement
aims at vindicating the Black man and not at promoting understanding.[11] The BPC and Saso regard Whites as irrelevant to the
Black man's struggle for identity and emancipation. For them the
movement appears entirely directed at increasing Blacks' awareness
of themselves and of their power potential.

For the Black consciousness movement the total involvement of
Blacks is an essential prerequisite for success. This exclusive Black
attempt at mustering Black efforts for realising Black political aspirations is referred to as Black solidarity, which implies a struggle
between White and Black for the resources of material and spiritual

livelihood, and for the power to impose a particular value system. Black consciousness could also be defined as a realisation by Blacks of the need for solidarity in order to achieve their objectives. It accepts Blackness as normal, a unifying element and a basis for planning and action. Black consciousness is therefore not just a state of mind, in spite of assurances that it is. It becomes a social criterion, a statement of policy, a political recruitment norm and, in the light of the qualities attributed to Black humanity and religion, an expression of a belief in Black superiority. Feelings of Black inferiority are eliminated, and belief in "certain unique characteristics associated with the Black life-style and philosophical outlook" is accepted by Blacks.[12] Self-indoctrination through slogans like "Black is beautiful" increases self-confidence,[13] while emphasising Black exclusiveness and superiority.

Because the economic underdevelopment of Blacks in South Africa is emphasised, the struggle for self-reliance, liberation and emancipation is largely directed at economic objectives. Wage discrimination, job reservation and influx control must be ended, the rights of Black workers through collective bargaining must be established and, most particularly, Africans must be taught that they can provide for their own material needs without White approval or assistance. Saso's Black workers' project, its educational projects, its attempts to promote Black fine arts and performing arts and its various community development projects are operational manifestations of Black consciousness.

The Black consciousness movement is overwhelmingly concerned with contemporary issues and has not so far been much concerned with defining what is "characteristic" or "unique" in the Black man's culture. The cultural diversity of those in South Africa who qualify to be termed "Black" makes any emphasis on culture impossible, lest diversity prove disastrous for the movement. Reference to "culture" often denotes nothing more than the fine arts and performing arts, while references to culture in the broadest sense is sometimes ambiguous. Gwala, for instance, regarded culture as one of the mainstays of the Black consciousness movement, and maintained that the domination of Black people was only possible by an alienation of Blacks from their culture.[14] Ndebele, on the other hand, advocated that the traditional African culture (i.e. customs, traditions and beliefs) should be destroyed because it was static and unable to contribute towards the economic development of Africans. It no longer provided a means for human expression and had made of Africa a human zoo and museum of human evolution.[15]

The problem of reaching consensus on the meaning and content of

Black culture is further compounded by the fact that especially the university educated Black finds himself the product of two cultural worlds: the Western and the African or Oriental, as the case may be.

The qualities of a Black culture are not defined, and it is perhaps unfair to expect such a definition at this stage of the movement, because the frustrations and uncertainty of the bi-cultural existence of the Blacks are among the root causes of the movement, and the search for "identity" is one of the prime objectives. In the meantime a common Black identity, consisting of common aspirations and common problems, is presumed without too close a definition. Several aspects of *African* culture are regarded as basic to Black consciousness, for example the following:[16] (a) African culture is man-centred, i.e. Africans have a concern for each other; (b) the formation of groups by Africans is characteristic of all their action; (c) an eagerness to communicate is emphasised by the Africans' love of song and rhythm, and it is maintained that all African songs are group songs; (d) land has always been owned jointly; (e) poverty was a foreign concept and it was normal to ask for help from one's neighbours; (f) while the Westerner has a problem-solving approach, the African's approach is situation-experiencing; and (g) Africans are deeply religious and religion is practised in daily life and not at given times in particular buildings.

Western values, which emphasise man's material well-being, are rejected and the African's contention that the cornerstone of society is man himself is re-emphasised. At the same time it is believed that Africa will make a major contribution to the world in the field of human relationships.[17] Black identity could, at least in part, be achieved through political fulfilment, which could contribute towards the legitimising of those human values and economic systems regarded as characteristic of Black culture.

The humanism of African culture refers, *inter alia*, to the "communalism" of African economics, i.e. the readiness to share possessions within a "corporate society" and a "collective way of life".[18] This characteristic is strengthened by poverty, and there is some fear that affluence would be contrary to this highly prized African cultural trait. This rather idealised conception of traditional African attitudes towards the acquisition of personal wealth is offset by the fact that, traditionally, individual wealth was well known in African society, though various factors encouraged the equalisation of income and possessions. The attitudes and values of Indians and Coloureds are apparently of no consequence in this connection – which underlines the dominance of African values in the "Black" movement.

The economic motive in Black consciousness is central to its rejection of separate development and even of the political involvement of Whites who are opposed to separate development. Apartheid is regarded as an economic principle, and Black people should concentrate on economic affairs rather than on debating multi- or non-racialism. The White liberals' involvement on behalf of Africans is rejected because it is based solely on ethical grounds, and is considered to be interested in a happy labour force and not in African political involvement.[19] White liberals who contend that the withdrawal of the Blacks into exclusive organisations is racist and immoral are suspected of wishing to maintain White racism and supremacy, wanting to exploit the Blacks and to be the only interpreters of Black attitudes. White liberals, as well as those Whites who support the South African government, are therefore all classed as White racists, and White power is regarded as a totality. In terms of the Hegelian theory of dialectical materialism, it is believed that White racism and Black unity should be the thesis and antithesis. The synthesis is not clear, but apparently it is believed that the Black system of values would ultimately appear as the truth.[20]

Black Consciousness and Human Relations

Although racism as a corollary of Black consciousness is denied by the leading exponents of the latter, overtones of racism are nonetheless present in the movement. A final stage of the movement is seen as the mobilisation of Black power, through which White political power and solidarity will be met on equal terms. The Black consciousness movement – with its involvement in cultural, economic, educational and social matters – leads up to this political crystallisation where attempts will be made to seek and maintain political power in Black hands. Dr. W. Nkomo, late president of the South African Institute of Race Relations, warned that Black power could have a fascination for young intellectuals, but with a racist bias. This was denied by exponents of Black consciousness, including Adam Small who said that skin colour was not a criterion for Blackness.[21]

The rejection of Whites and the Western values they represent, the refusal to acknowledge the good will of at least certain Whites, and cynicism and suspicion regarding Whites' motives towards Blacks testify to a racist bias: Whites who publish Black poetry only do so to salve their consciences, Whites like Alan Paton prescribe literary standards to Blacks only to capitalise on their position, White liberals try to control Black reaction to provocation only

to demonstrate the totality of White power, and as such form the
biggest stumbling-block to Black unity; and all Whites are inextric-
ably part of an exploitative society which perpetuates aggressiveness, misery and injustice.

Black withdrawal from multi-racial organisations occurred
first in 1969–70. It then evolved into a conscious strategy and has
led to the demise of at least one organisation, the University Christian Movement. For others, such as the National Union of South
African Students (Nusas), it meant loss of Black support and expulsion from the Southern Africa Students' Union. Scepticism among
Blacks towards multi-racial political discussion groups has increased,
and unwillingness to participate became marked in the early 1970s.
Saso declared (rather vaguely) that Whites in South Africa had
become a part of the problem, and (more explicitly) that they
should therefore be excluded from the Blacks' struggle to realise
their aspirations. In this process personal contact with Whites
should be discouraged. Also Blacks should first close their ranks so as
to act from a position of strength, oppose White racism, and then
join the open society which, Saso believes, can only be achieved
by Blacks.[22]

It was attitudes such as these which caused Alan Paton to ask
whether the White liberal should leave South Africa, keep silent
for ever, go north and be trained as a guerilla fighter, or just lie
down and die.[23] The White liberal establishment was obviously
stunned and horrified at the racist overtones in the Black consciousness movement, which were so overtly directed at themselves.
They were quick to put the blame on the South African government and its supporters, without noting the Blacks' viewpoint that
all Whites were equally responsible for the position in which the
Blacks found themselves. Not only the White liberals, but the new
cosmopolitan Afrikaners and the Indians were also, respectively,
the subjects of rejection and possible rejection. A warning was
sounded that the new type of Afrikaner, with his reduced race consciousness, was transferring White *baasskap* from the ideological to
the economic and military plane, and was therefore a dangerous
foe.[24]

Referring to Amin's expulsion of Asians from Uganda, an article
in the *Saso Newsletter*[25] warned Indian merchants and middle-class
Coloureds and Africans that everybody should get involved in the
struggle for emancipation or face the consequences. The Black
consciousness movement refused to consider the issue which had
dominated South African politics for centuries – racial integration
or separation – which was regarded, together with White people as
such, as irrelevant to the Black consciousness movement, and to have

been devised by Whites who saw all other people centring around themselves. It was thus a matter for Whites to put right if they had a problem in that respect. The White South African political parties' lines of division, based mainly on the racial issue, are by implication of no importance. By refusing to face White-Black relations as a contemporary problem, the racist basis of the Black consciousness movement was disguised and a debate on race relations within the movement (between Africans, Coloureds and Indians) was averted.

The BPC and Saso rejected participation in homeland governments, urban Bantu councils and the Coloured and Indian Representative Councils, and they are not prepared to use these bodies to attack government policy. Homeland leaders' arguments that they employ government-created institutions for their own ends were rejected. In 1972 Saso wrote to Chief Ministers in several homelands calling on them to resign – to be met by a blank refusal. This exclusivism of the Black consciousness movement is basic to its attempts to gain a monopoly for laying down leadership norms. This attitude probably earned it more opponents than followers and sympathisers – especially among the powerful homeland leaders. Realising this, the Saso president, Temba Sono, in July 1972 expressed his growing conviction of the necessity to co-operate with certain homeland leaders, and was immediately expelled from office. The widely read bi-monthly magazine *Drum* wrote of the homeland leaders: "What worries is that if the BPC is going to liberate even these guys, then the BPC can easily be charged with 'the same' arrogance as those who are trying to do good for the Blacks without consultation."[26]

Religious Involvement

At a missiological conference held at Umpumulo in KwaZulu on "A relevant theology for Africa" in September 1972, several exponents of Black theology were present together with representatives of various White or White-controlled churches. There was no unanimity among the Black delegates about the content and objectives of Black theology. Some also preferred to speak of "Africa theology" or a "relevant theology for Africa". There were also those who preferred to investigate Black theology in company with interested White theologians, and those, mostly younger members, who wished to do so without the Whites – the same exclusivist tendency found in Saso and BPC.

It was clear at this conference that Black theology was situation-bound and to a large extent existential. Some delegates, for example, doubted the relevance of the Old Testament to the Blacks in South Africa. Others saw a continuation of the traditional religion of the Blacks in the Christian faith, which for them was complementary to and a fulfilment of the traditional religion. Others saw Black theology as relevant only in South Africa and distinct from Africa theology. As soon as the social, economic and political situation in South Africa improved, Black theology as an aspect of Africa theology would disappear.[27]

Saso was probably one of the leading propagators of Black theology during 1971–2. According to its Commission on Black Theology,* which reported to the General Students' Council (GSC) in July 1971, Black theology is intimately related to Black consciousness. In a motion adopted by the GSC in 1971 (Resolution 57/71) Black theology was given the following definition, among others: "Black theology is not a theology of absolutes, but grapples with existential situations. Black theology is not a theology of theory but that of action and development. It is not a reaction against anything but an authentic and positive articulation of the Black Christians' reflection of God in the light of their Black experience" and further: "Black theology means taking resolute and decisive steps to free Black people not only from estrangement from God but also from slave mentality, inferiority complex, distrust of themselves and continued dependence on others culminating in self-hate."

The Black theologians' attitude to White churches was one of unanimous rejection and belief in the bad faith (in more senses than one) of the Whites. Like other aspects of Black consciousness the attitude towards Whites provided the firmest point of departure and the best material for cohesion. Accusations of apartheid practices in the Roman Catholic Church, Anglican Church and the Afrikaans churches gave substance to these attitudes.[29]

Because they did not concern themselves with problems like land distribution and with economic disparities, but rather with problems of interracial fraternisation, Saso believes that Christianity propagated by the White-dominated churches was designed to oppress Black people. It encourages theological students to emphasise their Blackness theologically by reviewing their history, culture, traditions and beliefs, by assessing the theological and secular realities

* The Commission on Black Theology was initiated at the Saso GSC of 1970, partly to involve religious organisations in popularising the concept. Initially Saso and the University Christian Movement would have undertaken the project jointly but the UCM abandoned it. New arrangements for a conference were then made in conjunction with Idamasa, Aica and Spro-cas' Black Community Programmes.[28]

of the present, and by observing their Christian goals. At its conference in 1974 it was also decided to infiltrate the churches "to
break their White-dominated power structures".[30]

While the activists in the Black consciousness movement regard
the debate on integration *versus* separation as irrelevant to their
purpose, other Blacks find it hard to reconcile the existence of
such a question with Christian brotherhood.[31] Black theologians
consider that man's secular experiences "colour" his religious
feelings. This viewpoint puts Black theology in the middle of the
political controversy over the Blacks' position in South Africa. It
also gives rise to the contention that Jesus was a Black, and that
conceptions of Him as a White cause the Blacks' feelings of inferiority when among White people. The liberating power of the
Gospel is, in fact, considered to apply to the Black man's struggle
for liberation from White oppression, and Black theology rejects
any religious doctrine which contradicts demands for freedom.[32]

While the established churches are regarded by some as obstacles
to Black consciousness, the African independent churches have
become of increasing interest to the exponents of Black consciousness and Black theology. This is shown by, among other things, the
co-operation between proponents of Black consciousness and organisations representing the independent churches, such as Idamasa
and Aica.

Schutte divides[33] the separatistic or independent churches in
South Africa into three "action-complexes" – escapist, adventist and
activist. The escapist churches are so-called Zionist churches
where the existing social order is replaced by a compensatory system
where status and active participation can be achieved by members
who have a low status in society. The church's aspiration for the
well-being of its members could result in a protest against the existing
order. The adventist churches postulate the coming of an ideal
state and try to prepare their followers for this event which again
could have political implications and repercussions.[34] The activist
churches believe in changing the existing order through direct
action, with obvious political consequences. These include the
Ethiopian churches.[35]

There are approximately 3,000 independent churches (of which
only about 10 per cent belong to Aica) with about 25 per cent
of the African population as members, and these constitute a clear
field for co-operation with the Black consciousness movement. The
syncretism of many of these churches is a further attraction to a
movement looking for a particular identity for its people. A repug-
nant aspect of these churches is their emphasis on the vertical dimen-
sion in religion as against the horizontal emphasis of the Black

heologians who feel that religion should involve man's entire exis-
ence, and in particular regulate his relations with his fellow-men
and assist in his secular aspirations.

Manifestations of Black Solidarity

Black consciousness is manifested in various ways and spread through
diverse methods. It has become popular recently among Africans
o use their African names instead of their Christian names and to
place the former before the latter. This is done, for example, in the
official minutes of the Transkei Legislative Assembly. A correspon-
dent in the letters column of *Weekend World* maintained that his
"Black name has a cultural and historical significance" and was a
"constant reminder of a proud ancestry".[36] No opportunity is lost
o further Black consciousness and in Saso and BPC the custom has
evolved of concluding press releases and letters with pithy slogans.
Thus the usual "Yours sincerely" was replaced by "Power and
Solidarity!", "Your Black Brother" and "Breaking the chains".
The term "Black" is used not only as a collective term for Africans,
Indians and Coloureds but to refer specifically to people who
identify themselves with a particular set of aspirations and
who occupy a particular legal position in South African society.
The term "Non-white" is used derogatorily to refer to those regarded
as collaborators, sell-outs and lackeys. As pointed out earlier, the
use of the term "Black" has been spread with considerable success,
bringing a measure of advantage for the Black consciousness movement by creating some involuntary solidarity on the basis of skin
colour.

To spread Black consciousness, Saso has launched several community development projects involving literacy classes, health
ervices, assistance with correspondence courses, provision of water
upplies, etc. Blacks should thus be involved in efforts at self-realisa-
ion and socio-economic development and learn that they are capable of doing such things for themselves. Few projects have so far
been completed, and the message of Black consciousness has not
been spread very widely in rural African areas.

Since the end of the 1960s various organisations have come into
being that stress Blackness as a common factor. We have already
discussed Asseca, which is opposed to Bantu Education, and,
in the religious field, Idamasa and Aica. In the field of sport, the
South African National Non-Racial Sports Organisation (SASPO)
was formed in Durban in September 1970; it is in favour of mixed
port at all levels, starting at club level. Then in March 1973 a
South African Council for Sport was established aimed at co-
ordinating all non-racial sport bodies in South Africa and obtaining

uniformity in sport policies. Consisting of Blacks, the Council purports to be non-racial and has rejected all racially organised bodies and "multinational" sport events approved by the South African government. At a Black inter-university sports meeting in 1972 at the University of Zululand, a South African Black Intervarsity Council was also established.[37]

Poetry, literature, drama, fine arts and music are all employed to demonstrate self-awareness by the Black man, and to propagate the idea that Blackness is synonymous with poverty and oppression and transcends the distinctions between Africans, Coloureds, and Indians. Several theatre and art societies sprang up within a short time. In particular the South African Black Theatre Union (Sabtu) was formed at Durban in 1972 to channel Black creativity towards the objectives of Black aspirations. Eleven local societie became affiliated to it, but these failed to meet their financial obli gations, and proper facilities for staging dramas were lacking The first national drama festival arranged by Sabtu, representing twelve theatre groups from various parts of South Africa, was held in Cape Town in December 1972. This left little doubt that the Black theatre was establishing its own norms, language and mes sage.[38] However, theatrical performances by Blacks are by no means in the hands of Sabtu only. Mrs. Doreen Lamb, who has assisted in the direction of Black drama in Soweto, has distinguished between two types of Black theatre, both of which obviously have no connec tion with Sabtu: namely, plays with a political message, mostly written by Whites and mostly about the pass laws; and morality plays without a "Black" message.[39] The Music, Drama, Arts and Literature Institute (Mdali), formed in Johannesburg in June 1972 has also propagated the expression of Black consciousness in art and drama, although it does not regard Whites as irrelevant At its own drama and art festival early in 1973, Mdali arranged exhibitions of sculpture, painting and photography by Blacks music and drama performances by Blacks, and poetry and speech reading from Black authors all over the world. Several local associa tions in various parts of the country arranged exhibitions and meetings.

After the May/June 1972 unrest at Black universities, Saso found it necessary to establish a Council of SRC presidents to co-ordinate and plan student action while leaving decision-making to the local student bodies. The need for such a co-ordinating body arose because during the student crisis a feeling developed at certain campuses that Saso failed to consult the SRCs adequately. In some cases Saso was seen as an outside force, and was called upon to keep out of local issues.

The absence of a newspaper to reflect the Black viewpoint and to communicate with Blacks exclusively has been a matter of concern to the movement. Saso's journal (*Saso Newsletter*, which appears ten times a year) is regarded as the beginning of a Black press, to promote which Saso set up a Black Press Commission at its 1972 annual congress. Only a seminar on the press in October 1972 has resulted so far. Another Saso move aimed at Black unity was the establishment of a Black Workers' Project at its 1972 annual congress. Under this project a Black Workers' Council was to conscientise Black workers and promoting Black trade unions.

Political solidarity among Blacks is the ultimate objective of the Black consciousness movement, and Saso's efforts in this direction were supplemented by the work of the Black People's Convention (BPC). Several meetings held by delegates of African welfare, religious, sports, and educational organisations, starting in April 1971, led to the establishment of the BPC in July 1972, since when it has grown into an exclusive Black political organisation based on the doctrine of Black consciousness. Heribert Adam's assertion that Saso was a "student wing" of the BPC and that "other branches" of BPC organised the Black Allied Workers' Union, or "concerned themselves" with Aica and Asseca, is incorrect. Those organisations are quite distinct, although there is co-operation between some of them.[40] Like Saso, the BPC rejected all co-operation with government-created institutions for Blacks such as homeland governments, and refused membership to Blacks who were prepared to work within the framework of separate development. While exclusively Black, BPC and Saso differentiate among the Black population. The BPC, for instance, with its stance that a teacher but not an inspector under the Department of Bantu Education can become a member,[41] is eliminating a great potential reservoir of supporters among the higher-paid ranks of African civil servants. Problems of recruitment are aggravated by the difficulty of putting across the philosophical and ideological content of Black consciousness, and thus the prospect of gaining meaningful support among "peasants" and "workers" – regarded by Saso as the most important potential power groups – does not seem bright.

The definition of society as an interaction of power groups is a key concept in the strategy of Black consciousness. If the relevant power groups are identified, activity aimed at political change and awakening can be directed towards such groups. Thus at least three distinct groups have been distinguished, namely the peasant group which includes labourers on White farms and inhabitants of the rural African areas; the semi-peasant group which includes the migrant labourers, who live from time to time in rural areas;

and the urban Blacks who are the professional and worker classes. The peasants and workers are regarded as groups with vast power potential which has been completely dormant. Urban Africans are further subdivided. In the past a Black middle class existed which consisted of the intelligentsia or élite who were the political leaders of the Africans up to the time of the banning of the ANC and the PAC. The Black middle class consists mainly of professional people, lacking creative imagination, who co-operated with the White liberals and thus assisted in the oppression of the Blacks. The second urban power group, the worker class, was very creative and showed considerable initiative in social life. The workers were more conscious of their political position than the peasants. The third power group was the numerous Black religious sects, which seek in religion the fulfilment denied them in politics; these are completely free from White control.[42]

Marginal Support

Cautious acceptance, intentional or unintentional, has been given to Black consciousness objectives and terminology by organisations and structures not explicitly connected with the movement, or even by those opposed to it. This has been manifested in commercial advertising, and the word "Black" has been increasingly used by the South African newspapers, the South African Broadcasting Corporation, and numerous African voluntary organisations instead of "Bantu" or "African". (In the first Saso constitution, however, the term "Non-white" was used and was only later replaced by "Black".)

Some interesting examples of Black consciousness were to be found in the African homelands the leaders of which are summarily rejected by BPC and Saso. For the KwaZulu government unity in KwaZulu was of the utmost importance in order to work towards Black unity in South Africa.[43] The ethnicity implicit in this approach was totally rejected by organisations such as BPC and Saso, who preferred to ignore the ethnic and racial diversity of the Black population.

Chief Kaiser Matanzima declared that the raising of a clenched fist would be the symbol of his Transkei National Independence Party, although he added that Black power was not the Party's slogan.[44] On his return from the U.S.A. in August 1972, Matanzima also reminded his followers that "Black is beautiful". His insistence over a number of years on a purely African Transkei can be understood in the light of his earlier Africanist tendencies. It was Chief Lucas Mangope, Chief Minister of Bophuthatswana, who came closest to the Black consciousness ideal in his expressions of African pride. Without doubt, he was expressing the sentiments of all other homeland leaders. At a meeting during his 1972 election campaign Mangope said that an attitude of self-reliance and determination to be independent was necessary and that there was nothing that the Africans could not do themselves. The best thing was self-knowledge and self-confidence: then you did not need to worry if you were called a stooge or a tribalist. A year later, in a newspaper interview, Mangope said that it was imperative for his people and all Black people to be rid of the inferiority complex that affected them so strongly. Improved education and economic development could provide the necessary impetus. Self-confidence could be built by acquiring skills and training.[45]

In another newspaper interview Chief Mangope said that to-gether with the land question and sacrifices by Whites, Black dignity and Black responsibility were two of the most important pillars of separate development. The Black people should use the available opportunities and prove to the White that, given the opportunities, they were not his inferiors.[46] Here Mangope differs radically from the proponents of the Black consciousness movement who maintain that the Whites are irrelevant in the Black man's struggle for advancement. Mangope's thoughts are nevertheless basically related to those of the Black consciousness movement.

There is close agreement among African leaders both in the homelands and in BPC and Saso on issues such as African dignity, political rights, job reservation, pass laws and education. Ideological differences over the institutions created under separate development and over the best political course for Africans in the present circumstances bedevil relations between the two groups of leaders and make communication impossible. The difference between homeland leaders and Black consciousness leaders over the value of interaction between White and Black leaders is deep-rooted. Unlike the Black consciousness leaders, all homeland leaders were firm on the necessity of negotiation between them and the South African government on various problems (especially those resulting from the presence of Africans in White areas), and that interracial co-operation was necessary for the maintenance of a peaceful South Africa. They also accepted that adversity among one racial group could be detrimental to the well-being of another in the long run – a viewpoint which contrasts sharply with that of the Black consciousness leaders who maintain that Whites are irrelevant to their destiny.

In the field of commerce, the buy-at-home campaign of the National African Federated Chamber of Commerce (Nafcoc) is, according to its president, essentially an effort "to restore Black money to Black people".[47] Not only has Nafcoc successfully negotiated the establishment of a Black Bank (although it complained of insufficient financial contributions from homeland governments), but it is also encouraging co-operation among small traders and the establishment of insurance companies, newspapers, factories, and printing works by Blacks.

After its establishment in 1964, the Chamber changed its structure in 1970 and became a federal organisation in order to accommodate regional chambers which took self-governing homelands into consideration. In spite of this partial compliance with government policy the national Chamber remained committed to the idea of Black solidarity and improvement through self-help.

There was sympathy with the Black consciousness movement in certain White circles, but it was firmly rejected by the Blacks, the most prominent example being Saso's rejection of Nusas. Not daring to condemn Saso or the right of Black students to follow their own way, Nusas decided at its 1970 congress to remain open to all, but instructed the executive to refrain from involvement on Black campuses unless requested to do so by Saso or the individuals or centre concerned, and to continue with the providing and gathering of information. Saso noted this decision and regarded it as of no consequence. When White students demonstrated in June 1972 in sympathy with Black students who were expelled at several Black universities, Saso was dismayed to find that the White students received greater news coverage, and rejected their actions as condescending and irrelevant to the Black students' goals.

In this way the exclusivistic character of the Black consciousness movement deepened, and a further practical contribution was made by Saso towards racial polarisation in South Africa. It was once again made clear that White assistance, however well meant, was unwelcome, and Black support from outside the movement could only be considered if the contributor was ready to meet certain ideological prerequisites. Undoubtedly many potential supporters were alienated in this way.

Support for Black consciousness in Indian and Coloured circles was not automatically forthcoming. Despite the support of several individual Coloureds and Indians, and a demonstration of Black solidarity by Coloured and Indian students, Black consciousness remained a largely African affair. A dispute arose between Saso and the Natal Indian Congress (NIC) over critical remarks by an executive member of NIC on Black consciousness and his comparison of Saso with PAC policies. The incident also strained the relations between NIC and BPC, whose delegates made NIC officials feel so unwelcome at the July 1972 BPC congress in Pietermaritzburg that they soon left.

The common purpose of Coloureds and Africans under the common banner of Blackness was questioned by the Federal Party (Coloured) in its journal, *Unity*. It rejected the classification of Coloureds under the term Black, and denied that colour was synonymous with oppression, poverty and deprivation: "The whole concept has racist overtones and is being unashamedly exploited by unscrupulous and irresponsible politicians and clergy." It contended that instead the question of equal opportunity and justice for all, irrespective of colour, in a common South Africa should be pursued.[48] In contrast with the Federal Party, the Labour Party (Coloured) saw a growing solidarity between the Blacks in South Africa. Its leader, Sonny Leon, said that there was a growing consensus among Coloureds that there should be a closer identity with Africans and Indians in striving for the removal of political, social and economic disabilities. On the other hand, the chairman of the Coloured Representative Council, Tom Swartz, encouraged Coloureds to identify with Whites rather than with Africans, because it was with Whites that they had religious, linguistic and cultural ties, and they had no prospect of independence in separate homelands.[49]

Conclusion

The diversity of population groups in South Africa faces the Black consciousness movement with a serious dilemma. While Africans, Indians and Coloureds are included in the "Black" population group by exponents of Black consciousness, references to a common "Black" culture are almost exclusively to African culture, of which descriptions tend to be idealised. For example, in an attempt to stress community spirit among Blacks, it is maintained that all African songs were group songs, and that traditionally land was owned jointly and possessions were shared. In reality not all African songs are group songs, there was a large measure of individual rights in land occupation, and acquisition of personal wealth was well known in traditional society. Similarly, Black theology does not account for oriental religions found among Indians and some Cape Coloureds. There is, in fact, a strong trend towards creation of ties with African separatist churches and organisations representing them, such as Aica and Idamasa.

Exponents of Black consciousness have not solved the problem of integrating the strains of African, oriental and White Afrikaner culture, represented by some Coloureds, into a common Black culture. Without such a cultural basis, one of the prime initial ob-

jectives of the Black consciousness movement, the search for identity, cannot be fulfilled. A further problem is posed by the relevance
of the traditional African culture to the search for cultural identity.
Traditional culture – especially traditional forms of government –
can be used in support of separate development, which is based
on traditional cultural differences.

Warnings against a latent racism in the Black consciousness
movement have been sounded by Chief Gatsha Buthelezi of Kwa-
Zulu and Chief Lucas Mangope of Bophuthatswana. Despite
denials of racism the exponents of Black consciousness reject
Whites and the Western values they represent, believe in the superiority of the Blacks' contribution towards solving the world's human
problems, and discourage personal contact with Whites. There is
also a racist bias in the rejection of discussions of segregation,
integration and multi-racialism, because the corollary of this
rejection is Black power.

Activities of organisations which explicitly adhere to Black
consciousness doctrines – namely Saso and BPC – are designed
to pursue the objective of Black solidarity. Community projects,
adult education, the Black workers' project, attempts at establishing a Black press and the promotion of Black drama, art and literature are aimed at inculcating a sense of Black achievement and
demonstrating the power potential of Black unity in every field.
To this end existing voluntary associations are penetrated where
possible, and new ones are set up. Religion is used for secular
purposes – there is a belief that religious fulfilment can only be
achieved together with, or after, fulfilment in other spheres of life.

"White" politics in South Africa needs to take serious note of
the objectives, grievances and techniques of the Black consciousness
movement. It is not something which can be countered by suppres-
sing specified organisations. It is a movement with psychological and
spiritual dimensions – at this stage still ill-defined and inadequately
understood – transcending organisational forms. Black exclusiveness
could prove disastrous in South Africa – as could a failure among
Whites to understand the reasons behind and apsirations of this
exclusiveness.

The most significant impact of the Black consciousness movement
in South Africa is on homeland politics. Despite serious differences
between homeland leaders and Black consciousness exponents over
political strategy, there is much common ground – as we have
shown above. The common approach to African problems advocated
by homeland leaders, their support for a federation of homelands,
and increasing belief among them in the necessity of African unity
for political action (see Chapter 11) coincided with the granting of

self-government to several homelands in the early 1970s and is a function of the political interaction among homeland leaders. Also the sudden emergence of parochial homeland politics on to the national scene coincided with the rise of Black consciousness in South Africa. It cannot be asserted that changes in the styles of homeland politics were a function of rising Black consciousness; the simultaneous upsurge was probably a natural revival of African political consciousness from different sources.

Homeland leaders have not succeeded in gaining massive support from Africans in White areas. This is reflected in the low percentage participation of urban Africans in homeland elections. It is especially in this field that the homeland politicians and the Black consciousness movement vie for the support of the African population. The homeland politicians are at a disadvantage here in the sense that they can neither promise nor do anything for urban Africans who are outside their fields of jurisdiction. They can, however, compete with Black consciousness leaders if they depart from separate development platforms as bases for political action. In this connection Buthelezi, closely followed by Mangope, Ntsanwisi and Matanzima, has been spectacularly successful in expressing the aspirations and problems of urban and rural Africans. Saso and BPC, on the other hand, are at the disadvantage of being subject to frequent banning of leaders by the South African government, and they are caught in the web of a puritanical ideological approach.

The Black consciousness movement is essentially a middle-class movement. It can be regarded as largely the function of three important interrelated factors, namely African material insecurity, White paternalism and exclusiveness, and the increasing socio-economic mobility and progress of the African community. It is unnecessary to labour the point that White paternalism and exclusiveness drew a reaction from the Africans and other Blacks, but a few words will be in order on the remaining two factors. In spite of material insecurity many Africans achieved relative prosperity in commercial and professional fields, particularly in urban areas. However, their position as temporary sojourners in White areas (in terms of government policy) renders their material position relatively insecure, and restricts their possibilities for capital investment and material progress. Because it would be impractical from various points of view for the South African government to deprive Africans in White areas of existing wealth and rights, Africans can materially afford involvement in the Black consciousness movement. This is no doubt qualified by the knowledge that upon their demise the dependent members of their families could legally be required to move to a homeland in terms of influx control regulations. It becomes all the more necessary for them to break down separatist measures. On the other hand, it could be argued that the homelands provide security against total closing of financial, professional and social avenues in White areas and it could be fallen back upon if the need arose.

The middle-class nature of the Black consciousness movement is illustrated by the supporting organisations of the Black consciousness convention of 16 December 1974. They include various churches, church associations, chambers of commerce, leading figures in education, students, and homeland politicians. Also relevant to its middle-class nature is Saso's failure to instil Black consciousness ideals among peasants through literacy programmes. These Africans have achieved their positions by successfully exploiting the individual competition principle of Western society as its guiding value. One of the important objectives of their Black consciousness ideals is, however, the instilling of a co-operative ethic[50] which finds expression in the promotion of Black communalism and the active discouragement of a middle-class mentality. This would in fact imply a social and economic revolution, but until the details of communalism are spelled out as a social and economic programme, it must be accepted as a perpetuation of traditional forms of mutual assistance on the basis of the extended family. It also remains doubtful whether middle-class leaders of the Black consciousness movement are seriously contemplating such revolutionary changes as their material position would be most seriously affected thereby. Communalism, as a form of traditional mutual assistance, does however link Black consciousness in at least one respect with homeland-oriented Africans.

As a middle-class intellectual movement with strong emotional appeal to the masses, the Black consciousness movement has the potential of politicising the needs and aspirations of Africans in White areas. In this respect its strategy is theoretically sound: the establishment of a political organisation (BPC) and the penetration of voluntary associations, mainly through the wide-ranging activities of Saso. Future success will depend on organisational abilities, South African government pressure, the general socio-economic conditions of Africans, and the ability to combine greater pragmatism with a coherent ideology which, if necessary, must sever all ties with Coloureds and Indians, and seek the co-operation of homeland leaders and moderate urban African spokesmen for African civil rights.

REFERENCES

1. *Weekend World*, 3.12.72
2. Philip Frankel, "Black power in South Africa", *New Nation*, October 1972, p. 3.
3. N. C. Manganyi, *Being-Black-in-the-World*, Johannesburg, Spro-cas, 1973, pp. 18–21.
4. "Understanding Saso: Introduction to Formation School", paper delivered at Formation School on Black consciousness and community development, Edendale, 3–9 December 1971. Author unknown.
5. *Weekend World*, 3.12.1972.
6. "Understanding Saso . . .", op. cit.
7. Saso policy manifesto.
8. Adam Small, Book review in *Deurbraak*, 2, 2 (Feb. 1973), p. 9.
9. Adam Small, "Universiteit van Wes-Kaapland: Dramatiese denke nodig", *Deurbraak*, 2, 2 (Feb. 1973), pp. 13–15.
10. Interview with *Rapport*, 16.7.72.
11. *Weekend World*, 3.12.72.
12. Philip Frankel, op. cit., p. 5.
13. Cf. Allister Sparks in *Rand Daily Mail*, 22.7.72.
14. M. P. Gwala, "Priorities in culture for creativity and Black development", in *Creativity and Black Development*, Durban, Saso Publications, 1973, pp. 41–2.
15. N. Ndebele, "Towards the socio-political development of the Black Community in South Africa", in *Creativity and Black Development*, op. cit., p. 81.
16. Saso, "Some African cultural concepts", roneoed, n.d.
17. Ibid.; and M. T. Moerane in *Weekend World*, 3.12.72.
18. Saso, "Old values, concepts and systems", roneoed, n.d.; also Manganyi, op. cit., p. 20.
19. Ndebele, op. cit., p. 75.
20. "Definition of Black consciousness", MS., author unknown, n.d.
21. *The Star*, 16.2.1972.
22. Saso policy manifesto.
23. *The Star*, 16.3.1972.
24. Gwala, op. cit., p. 48.
25. "Focus: Ugandan Asians and the Lesson for us", in *Saso Newsletter*, Sept./Oct. 1972, p. 8. Author anonymous.
26. Stanley Motjuwadi in *Drum*, 8.2.1973, p. 44.
27. Information derived from notes made at the conference by Dr. J. du Preez, Decoligny Theological School, Umtata.
28. Saso executive report to General Students' Council, 1972.
29. Cf. *Weekend World*, 20.12.70 and 16.4.72; *Daily Dispatch*, 25.10.72; *Rapport*, 29.4.73.
30. Resolution No. 57/71 of General Students' Council, July 1971; *Drum*, 8.9.1974, p. 34.
31. Cf. Gatsha Buthelezi in *Natal Mercury*, 30.6.1971; and C. M. C. Ndamse in *Daily Dispatch*, 26.7.1972.

32. "Black theology in a plural society", author and date unknown, Saso leaflet.

33. G. Schutte, "The political function of some religious movements in South Africa", paper read at seminar of Dept. Social Anthropology, University of the Witwatersrand, 28.7.1972.

34. An example was the Bulhoek incident in 1921 when a sect called the Israelites believed that the Whites would be destroyed in a world war and then occupied Crown land from where they refused to be removed, followed by a battle with government troops in which 183 Israelites died – Schutte, op. cit.

35. Some years ago the Ethiopian Church in South Africa associated with the ANC against discriminatory laws – Schutte, op. cit.

36. Ngoako Thebehali, *Weekend World*, 24.1.1971.

37. *Rand Daily Mail*, 29.3.1973; *Drum*, 8.5.1973, p. 13; and Report of University of the North's centre to the Saso General Students' Council, July 1972.

38. Dr. R. E. van der Ross in *Rapport*, 31.12.1972.

39. *Rapport*, 31.5.1973.

40. Heribert Adam, "The Rise of Black Consciousness in South Africa", *Race*, XV, 2 (1973), p. 151.

41. President of BPC in *Drum*, 22.3.1972, p. 10.

42. Ndebele, op. cit., pp. 70–9.

43. Interview with B. Dladla, KwaZulu Executive Councillor for Community Affairs; and also Buthelezi at a meeting of Nafcoc, *Daily News*, 13.5.1972.

44. *Daily Dispatch*, 8.6.1973.

45. *Rand Daily Mail*, 1.8.1973.

46. *Daily News*, 26.1.1973.

47. Nafcoc, presidential address, 8th national conference, Durban, 13.5.1972.

48. See *Rand Daily Mail*, 31.8.1973.

49. *Rand Daily Mail*, 23.2.1973 and 19.4.1973.

50. See James V. Downton and David K. Hart (eds.), *Perspectives on Political Philosophy*. Vol. III: *Marx through Marcuse*, Hinsdale Ill., Dryden Press, 1973, pp. 4–6, for a discussion of the competition principle and the co-operative ethic.

6

ORGANISATION

Introduction

Formal constitutions provide the bases for all African political organisations in South Africa, most having been formally accepted and ratified by a general meeting and thereafter accepted as legitimate. Constitutions vary in the amount of attention given to particulars, but all of them cover organisational structure, membership, division of functions among office-bearers, discipline and financial regulations, and briefly summarise the principal objectives. The Venda Independence People's Party (VIP), the Ciskei National Independence Party (CNIP), the Ciskei National Party (CNP) and the Democratic Party (DP) of the Transkei have elaborate constitutions, whereas the constitutions of the Bophuthatswana National Party (BNP) and the Transkei National Independence Party (TNIP) are skeletal. In lay-out and phraseology the constitution of the Seoposengwe Party (SP) in Bophuthatswana resembles to some extent that of Saso, which preceded it. No constitutions exist for the Tswana National Party (TNP), the Zulu National Party and its successor the Umkhonto KaShaka, nor did they for the Transkei People's Freedom Party (TPFP), Lebowa National Party (LNP), Transkei People's Democratic Party (TPDP), Pondoland People's Party, and Umlazi Zulu National Party all of which are now defunct.

Of all the homeland-based parties, only the TNIP has an office and a permanent secretary-general, assisted by a typist. All other parties rely on voluntary support, the result being poor record-keeping and a degree of inefficiency at all levels. Lack of finance is the main cause of the poor staff situation, but the sporadic nature of organisational efforts at grass roots level is also responsible. Income is derived solely from dues, donations and special fund-raising functions. The hierarchical structure prescribed by the constitutions is not always adhered to, and dues-paying members are relatively few. Organisations opposing government policy and working outside its framework, like Saso and the Black People's Convention (BPC), have well-staffed head offices, with Saso also maintaining a branch office in Johannesburg and two regional offices. These organisations lavish attention on grass-roots organisation and, unlike the homeland-based parties, on their relations with voluntary associations. As a result their fund-raising capacity is probably higher than that of the homeland-based parties. The extent of their membership and sources of income is not generally known: they are secretive in the face of government opposition.

Homeland-based parties largely rely, within the homelands, on existing traditional structures for organisation and recruitment, particularly on the chiefs and headmen and their councils. All parties, including Saso and BPC, strive towards the establishment of branches as the bases for their organisation. Homeland-based parties often appear to be better organised outside than inside the homelands, but they have achieved greater recruitment successes within the homelands through effective use of traditional structures. In such circumstances strong party organisations do not result because traditional loyalties remain paramount and unaffected. Not surprisingly, tribalism is one of the greatest divisive influences in homeland politics and each party is watchful for manifestations within its own ranks. Although provisions for disciplining party members exist in all constitutions, they are seldom enforced. Only in the case of the TNIP, DP and BNP have leadership disputes led to explusions. The overall trend is rather towards conciliation.

Formal Framework

The constitutions of all African political organisations open with brief statements of policy. Every one of the homeland parties is critical of separate development, and the DP rejects it outright, but all are prepared to operate within its framework, and the LNP, CNP and SP affirm this in their constitutions. Generally they express a willingness to engage in negotiation and dialogue with the South African and any other friendly government, adherence to the values of democracy, the rule of law and Christianity, national unity within the homeland and ultimate independence for the homeland, economic development, improvement in educational and social services, satisfactory land consolidation and expansion, maintenance of enlightened chieftainship, recruitment of voters and members, and the study of local and national issues.

The Ciskei opposition CNP, established in April 1973, was one of the first homeland-based parties to show universalism in its outlook by using the word "Blacks" in its constitution in place of the time-honoured "Bantu", and by expressing explicit support for an "amalgamation" of Black states in South Africa. BPC and Saso have ideological and universalistic objectives in their constitutions. That of the BPC expresses the conviction that a need and a right exist for a political movement to express the ideals, aspirations and goals of the Black people, and that the BPC will unite and "solidify" the Black people. It states the BPC's acceptance and promotion of Black consciousness and solidarity, its intention of formulating an educational policy, of creating and maintaining an egalitarian society and an equitable economic system, applying the principles of Black communalism ("the philosophy of sharing equally"), and reorienting the theological system to make religion relevant for Black people. The BPC's "object" was to unite the Black people in order to "realise their liberation and emancipation" – outside the framework of separate development. Though much shorter, the Saso constitution expresses much the same objects. The belief is stated that the Black students in South Africa have unique problems and aspirations, and to satisfy them requires consolidated effort and a reassertion of pride and group identity. Saso therefore aims at promoting contact and co-operation among Black students, in order to represent them nationally and internationally.

The usual minimum age limit for members of all the above organisations is seventeen or eighteen years. The SP, clearly in an attempt to attract members for its proposed youth league, sets the limit at sixteen years. Homeland-based parties recruit only among citizens of the homelands, whereas Saso and BPC accept all Blacks – i.e. Africans, Indians and Coloureds. BPC, however, does not enrol supporters of South African government policies.

All African political organisations employ branches with a minimum of ten to twenty members as their basic unit. Branches are all supposed to meet regularly and elect governing committees. In the homeland-based parties, committees are responsible for recruitment of members, registration of voters, organising lectures or seminars for discussion, raising funds, distributing party publications, assisting party candidates at elections, countering hostile action by opponents of the party, carrying out instructions from the higher echelons of the party, and making regular reports to the regional committee of the party concerned.

A youth league is proposed in the constitution of the SP, whereas the DP envisages a women's and youth wings respectively. Neither party has succeeded in actually establishing these organisations.

All political organisations have hierarchical organisations, with branches repesented on regional committees, which are again (except in the case of the CNP) represented on the national executive. Between the branch and regional committees the TNIP and DP also have district committees. The duties of the regional and district committees are of a supervisory and co-ordinating nature.

The national executives of all organisations are responsible for the implementation of the principles, goals and objectives of the organisations. The presidents of Saso and BPC have the threefold function of chief executive, leader and chairman at meetings. The homeland-based parties tend to disperse these functions to a small extent, with the exception of the SP where the chairman, and not the leader, is the chief executive officer. The functions of other national executive members are always carefully delineated.

National executives of Saso, BNP and SP are two-tiered bodies, consisting of a larger executive council, meeting once or twice annually, and a smaller executive committee, meeting more regularly and often. Regional representatives are excluded from the smaller executive committees. All other parties have a small single executive committee.

Annual congresses (called students' general council by Saso) are held by all organisations. All have representatives from branch level upwards, and are regarded as the highest governing and policy-making bodies. Membership fees provided for in the constitutions range from Saso's 20c annually to the 50c annually of the SP. Branches are allowed to take a percentage of fees collected.

Very little changes have occurred in constitutions. Saso replaced "Non-white(s)" with "Black(s)"; and the TNIP brought greater clarity to financial regulations.

Administration

The administrative arrangements of African political organisations depend mainly on voluntary effort by supporters and are greatly deficient in relation to the obligations brought by normal party activities. Among the homeland parties, only the TNIP has a permanent office.

The constitutional requirement of homeland parties that secretaries-general, treasurers and national organisers be elected at annual congresses would have inhibited the appointment of career officials if this had been financially possible. Only the TNIP, among the homeland parties, has a permanent secretary-general. During elections parties usually appoint part-time honorary organisers in urban areas and those homeland areas where it is impossible to work through chiefs and headmen. Pretensions of homeland parties to mass-party status cannot be sustained by their inefficient, small-scale organisational efforts.

The decline and present languishing position of the DP could be ascribed at least partly, to the fact that it has never made a consistent and integrated organisational effort. In April 1972 it elected for the first time a national organiser, who was supposed to work on an honorary, part-time basis, but this appointment had no effect on the party's organisation. In the largest White urban areas, and in those Transkei districts where the DP is relatively strong, supporters perform certain voluntary services for the party, such as organising meetings for the discussion of party problems, to hear visiting party leaders, and so on. Within the DP the post of secretary-general has always been honorary. Archives, records and minutes of meetings are kept in a haphazard way, and old documents are often discarded or lost. There is no co-ordination of effort within constituencies, regions, the Transkei, or among branches outside the Transkei.

Apart from the two paid members of the TNIP's head office staff, all other functionaries are voluntary, part-time workers. The activities of most of these workers are haphazard and intermittent, but more purposeful and manifest than those of the DP.

The TNIP's secretary-general, G. M. Mwanda, a matriculated former civil servant and attorney's articled clerk, was appointed in 1965 as assistant in the TNIP-office in Umtata and shortly afterwards as secretary-general. He is responsible for all the party's administrative work, prepares agendas and minutes of national meetings, supervises financial and ordinary administration of the party on a national basis, maintains contact with regions, districts and branches of the party all over South Africa, disseminates party pamphlets and visits areas where his assistance is required. His visits to Transkei districts are not according to a planned schedule, and between the elections of 1968 and 1973 he had not visited some districts at all. His visits to urban areas outside the Transkei are even less frequent, causing dissatisfaction among urban followers who feel that a more dynamic approach would benefit the party. Finances would not allow this, however.

Although constitutionally required by the TNIP, organisers are not elected to all branch, district and regional committees of the party in urban areas. They occasionally arrange local meetings including meetings addressed by TNIP national executive members, arrange film shows to assist recruitment efforts, disseminate party propaganda, and explain procedural and policy matters as and when necessary. Within the Transkei honorary agents were appointed in every district as contact points for the party. They keep membership cards and are communication channels for the party with chiefs and headmen. In exceptional cases chiefs were appointed as agents.

Saso is the best-staffed Black political organisation in South Africa. At the outset a permanent organiser was appointed to liaise between the executive, the various centres (branches) and the members: he co-ordinates community projects, assists in their planning and is research officer. He was also given the task of investigating the establishment of a Black workers' council to promote solidarity among Black workers. A field worker was appointed in 1972 to assist him in this task and to organise a national workers' seminar. Public relations work is undertaken by the general secretary. A permanent administrative assistant was appointed in December 1971 to provide greater continuity in the administration of the head office in Durban. The general secretary and permanent organiser were appointed for three-year terms.

Administrative and financial decisions are highly centralised in all political organisations; branches are accountable to the national executive and annual congress, and the Transvaal and Western Cape branches of the TNIP have successfully objected against rulings by regional committees. Co-ordinating work by unpaid honorary regional organisers has proved indispensable, though not nearly sufficient, for the oldest homeland-based party, the TNIP.

Procedures for accountability are less well-developed in homeland-based parties than in Saso. Informal contact with regional and lower committee members provides important sources of information, and regular informers operate in certain areas. At least one possible rival for the leadership of the TNIP was known to be "smelled out" in this way. Needless to say, such practices are deterimental to innovative thinking, and strengthen strict central control.

The public use of slogans and symbols is not popular among African political organisations. Only the CNIP made constitutional provision for the adoption of a symbol – the leopard (erroneously referred to in the constitution as "tiger"), whereas through constant use Saso and BPC have adopted, respectively, a raised clenched Black fist and a broken chain as symbols.[1] The BNP has a circular emblem depicting two clasped hands against a background of the rising sun (symbolising the future), with the inscription *Tswaraganang lo dire*, meaning "support and work".

Finance

The financial position of all African political organisations in South Africa is, on their own admission, precarious. Homeland-based parties rely mostly on membership fees, donations, levies on legislative assembly members, special fund-raising efforts like film shows, concerts and dinner parties, the sale of identification marks or (in the case of the BNP) the party emblem. Saso also derives income from the sale of its publications, notably the *Saso Newsletter*. The BNP also succeeded in raising a loan of R6,000 to finance part of its 1972 election campaign in Bophuthatswana. According to the BNP's calculations, this campaign required about R15,000, which was met, apart from the loan, by donations of more than R6,000 and income from membership fees, functions and the sale of emblems.

The Transkei DP, the oldest homeland-based party, is in worse financial straits than any other. Without formal membership, it has no regular source of income. At its congress of 16 September 1972 the DP resolved to improve the position. It was also resolved that the area committees (branches) would be the "mainspring" of the party's finances, and they were empowered to keep the exceptionally high quota of two-thirds of the amount raised, and return one-third to the national executive. Nothing was done to implement these decisions. Generally fund-raising efforts by homeland-based parties are determined by the needs of the moment, and there is no advance financial planning.

The income of Saso is much higher than that of any other political organisation – as indeed is its expenditure on its many projects. Foreign grants and a commitment by branches and affiliated centres to contribute a certain amount for every member they represent account for most of its income. Thus Pretoria, the Reef, and the University of the North committed themselves in 1972 to R1 per member annually, whereas other branches and centres paid 50c per member annually. Scholarships and contributions for specific projects were received from several students' organisations in Europe. Grants were also received from the World University Service and the International University Exchange Fund. No assistance was received from Unesco on the grounds that South Africa was not a member of the organisation – a fact for which Saso felt it should not be held responsible.

The TNIP experienced some difficulties in establishing satisfactory financial procedure at all levels. Initially, money collected by branches reached the secretary-general through the district and regional committees. Following suspicion of misappropriation in the intermediate levels, the party constitution was amended and circulars were issued to all committees in 1971 to the effect that branch committees should send all membership fees and donations directly to the secretary-general by bank draft; all other monies collected by branch, district and regional committees could be appropriated by them as they saw fit. The Transvaal regional committee of the TNIP failed to hold annual elections of committee members in 1968–71, and contrary to instructions continued to handle money from branches. It was necessary for the party leader, Chief Kaiser Matanzima, to pay a visit to the Witwatersrand personally in order to straighten the matter out. A new nominated interim executive was appointed and the financial procedure brought in line with the constitutional requirements. Similar problems have not been experienced by other parties.

Structure

Unlike BPC (which had branches in Johannesburg, Pretoria, Durban, Cape Town, Natal South Coast, and Pietermaritzburg before the first full conference in December 1972) and Saso, the homeland-based parties were relatively slow to establish their grassroots organisation, and several months invariably elapsed after their establishment before any of them made significant efforts to this end. Structures proposed in the respective constitutions are never closely adhered to, which causes organisational weaknesses but no great worry among the party leaders. In this respect too Saso appears the most efficient and tightly organised. Various commissions, without decision-making powers, form part of the top structure of Saso, and projects of a continuing nature are entrusted to them, such as the Literacy Commission, Planning Commission, Cultural Commission ("Cul-com") and Advisory Council for Publications.

Meetings of the executive committee and staff of Saso are held monthly, thus promoting familiarity and regular consultation among members. The executive council meets in May and December each year to review planning, administration, projects and the next conference. The annual intervarsity sports meeting on 7 April 1972 at the University of Zululand was used by the SRC presidents and other campus representatives to report on progress since the executive councils' previous meeting in December 1971.

In Bophuthatswana branches had been formed by the BNP at Odi, Mabopane, Mothutlung and Ga-Rankuwa before the party's constitution was confirmed by its first congress, held in February 1973. Further branches were established later, but certain difficulties were encountered, as in Bloemfontein, a BNP stronghold, where no branch could be established when respectively six and seven people turned up at meetings. The BNP assembled only two regional committees, each assisted by two regional organisers. The Bophuthatswana opposition, the Seoposengwe Party, was still struggling to establish a grass-roots organisation months after the general election of October 1972. In the Ciskei, the CNP and CNIP made a start with the establishment of branch committees in the second half of 1973.

The constitutional provisions of the Transkei Democratic Party (DP) regarding its structure are largely formalistic and the party's actual structure is informal. There were none the less early attempts to comply with the constitution, and in January 1965 the DP declared that the organisation was taking shape, and that committees had been established in East London, Cape Town, Durban, the Witwatersrand, and in most of the nine constituencies of the Transkei. Enquiries were received from various White urban areas. Dissent in the East London committee, when subjects of Tembu Paramount Chief Sabata Dalindyebo tried to gain control, soon made it powerless. Since 1968, when the DP suffered a serious setback in the general election, its organisation has steadily declined. The previously strong Durban area committee dissolved when the DP members of the Legislative Assembly from Eastern Pondoland, who had been mainly responsible for its vitality, all lost their seats. The Johannesburg committee suffered when the DP executive insisted that prospective committee members declare their previous political affiliations; the executive feared that members of banned organisations might gain control of DP committees for their own ends. In Port Elizabeth the DP has never established a viable committee. The only active area committee which remained outside the Transkei is in Cape Town, while a recalcitrant regional committee gained a foothold in East London.

Within the Transkei there are a few informal local and area DP committees, and one regional committee in the Emboland region. DP supporters in the Transkei often meet for political discussion and for the informal election of a local area committee. Each of these groups consists of ten to fifteen people, and depends entirely on local initiative. A general decline in enthusiasm for committee service since the DP's defeat in the 1968 election is evident in all parts of the Transkei, and is also partly ascribed to fear of victimisation by TNIP-oriented chiefs. The paucity of area committees, which caused concern at the 1971 DP national congress, was ascribed by the party Secretary, H. H. T. Bubu, to the DP's poor financial position.[2]

The TNIP's organisational drive was launched at about the same time as that of the DP, namely towards the end of 1964, continuing during February 1965 in Bloemfontein, Welkom and Odendaalsrus in the Orange Free State. Interest in the TNIP was also demonstrated at this stage in Durban and Pietermaritzburg in Natal. Only in 1965 did the leader of the party issue a circular to his supporters among members of the legislative assembly, requesting them to hold meetings in their constituencies to explain TNIP policy, and with a view to opening party offices in each constituency, a suggestion which never materialised. He also suggested that chiefs and headmen be invited to these meetings.

Branches are not found in all Transkei constituencies, not even in some TNIP strongholds, such as Eastern Pondoland and Unzimkulu. Western Pondoland, until 1973 a DP stronghold, also had no branches. On the other hand, relatively strong branches exist in Umtata and Qumbu where the DP is quite strong (Umtata was captured by the TNIP only in 1973 whereas Qumbu remained in DP hands). Due to poor attendance at meetings, branch committees can sometimes not be properly constituted, and co-option of members is then resorted to. In most large White urban areas branches have been established. District committees are sometimes not established, and branches are then directly represented in regional committees, for example in Emboland in the Transkei, the Orange Free State, and some Witwatersrand and Transvaal districts. The actual organisation of the party in the Transvaal only broadly corresponds to the boundaries laid down in a circular by the party's secretary-general dividing the Transvaal into nine districts for organisational purposes. In Eastern Pondoland, since 1968 held in the Legislative Assembly by TNIP members and one independent, branch and district organisations are non-existent, and a regional committee manages all party affairs. The best-developed district organisation is perhaps that of the Western Cape where five districts are viable and in regular contact with the regional executive.

Characterised by slackness, the TNIP structure has an advantage over that of the DP only because the latter is even more inefficient and lacking in energy. In tribal areas the TNIP and DP, as well as all other homeland-based parties, rely largely on traditional chiefs and headmen for recruitment of support. Tribal loyalty remains foremost and party loyalty accordingly suffers. The TNIP, however, does not allow chiefs to serve on party committees in order to protect them from political exposure which might affect their dignity, and to protect the party from the possible inefficiency of life-long chiefly members. This decision resulted from early experiences of the party when the organisational assistance of some chiefs proved worthless.

A caucus was formed by all TNIP members of the Legislative Assembly, mainly to prepare motions to be tabled by TNIP-members and to determine the party's approach to matters before the Assembly. The caucus has no committees and it meets four times a week. Without formal status in the party, it is completely dominated by the party leader, Kaiser Matanzima. The caucus of DP members in the Assembly has similar duties, but has also established

study committees under the chairmanship of six shadow ministers
to make participation in debates more effective. Indications are
that homeland-based parties established in 1972 and 1973 are following the example of the two older parties in the Transkei in establishing parliamentary caucuses with similar functions.

Recruitment and Membership

An important difference between the homeland-based parties on
the one hand, and Saso and BPC on the other, is that the latter,
through their intention to penetrate voluntary Black organisations
and establish new ones, are able to draw on a variety of interest
groups for recruitment purposes. Saso's affiliated centres also rapidly
increase that organisation's paid-up members through mass enrolment of entire student bodies. The homeland-based parties
rely exclusively on recruitment of individuals, and so far have made
no effort at establishing relations with voluntary associations. The
women members of the TNIP in Bloemfontein established their
own branch when they found it difficult to attend meetings which
were mainly in the evenings. This branch, the "Women's League",
has permission from the TNIP head office to function independently.
Similar efforts by TNIP women in Johannesburg and Cape Town
were soon abandoned.

Homeland-based parties established in 1973 – namely the LNP,
LPP, CNP, CNIP, VNP and VIP – allowed several months to
elapse before starting to recruit members and establish branches.
In Venda the ruling faction relied almost exclusively on chiefs and
headmen for recruitment of support before it established the
Venda National Party. The KwaZulu government enjoys great
loyalty and support, although there is no party or other organisation behind it. Its success stems partly from the support it receives
from the majority of chiefs in the Legislative Assembly, and partly
from the great personal popularity of the executive councillors –
particularly Chief Gatsha Buthelezi – in urban areas.

There are several problems confronting the recruitment efforts
of homeland-based parties. Many people, especially in the rural
areas, have never belonged to a political party and see little need to
change this habit. To apathy can be added a deep-rooted suspicion
among many Africans of all political activity. In rural areas, where
a parochial political culture predominates, people tend to be
suspicious of universally-oriented political organisations, often
with leaders who, in many localities, are total strangers. In
the urban areas, economic experience, education and, in frequent
cases, experience of the activities of the African National Congress

and Pan African Congress and their banning, tend to widen political horizons, and political awareness is greater. Memories of the long-
drawn-out confrontation between African political organisations
and the South African government in the 1950s and early 1960s
are sufficiently fresh to cause a fairly pervasive reluctance to be
associated with overt political activity. However, the greater political awareness of urban people, and the higher population density
and better transport facilities in urban areas contribute to the fact
that branches are more easily formed in urban areas than in rural
areas.

The parties try to overcome recruitment problems in various ways.
The most overt measure in rural and urban areas is the appointment
of part-time honorary organisers, and sometimes of part-time paid
organisers, who are well versed in their party's aims and its constitution. Apart from dealing with new members, they try to identify
grievances, but opinion surveys are only seldom undertaken,
and depend entirely on the initiative and effort of the local organiser. All parties agree that the most effective method of enrolment
is to rely on individual members to recruit their friends. The secretary-general of the TNIP, a full-time official, sometimes visits areas
where membership is lagging and tries to invigorate the local supporters – often unsuccessfully. From his office in Umtata he is in a
position to communicate with the Transkei government on behalf
of many people in connection with their complaints and problems.
He thus builds up goodwill for the party and has enrolled many
new members.

In urban areas the support of influential local people has favourable effects on recruitment. In Bloemfontein, for instance, the
BNP failed to form a branch, supposedly because no influential
person was known to be an active supporter of the party. Para-
doxically, the majority of Tswanas in Bloemfontein supported the
BNP in the 1972 general election, underlining the difference between support recruitment and membership recruitment.

Another urban recruitment problem stems from the South African
influx control system. Many urban Africans qualify in terms of
Section 10 of the Bantu Urban Areas (Consolidation) Act, 1945,
for quasi-permanent residential status in White urban areas, and
many have lived in urban areas since birth. Some have no desire
to participate in the governmental affairs of a homeland, whereas
others are interested but do not wish to be too closely identified
with a homeland politically because of an unfounded fear that they
might lose their "permanent" status in the urban area. Another
urban group realises that homeland-based parties are oriented towards homeland governments without jurisdiction in White urban

areas, and regards membership of these parties as a waste of time. The position is slightly different, however, in KwaZulu and Bophuthatswana, where large African townships near Pietermaritzburg and Durban, and near Pretoria, respectively, are inside the homelands, and the jurisdiction of the homeland governments. In the Ciskei, Zwelitsha and Mdantsane townships and, in Lebowa, Seshego township, are also inside the homelands.

A common problem experienced in the Transkei, by the TNIP as well as the DP, was that membership cards have sometimes been sold by unknown people under false pretences, for example that they would give exemption from taxes or influx control. At the time of the establishment of parties in the Transkei, there was still unrest in certain areas due to the activities of the underground, violence-oriented Poqo organisation. The DP, as well as Poqo, had a 25c membership fee and both opposed South African government policy. This caused some confusion over the DP's identity, which in turn led the DP to stop formal recruitment of members. The private and illegal sale of membership cards to TNIP and DP supporters still continues, and is made possible through the widespread ignorance in tribal areas about the functions and activities of political parties.

Africans in White rural areas are left out in the cold by all the homeland-based parties. Only in the Western Cape is some attention given by the TNIP to the recruitment of farm labourers. It is made possible by the smallness of the farms and the high population density, but even so the distance from farms to urban African townships, the long working hours of farm labourers and the unfriendly attitude of some farm owners are inhibiting factors.

The fact that the conditions of service of government servants and teachers in the homelands prevent them from joining political organisations and publicly commenting on their employer excludes most of the rural élite from belonging to political parties. Although they can and do exercise influence in many covert ways, their overt support would have stimulated the parties considerably.

Membership and support are also affected by particular policy issues and leadership disputes. When in August 1972 Kaiser Matanzima announced changes in his party's policy on White citizenship in the Transkei, and on a federation of self-governing territories, without first consulting the executive of his party, the TNIP, great confusion resulted in the party at all levels.

It gradually became clear that Matanzima had not been wooing DP supporters, but rather marginal elements adhering to the more universalistic values of African unity and non-racialism. Matanzima probably knew well enough that his remarks would have no impact on the rank and file tribal voters, and it is quite possible that he addressed them principally to White South Africans to impress upon them certain possible alternatives to separate development.

It is the continuation of leadership disputes, rather than the TNIP's policy changes, which is draining the DP of supporters. Important DP members have left because of dissatisfaction with the party's leadership. Thus, Dr. H. P. Bala resigned in April 1968 because of "vaccilating leadership";[3] Cromwell Diko, who had been (like Dr. Bala) a DP member of the TLA between 1963 and 1968, resigned for the same reasons in 1968 and joined the TPFP, later joining the TNIP because he supported Matanzima on independence and the land question. Dissatisfaction over leadership also caused Mr. Vanqa, who established the TPDP, to leave the DP in 1968. Dr. Bala remarked, on leaving the DP, that his own viewpoint on non-racialism could no longer be accommodated within the multi-racialistic DP. He could also no longer reconcile himself with the DP's support for chieftainship, which was obsolete in the twentieth century; the party was inconsistent over the apartheid issue, and he could no longer tolerate the continuous disputes between party members.[4] Many of the DP's early supporters joined solely because it presented the first legal opportunity, after the banning of the ANC and PAC, for opposing South African Government policy, but they became disillusioned by the extremely moderate multi-racialism preached by the DP and its essentially rural character.

The TNIP also suffered from leadership disputes at all levels. In the Witwatersrand and Western Cape regions, entire regional committees had to be suspended for not abiding by constitutional provisions and directives from the secretary-general. Suspicion over the financial administration in these regional committees scared away many prospective members. Disputes at regional level led to rival factions in the underlying district and branch committees, with a further loss of members.

At national level three serious divisions occurred, respectively in 1966, 1968 and 1971. Only the latter caused the TNIP substantial loss of support and the loss of one seat in the 1973 general election when a former cabinet member, C. M. C. Ndamse, beat the TNIP candidate in Mt. Ayliff constituency.

Urban-based political organisations reveal little about their recruitment efforts. The BPC is open to all Africans, Indians and Coloureds, but apart from the fact that several branches have been established, no membership figures are available. The BPC does not believe in mass political rallies, but rather in private discussions and contribution to the improvement of the Black communities. Re-

cruitment among Indians received a setback when the Natal Indian Congress expressed its oposition to Black consciousness in 1971.

When the BPC was established in 1972 a decade had passed in
which homeland leaders filled a need for African political leadership.
If the BPC and Saso had appeared on the scene earlier, they might
have filled this vacuum more effectively. Significant in this respect
is the refusal by students at the University of Zululand in July
1971 to affiliate to Saso as a result of its president's criticism of
Gatsha Buthelezi's conditional support for separate development.[5]

As a result of the parochial orientation prevalent among the
African workers and rural population, the broad ideal and philosophical content of Black consciousness is often regarded by them
with little comprehension, and at worst suspected as a sell-out to
other ethnic groups. Failure to offer simpler explanations retards
expansion of BPC as well as Saso. Both organisations have their
origins among intellectuals and their roots in idealism, and in
consequence are regarded as snobbish, élitist and exclusive[6] not
only by homeland leaders but by an increasing number of potential
supporters, especially among the less well educated. This, however,
does not detract them from their ideological commitments and
policy objectives.

Saso's total membership rose from about 4,000 early in 1972
to about 7,000 early in 1973. Affiliated centres account for the
largest contributions to this number. Thus, early in 1972, 1,300
members affiliated from the University of the North, 750 from the
University of Zululand, and 481 from the University of Natal
(Black section) and 102 from the Federal Theological Seminary.
Branches consisted of between 100 and 150 members, with only 20
members in the Lutheran Theological Seminary.[7] Membership
increased after the decision to expand the organisation into the
White urban areas and African rural areas: this was done by
establishing branches and launching self-help projects. Furthermore,
the definition of "student" was widened to include almost anybody;
"studentship" was defined by former Saso president Temba Sono
as "a state of mind, a particular ambition, a particular awareness
of one's social role".[8] Strong opposition was encountered in secondary schools, especially in self-governing African areas. School
principals generally are not sympathetic to Saso, and the homeland
governments' opposition was aroused by Saso's rejection of them.

The banning of Saso and BPC leaders will undoubtedly deprive
both organisations of strong leadership at a vital stage of their
development and this will have long-term consequences. In the
short term it is almost certain to cause many prospective members
to fade away. There is also reason to think that bannings have a

splintering effect by causing many small, localised organisations to be established with the ideal of Black solidarity and consciousness as their point of departure. Such splinter groups could work for a long time in isolation before finally joining forces when it is opportune.

Among the homeland-based parties, only the TNIP has significant membership figures. Mostly these parties are too young to be able to present membership data. For several years the DP had no dues-paying members, and a decision of its annual congress of September 1972 to resume the formal recruitment of members remained a dead letter.

Because of the mobility of urban Africans within urban areas and between urban areas and homelands, it is difficult to keep track of party supporters. As a result of this, and of poor records, neither the TNIP nor the DP has a clear conception of the distribution of its followers in urban areas outside the Transkei, and canvassing for elections has in several cases been misdirected.

The number of enrolled members claimed by certain district and regional committees of the TNIP in urban areas does not agree with figures given by the secretary-general of the TNIP. Figures are mostly based on estimates. The Orange Free State, Witwatersrand, and Western Cape regions of the TNIP had no reliable statistics on membership. In all cases they were "in preparation" at the time of research. Information on individual branches and districts was given by branch and district committee members. In the Southern Orange Free State there were five branches in 1973 with membership ranging between 5 and 200, with a total of approximately 266. In the Northern Orange Free State the number of branches and their members were not known to the regional organiser in Bloemfontein, but it was ascertained that at least two fairly large branches existed in Odendaalsrus and Welkom. The estimate of 1,000 members for the entire Orange Free State by the secretary-general exceeds those given by the committee members.

The Western Cape regional membership, given by district committees in 1973, was approximately 1,000, of whom 611 were in the Cape Town district. The estimate for the Western Cape by the secretary-general was 3,000.

In the Witwatersrand region no figures could be given by several regional committee members, but viable branches existed in at least two districts, namely three in Tembisa and two in Vereeniging (Sharpeville), with respectively 500 and 60 members. The estimate for the Witwatersrand by the secretary-general was 3,000 members.

According to the secretary-general of the TNIP the total membership figures for only the Transkei at the end of 1971 and beginning of 1972 was 6,000. This was regarded as particularly low and it had been as high as 15,000 in some years. The highest enrolment was in the Cofimvaba district – home of the Chief Minister – and the lowest in the Libode district where the former DP leader, Victor Poto, lived.

In the constitutions of Saso and BPC, no provision for disciplinary measures is made and no offences are specified. However, the 1972 annual congress of Saso censured its president, Temba Sono, for advocating contact with homeland leaders, and unanimously called on him to resign – which he did.[9] Although the constitutions of homeland-based parties refer to offences and discipline, these are not clearly defined. Final decisions rest with the national executives, while lower committees are sometimes expected to submit reports on disputes and alleged offences. Punishment is either through expulsion, or steps determined by the national executive.

Generally reconciliation is sought by national executives, except where the interests of the party could be harmed irreparably. Steps against members have almost invariably been taken only when they had decided to oppose official party candidates at elections. Repeated flouting of party directives by the Witwatersrand and Western Cape regional committees of the TNIP always led to dismissal from office, but retention of party membership. In the Witwatersrand, for instance, the first TNIP agents, R. Nkopo and J. G. Mtwesi, were dismissed in November 1964 by the party leader because of unresolved differences. The second and third regional committees had to be dismissed from office as a result of maladministration and inefficiency, and a fourth committee was appointed in 1972. Always the persons concerned remained members of the TNIP.

REFERENCES

1. *Daily Dispatch*, 8.6.1973.
2. Official minutes of 1971 annual DP congress.
3. *Daily Dispatch*, 27.4.1968.
4. *Daily Dispatch*, 20.4.1968.
5. Saso, Executive Report to 3rd General Students' Council, 1972.
6. Cf. Asseca, Report of General Secretary for 1970–2.
7. Saso, Executive Report to 3rd General Students' Council, 1972.
8. *The Star*, 29.6.1972.
9. Saso, Minutes of 3rd General Students' Council, 1972, Motions Nos. 6/72 and 7/72.

7

PARTY LEADERSHIP

Introduction

African political organisations in South Africa place great value upon educational and professional achievement in their recruits. Within the parties and legislative assemblies, such achievement is almost as important as acceptance of the parties' policies. In the homeland parties, tribal status also plays a role, and where prominent traditional leaders have achieved no leading party or governmental position, their more prominent subjects are accommodated – invariably people with educational and professional status in their own right or personal prestige in their localities. Those who aspire to advance themselves in politics are not expected to have a great aptitude for politics. Most leadership disputes in the past have stemmed from the aspirations of political activists who pursued their objectives ruthlessly and sometimes deviously. The national leader is required under all circumstances to maintain an unchallenged supremacy while his sole right to interpret policy is jealously guarded.

All African political organisations are exclusive of Whites, either in terms of their support for separate development, or in terms of their pursuit of Black consciousness as the way to self-reliance and political emancipation – quite apart from segregationist requirements imposed by the Prohibition of Political Interference Act. The populations of the respective homelands are by no means ethnically exclusive, although in each a particular ethnic group is dominant. Thus, in the Transkei and Ciskei, which are predominantly Xhosa, the fairly large but minority Basotho population was accommodated in the leadership of the governing parties (TNIP and CNIP) and the cabinet, in order to recruit Basotho support. In other homelands minority groups, such as the Pedis in Bophuthatswana and the Ndebele in Lebowa, are too small to enforce significant representation.

Tribal, as distinct from ethnic, affiliation is a fairly important leadership norm in homelands where large tribal groups co-exist. In the Ciskei, for example, the Rarabes, Tembus and Fingos and in the Transkei the Tembus, Emigrant Tembus, Western Pondos, Eastern Pondos, Fingos and Gcalekas were able to influence decisively the polarisation of leadership immediately before and after the establishment of the first political parties, laying down a pattern of loyalties which persisted later. On the other hand, the geographical and tribal dispersal of people in Lebowa and KwaZulu make particular tribal pressures difficult to exert. No clear trend developed in Bophuthatswana, although leading party posts in the BNP and cabinet posts went to people who were widely dispersed geographically and who also belonged to various tribes where they respectively occupied leading positions.

Businessmen, chiefs and headmen, farmers and teachers form the majority of candidates and elected members in the homelands, with a smattering of participants who are attorneys, university lecturers, clerks, nurses, labourers, builders, etc. In the case of chiefs and headmen, no particular trend is discernible: they seem moderately successful candidates in elections. Constitutional attempts to ensure leading positions for chiefs have obliged the Chief Ministers in some homelands to appoint chiefs to cabinet rank. The Transkei and Ciskei are the only homelands without such stipulations. In the Ciskei no chief holds cabinet office, and of the four chiefs in the Transkei cabinet of seven, three possess degrees and pursued other occupations before assuming the chieftainship, the two Matanzimas as attorneys and Ndabankulu as a school principal.

Although purporting to be national organisations, the BPC and Saso leadership consists almost exclusively of urban people, which has given rise to special attempts at extending their influence to homelands. (Homeland-based parties recruit leaders almost exclusively from among homeland residents.) There is no doubt of the élitism existing among Saso and BPC leaders. Saso and BPS accused the ANC and PAC of élitism and of having been out of touch with the masses, but they seem to have assumed the same characteristics. This trend no doubt gives them an intellectual advantage, especially in leadership ranks, but seriously hampers membership recruitment among the parochially oriented and less educated masses.

Homeland-based parties such as the DP, CNIP and CNP, and even those without constitutionally prescribed procedures for nomination of election candidates (e.g. TNIP, BNP, SP), leave the first stage of nominations in the hands of local followers or members, with a final decision by the national executive. Nomination procedure has caused more dissatisfaction in homeland-based parties than any other factor and generally they have not succeeded in achieving consensus on the legitimacy of procedures and results.

The greatest success at nomination was achieved by the tightly knit Sebe faction and the embryonic VIP, respectively in the Ciskei and Venda, employing completely centralised methods of nomination for their respective general elections in 1973. Their selected candidates were remarkably successful and were not opposed by disgruntled unsuccessful candidates. In contrast the TNIP, DP and BNP contended with numerous dissatisfied candidates who had been eliminated at lower levels of nomination procedure. All three parties were opposed at elections by some of these candidates who then persisted in propagating the party policy. The TNIP and the DP on several occasions received back into their fold some of the independents who had thus been successful. In the case of the TNIP and DP, the three Transkeian general elections after 1963 and several by-elections showed a decreasing number of independents, indicating greater success in imposing party discipline at nominations – but a larger number of election successes by independents, indicating increasing flaws in the nomination procedures. However, party affiliation remains the most important leadership recruitment norm in homeland politics.

The position of chiefs in homeland politics remains controversial. On the one hand there is a feeling that chiefs should be accommodated in a house of chiefs as a kind of chamber of review to a lower house of elected members, and on the other it is recognised that chiefs still have an important role in daily politics and that their segregation from elected members could lead to an undesirable polarisation of political interests. Several factors in the South African homelands contribute to the continued recognition of chiefs as leaders by a large section of the African population. The relatively undifferentiated social and economic structure in the homelands helps to perpetuate the tribal organisation and its leadership norms, whereas local government policy (applied in the form of Bantu authorities) enhances the status and powers of chiefs and headmen by conferring on them minor administrative and judicial powers. The influence and status of chiefs are recognised by the political parties, who tend to rely on their support in the recruitment effort, rather than by-passing them with their own independent efforts. In the Transkei, the chiefs in the Legislative Assembly are largely harnessed by party discipline, which neutralises their influence as a majority group. This was achieved at first by institutionalising tribal differences in political parties, and the discipline was later strengthened when the increase in the number of chiefs made possible the omission of recalcitrant chiefs at the election of chiefs to the Legislative Assembly.

In all homelands the chiefs form a majority in the Legislative

Assembly, and without exception they have been wooed by every aspiring candidate for chief ministership. Support for a candidate indicates a chief's subsequent support for the governing or opposing party. After the election of a Chief Minister, all legislative assemblies pass through a phase where chiefs and elected members re-align their political affiliations – mostly in favour of the government, except in Venda where Chief Minister Mphephu had difficulty in retaining his support among chiefs and headmen. At the end of this phase the voting power of the chiefs is harnessed by the respective parties – except in Gazankulu where no parties are represented in the assembly.

Leadership disputes are found at all levels of the homeland parties and are of frequent occurrence. This is not true in the case of Saso and BPC, where a quick turnover of leaders was ensured by their successive banning in 1973; this at the same time demanded solidarity at all levels of the organisations. Only disputes at high level – within national executives of homeland parties and among aspiring election candidates – have given rise to expulsions and resignations. In only three cases were disputes the result of clear policy differences; the first between the TNIP and Sinaba over the independence issue in 1966; the second between Saso and Sono over co-operation with homeland leaders in 1972; and the third between Bubu and the DP over co-operation between the TNIP and DP on certain policy issues in 1973. Other leadership disputes arose mainly from leadership aspirations among prominent party members (e.g. between respectively Ndamse and Sobahle, and the TNIP), and dissatisfaction over the style of leadership (e.g. between Guzana and sections of the DP, and Mangope and sections of the BNP). These disputes mostly had little effect on the parties, except in the case of the DP where continuous disputes after 1966 depleted the membership of the party and made it almost powerless, and the BNP where dissatisfaction culminated in a no-confidence motion in the Legislative Assembly in 1974, narrowly averted by Mangope, who then unsuccessfully tried to expel his main opponents from the party – a failure which led to his establishment of a new party.

Leadership in all political organisations is highly centralised. In the case of the homeland-based parties the national leader maintains almost absolute control over all aspects of organisation and policy, nominations, tactics and parliamentary approach. He dominates caucus meetings, while the extra-parliamentary parties are invariably too weak to influence the caucuses in any way. The political skill, sophistication, experience and educational level of party leaders – especially in governing parties – place

those leaders in a position far above most of their followers and
enable them to exercise decisive influence. Infringement or any
threat of infringement of this ascendancy is ruthlessly dealt with.

Saso and BPC show a greater tendency to share control and co
ordinate activities through delegation of power to members of the
national executive, spadework by committees, co-ordination through
regular executive meetings, and accounting of activities through
detailed written reports.

Party Leadership

The first leaders of the Transkei National Independence Party
were formally elected at the party's inaugural congress on
23 April 1964 at Umtata. The congress was attended by about
seventy delegates from all parts of the Transkei, and eight from
the Witwatersrand.

The first regional committees of the TNIP in urban areas were
appointed by the secretary-general, who nominated chairmen and
secretaries on the recommendation of local supporters. They
were then left with the task to set up elected district and branch
committees, cause further regional committee members to be
elected, and arrange elections of all regional committee member
after the first year.

Policy and leadership disputes forced the TNIP executive to take
drastic steps against leading members in 1966 and again in 1968
and it was unable to act decisively in a third case in 1972. The
first case occurred when S. M. Sinaba, member of the first
national executive, tried to force the party to request immediate
independence for the Transkei. At a TNIP regional conference
arranged by Sinaba in the Maluti region on 18 December 1965 a
motion to this effect was introduced by J. Z. Kobo, a member of
the TNIP Witwatersrand regional executive, and unanimously
adopted. After the conference George Matanzima said that he
had never before heard of Kobo, whom he called an extremist and
a stooge of the (White) United Party. He also said that the
regional conference decision had not been submitted to the national
executive. The TNIP committees in the Witwatersrand and East
London thereafter dissociated themselves from the motion, fol
lowed by a meeting of voters, chiefs, headmen, and members of
the Maluti regional authority. Sinaba was forced to resign from the
TNIP soon afterwards.

Next, a rising personality and TNIP front-bencher, and former
chairman of the Transkei Public Service Commission, P. M
Sobahle, was dismissed from the party for "flirting" with the DP

There was also some suspicion among the TNIP that Sobahle could have been the spearhead of tribally motivated aspirations of the Eastern Pondo supporters of the party to obtain a greater voice in government. In a similar case, former cabinet minister Ndamse was accused of being self-seeking, flouting party decisions, opposing policy decisions, and violating the confidentiality of party material. At the root of these accusations lay a belief that Ndamse was actively aspiring towards the party leadership. At the TNIP's annual conference in 1972 he successfully challenged these accusations. In an abortive attempt to expel him from the conference it became clear that a serious rift in the TNIP would follow, and the matter was referred to the caucus and national executive. After frank discussions in the caucus Ndamse was allowed to remain a member of the TNIP. The party leadership pointedly ignored him at the 1973 conference, and eventually he was forced to resign when his candidature in the Mt. Ayliff constituency was not accepted by the national executive for the 1973 general election.

The first national executive committee of the DP was elected on 5 April 1964. From the start the DP attracted supporters of various convictions, with opposition to separate development the only common factor. By 1966 the moderates (i.e. those in favour of multi-racialism and partnership between White and Black) had gained control of the party. In April 1966 Poto decided to relinquish the leadership, being sixty-nine years of age and in poor health: he was succeeded by K. M. N. Guzana. Poto's resignation came shortly after five DP members, who were also prominent members of the Legislative Assembly, had been arrested on charges of conspiracy to murder the Chief Minister. Although Poto's resignation was said to have no connection with these events, they illustrated the divergent streams within the DP and the difficulties of leadership at that early stage. Poto remained an honorary member of the national executive and retained great influence behind the scenes. His continued interest in the party and personal intervention at crucial stages helped to stabilise the moderate image of the DP, and it was mainly due to his support for Guzana – and Guzana's tenacity – that the latter remained leader of the DP.

Disloyalty in certain DP circles towards the leader and national executive has continued throughout Guzana's term of office as leader, reaching a climax in 1971 and 1972. In February 1971 the Tembuland regional committee (including Tembu Paramount Chief Sabata Dalindyebo who is constitutionally an *ex-officio* member of the DP executive) forced the national executive to relinquish its official candidates for the Umtata by-election in favour of its own candidate. A committee member also called for the rejection of Guzana as leader. In the face of the by-election of of 1971, the DP's annual congress in that year decided to postpone the election of a national executive until 1972. The flames of the resulting controversy were fanned by the news that the April 1972 congress would be held at Qumbu, the constituency of S. S Majeke, a staunch Guzana supporter. With its largely informal organisation, DP conferences are attended mostly by volunteers at their own cost. Afraid that this would put Guzana at an advantage in Qumbu, the Tembuland regional committee objected to this venue. In the meantime the Tembuland and Border regional committees had advised Dalindyebo to assume the leadership of the party and to suspend Guzana.* After the attempt to oust Guzana a meeting attended by the rebels and the national executive committee was held at Poto's Great Place, Nyandeni, and it was agreed with Poto's full support, that Guzana would remain party leader but that the venue for the congress would be moved from Qumbu to Umtata. Dalindyebo subsequently denied his involvement in a leadership contest and said that he had merely been approached by regional committees of the party to assume leadership in order to prevent a split in the party. However, the committee member continued their campaign against Guzana on the grounds that he was neglecting his duties as leader.

At the congress of April 1972 Dalindyebo refused nomination for any office and remained an ordinary *ex-officio* member of the national executive. None of the rebels or their supporters gained election to the national executive. At this congress it became evident that out of the DP's twenty-three Legislative Assembly members only six supported the rebels. The complaints against Guzana were not discussed or investigated. Some of the rebel continued their struggle against Guzana, but without the support of Dalindyebo and Mgqweto. By the beginning of 1973 Kobo was chairman of the Tembuland regional committee and tried unsuccessfully to have Guzana rejected as official party candidate in the Mqanduli constituency for the 1973 general election. Guzana's leadership had indeed been tottering at the beginning of 1971 but his position was strengthened through the very rashness and arrogance of the rebellion against him. However, he failed to consolidate his position, and did not call a meeting of the new executive for at least seven months after the April 1972 congress only maintaining contact with individual members, and was con

* Leading members of the regional committee were G. G. Kut (Engcobo), L. Mgudlwa (Engcobo), N. Nkosiyane (Mqanduli) and S Mgqweto (Umtata) (all members of the legislative assembly) and J. Z Kobo, who in 1966 became deputy leader of the TPFP.

tent with meeting them at a special party conference in September 1973.

It seems as if the DP expends the greater part of its energy on internal squabbles, and that the alternative leaders present a choice between impetuosity and timidity. When some of the Tembuland rebels contested and defeated official party candidates in the Engcobo constituency in 1973, Guzana adopted a new hard line towards them and at first refused to have them back in the party, but was later reconciled with some of them. However, by then the entire DP had been almost completely dissipated, and Guzana's personal support in the Legislative Assembly had become depleted to eleven members out of 110, while outside the Assembly attitudes of DP supporters were hardening against him.

Leadership disputes occurred in other homeland-based parties, and had much the same origins as those in the Transkeian parties. In Lebowa, dissatisfaction within the opposition Lebowa National Party with the leadership of Chief Matlala, coupled with the similarity of its policies with those of the ruling Lebowa People's Party, caused the party's leading members to pressurise Matlala into amalgamating with the LPP in March 1974. Since being defeated in his bid for the chief ministership, Matlala has been unable to forge his LNP into an effective opposition. Being short of members who could form a shadow cabinet or provide expert advice in respect of the various ministries, and deprived of the advice of permanent heads of government departments, Matlala made an increasingly poor impression as leader of the opposition. Given to following his own counsel, his popularity within his own party soon dwindled. Meanwhile, Phatudi's control over his party remained firm. At one stage his outspoken Minister of the Interior, Collins Ramusi, who openly advocated the rejection of separate development in favour of an integrated society, looked like a possible contender for the leadership, but it seemed in effect that his wide-ranging criticisms were welcomed by the LPP as a test of public opinion.

The leaders of the parties in Bophuthatswana value the unity of the Tswana people – those in White areas together with those in Bophuthatswana – and are convinced of the potential political strength of a unified Tswana nation. They are convinced that they have sufficient credibility among their people for effective leadership. Mangope explicitly rejected the interference of his "brethren in the North" who wish to "liberate" the people of Southern Africa. In a world which "arrogates to itself the right to decide what is best for us, never mind what we ourselves wish", Mangope prefers to be "a stooge of my own people rather than of popular world opinion".[1] Though not equally explicit, leaders in other homelands have similar views.

Starting with Mangope's attempts between November 1973 and March 1974 to remove the deputy leader of the BNP, Minister H. Maseloane, from the cabinet, a split developed in the ruling BNP. When a party conference in February 1974 decided (by 112 votes to 86) to sack the influential general secretary, S. T. Mogotsi, the quarrel burst into the open and in March 1974 Mangope came under severe attack in the Legislative Assembly. The attack was led by two prominent chiefs in the BNP, and two cabinet members – Chiefs H. Maseloane and J. D. Toto. Characteristic of the debate over Mangope's leadership was the prominent participation of chiefs, on both sides. Complaints against him were that he acted without consulting or informing his cabinet and party executive, that he interfered in the affairs of the Madikwe regional authority, that he divided the Tswana nation into social classes by allowing an exclusive private school to be established, and that he discriminated against non-Tswanas. The motion requesting Mangope's dismissal was withdrawn in response to appeals by the Commissioner-General for a reconciliation. Mangope immediately afterwards retaliated by trying to secure the dismissal of Maseloane and Toto from the BNP. After a successful application to the Supreme Court in September 1974 they were, however, reinstated as members. Mangope then reverted to the unusual step of resigning from the BNP and establishing the Bophuthatswana Democratic Party. At a special session of the Legislative Assembly he succeeded in obtaining a motion of confidence (which also requested the dismissal from the cabinet of Maseloane and Toto) by 35 votes to 23. Maseloane took over leadership of the BNP and allied with the SP against the BDP.

A similar situation developed in KwaZulu where increasing differences developed between Buthelezi and his Councillor for Community Affairs, Barney Dladla. Dladla was removed to the Dept. of Justice, but when he proved recalcitrant in certain respects and openly opposed Buthelezi, the latter called a special meeting of the Legislative Assembly which then adopted a motion for the dismissal of Dladla.

Within the South African Students' Organisation and the Black People's Convention, leadership crises have been caused by the banning of several of their elected office-bearers and officials. Through banning orders these organisations have been deprived of important organisational and ideological talent and drive, affecting the entire Black consciousness movement in South Africa. In March 1973 the first eight Black student leaders were served with banning orders.* They were then replaced at an emergency meeting by temporary appointees, who were confirmed at the 4th General Students' Council (GSC) in July 1973. Shortly afterwards the new president and vice-president, respectively Henry Isaacs and Mervyn Josi, received similar orders, followed by Johnny Issel (Western Cape regional secretary), Ben Langa (secretary-general) and the Rev. H. Qambela (acting president).

Africans predominate in the leading ranks of Saso and BPC, although Coloureds and Indians – e.g. Isaacs and Josi – have been elected to high offices in Saso. Important recruitment norms are the militancy with which Black consciousness is propagated by an aspirant, a "Black" skin colour and African descent. At his first sign of accommodating aspects of separate development, a former Saso president, Temba Sono, was expelled from office, and rigid ideological conformity has since characterised the organisation.

Nomination of Candidates

Most of the political parties under discussion have participated in one election only, or have been established after the only election that had so far been held. In the Transkei where three general elections and several by-elections have been contested by the TNIP and DP, uncertainty grew among prospective candidates about the parties' procedure for nomination of candidates. The national executive of the DP, who has the final authority in the appointment of party candidates while acting on the advice of area and regional party committees, consistently failed to supervise the activities of these committees. As a result local dissensions and aspirations produced disputes over selection of candidates in almost every election since 1963. The chaotic conditions in the DP are well illustrated by the nomination of candidates for the 1973 general election in the Dalindyebo region (Tembuland). The Tembuland regional committee of the DP (not recognised as such by the national executive), under the chairmanship of J. Z. Kobo, opened its campaign in March 1973 by naming its candidates in an attempt to secure the DP nominations for the three Tembuland constituencies. In May 1973 a meeting of Tembus at Sithebe selected a

---

* These were: Strini Moodley (Saso administrative assistant and editor of Saso publications), Saths Cooper (public relations officer of BPC and Saso member), Jerry Modisane (Saso president), Harry Nengwekulu (Saso permanent organiser), Bokwe Mafuna (employee of Black Community Programme and Saso member), Steve Biko (former Saso president), Barney Pityana (Saso general secretary) and Drake Koka (general secretary of Black Allied Workers Union and founder member of BPC).

slightly different slate of candidates, with the backing of Dalindyebo, who added the proviso that the candidates had to be confirmed by the national executive. Ultimately the national executive selected a third slate of candidates, omitting the rebels of 1972. The three slates of candidates were as follows:

Constituency	Regional committee list, March 1973	List by Tembu meeting, May 1973	Actually nominated, August 1973
Umtata	J. Z. Kobo F. S. Twala	S. F. Mgqweto F. Twala	S. F. Mgqweto B. P. Feke
Engcobo	L. Mgudlwa G. Kutu H. M. Xuma	L. Mgudlwa G. Kutu A. Xobololo	Z. L. Majija H. M. Xuma
Mqanduli	N. P. Nkosiyane W. Z. Nkosiyane	N. P. Nkosiyane K. Guzana	N. P. Nkosiyane K. Guzana

Twala, Mgudlwa, Kutu, Xobololo and W. Nkosiyane were nominated as independents, but Kobo not at all. In Engcobo constituency, Mgudlwa, Kutu and Xobololo defeated the official candidates; and in Umtata, Mgqweto teamed up with Twala against Feke, and all three were defeated by TNIP candidates. In 1974 Kutu joined the TNIP and then, together with Mgudlwa and Xobololo, rejoined the DP. Nomination of DP candidates in the Eastern Pondoland constituencies was hampered when the national secretary resigned from the party two days before the official nomination day, and on the same day (25 August) the national executive met to confirm party candidates. The secretary, Bubu, who lived in Lusikisiki in Eastern Pondoland, had been responsible for arranging party nominations in that region.

The constitution of the TNIP does not prescribe a procedure for selecting election candidates, which is determined by the national executive to suit circumstances and experience. Before the 1963 election, when no parties existed, Chief Kaiser Matanzima was directly involved in the selection of a number of candidates, but after the party was established, this duty was transferred to the party supporters. For the 1968 general election, and by-elections up to 1971, prospective candidates were invited, by circulars from the secretary-general and the party leader, to submit applications for candidature in writing to the national executive. These aspirants were then required to address a series of meetings, usually chaired by the local chief or a neighbouring one. Supporters then selected their favourite candidates by voting. This procedure was followed in most districts.

Prospective TNIP candidates for the October 1973 general election were reminded by circular at the end of 1972 to submit their applications, and some had indeed been submitted by November 1972. The final number of aspirants was 107. At the March 1973 annual congress of the TNIP, district committees were instructed to make recommendations before 31 March. The selection process began in the first week of June, by "nomination courts" (not the district committees), comprising the heads and members, excluding DP members, of the local tribal authorities, all sub-headmen loyal to the TNIP, and a number of women equal to that of the sub-headmen. The ballots submitted by each nomination court were sealed in envelopes with the signatures of high-ranking party officials, and counted in Umtata in the presence of the national executive on 19 July. Some of the ablest TNIP members in the legislative assembly were eliminated, such as Messrs. Cemane, Ndamse, Vika, and Canca. There were great dissatisfaction over the nomination procedure, and 10 rejected candidates, in 9 constituencies, decided to stand as independents.

In effect the nomination procedure eliminated the party's grass-roots organisation to a large extent. Selection of cadidates was in the hands of people who sometimes were not strongly committed to the party and easily amenable to persuasion. The frequent changes in nomination procedures caused uncertainty among aspiring politicians and when the high rate of nomination failure among the sitting members is considered, it has disturbed continuity in the party's top structure.

Strict control over nomination of candidates has been exercised by the SP in Bophuthatswana, the VIP in Venda, the Sebe faction in the Ciskei and the Mphephu faction in Venda. Nomination by these factions and parties was highly centralised in the hands of a national executive or leading person. In no cases was there need to consider the wishes of grass-roots organisations and aspiring members from lower levels, because no such organisation had at the time been established. Both the Sebe and Mphephu factions have meanwhile established parties and expanded their organisation.

In the first general elections in Lebowa and Gazankulu in 1973 no parties or clearly defined factions existed, and as a consequence nomination was largely on an individual basis. In multi-member constituencies slates of candidates were formed – mostly unrelated to slates in other constituencies. These slates were based on bonds of friendship, mutual trust, family relationship and political agreement. In the Bochum constituency in Lebowa, the candidate was determined through a tribal meeting.

Factions under the leadership of Chiefs Mangope and Mabandla in Bophuthatswana and the Ciskei respectively, played no role in the nomination of candidates in the first general elections. After nomination day Mangope established the BNP and then commenced with the selection of official party candidates from the candidates already nominated. The selection was made at a meeting consisting of 41 appointed members of the Legislative Assembly and all candidates who supported Mangope. In the Ciskei Mabandla only established the CNP after the election and made no attempt to obtain closer organisation among the candidates supporting him during the election campaign.

Generally, candidates from White urban areas in all homeland elections were scarce and were sometimes even discouraged by homeland parties. The TNIP referred prospective candidates from urban areas to the constituency concerned, where they were all rejected. No urban candidate had been prepared to follow a suggestion by the secretary-general of the TNIP that they reside inside the constituency for at least a month before seeking nomination. In several other homelands candidates from White urban areas who were also well known in the homelands were successful in the elections. They include several prominent people, such as Messrs. Sefotlhelo, Mokale (Bophuthatswana), Mageza (Gazankulu), Maqomo (Ciskei), Ramusi (Lebowa), and Mudau (Venda). Successful candidates from urban areas were invariably occupied as professional people or in administrative positions.

Party affiliation in local government played a minor role. For the Transkeian towns African advisory and local committees are appointed by the Transkei Townships Board after consultation with the Transkei government, the local magistrate and the White local committee (in the case of advisory committees). Transkei government nominations are made by the Transkei cabinet. Cabinet nominations during 1972 for ten out of the nineteen towns included members of the Legislative Assembly, including four DP members (in Mqanduli, Willowvale, Ngqeleni and Mt. Fletcher). The size of committees varies between 4 and 10 members, but the cabinet nominated only three people in each case. Party affiliations of nominees were as follows: TNIP: 30, DP: 10, Independent: 14, Unknown: 4. No definite pattern could be discerned, except that the majority belonged to the ruling party. In certain districts the nominations tended to follow election results, namely in Libode, Ngqeleni, Mt. Frere, Cala, Mt. Fletcher and Elliotdale; whereas in other districts the election results were apparently not fully considered, namely Cofimvaba, Flagstaff, Lusikisiki, Mt. Ayliff and Mqanduli. In most cases only some of the cabinet nominees have been appointed by the Townships Board.

In urban areas outside the Transkei, the Transkei political parties have not participated in the election of members of advisory boards or urban Bantu councils. However, TNIP supporters have been elected in greater numbers than the DP on the advisory boards of the Transkei government representatives in urban areas in Cape Town, Bloemfontein and the Witwatersrand. In these urban areas the TNIP more than the DP is therefore concerned with the channelling of urban grievances, problems and needs to Transkeian and South African authorities. At the time of research other home-land parties were still establishing themselves in White areas and had not yet commenced participation in local politics in White areas. The same applies to township councils for urban areas inside the homelands, although there is a tendency among homeland governments to frown upon opposition membership of these councils.

In the homeland rural areas political parties take no part in the election of tribal authority members. Here and there party affiliation is beginning to play a role in the election of office-bearers of tribal and regional authorities. The most positive role by tribal authorities in party affairs is in the Transkei where the TNIP uses tribal authorities for issuing membership cards and also employed some tribal authority members in its nomination structure for the 1973 election.

Voters' interest is low in the election of advisory and township councils in urban areas inside White area and homelands. Local parties (mentioned in Chapter 4) often participate, but tend to be unstable and short-lived. They provide, however, the main machinery for the nomination of candidates.

Legislative Assembly

Nominating his candidates for the first cabinet election in 1963, Matanzima took two factors into consideration: qualifications and geographical distribution. The latter was as follows:

Moshesh: Maluti (Matatiele district)
Mvusi: Umzimkulu (Umzimkulu district)
Madikizela: Qaukeni (Bizana district)
Mdledle and George and Kaiser Matanzima: Emigrant Tembuland (St. Marks district)

Thus half of the first cabinet came from Emigrant Tembuland – the Chief Minister's region. Some of Matanzima's best qualified followers, were, however, in this region. Ethnic and tribal considerations also played a role. Moshesh, as the most prominent leader of the Basotho in the Transkei, ensured substantial support for the TNIP from the Maluti region. Difference of opinion among the Basotho on the advisability of the institution of a paramount chieftainship for the Basotho, and on who the first incumbent should be, is potentially divisive, and could become a thorny problem for Matanzima if Moshesh actively aspired towards the paramountcy. The Ministry of Agriculture and Forestry went to the Eastern Pondo with the appointment of Madikizela, a trusted and prominent follower of Paramount Chief Botha Sigcau, whose area has since produced the largest single block of support for the TNIP. When Madikizela left the cabinet in 1968 he was replaced by Paramount Chief Botha Sigcau's daughter Stella Sigcau. Other ministers from Eastern Pondoland were Ndamse (1968–71) and Chief George Ndabankulu, appointed in 1973. Also, the appointment of Mabandla, first when Mvusi died and a second time when Ndamse was dismissed, was to consolidate the doubtful support for the TNIP in the Emboland region.

The first Transkei cabinet consisted of the best qualified men the TNIP then had in the Assembly. The Matanzimas both held Baccalaureus degrees and, like Mvusi, were qualified attorneys; Mdledle was a B.A.; Columbus Madikizela held a teacher's certificate and a Diploma in Bantu Studies; and Moshesh possessed a matriculation certificate. Mvusi's successor, Mabandla, had matriculation and a Diploma in Agriculture. Of subsequent cabinet members, Ndamse held two M.A. degrees, Stella Sigcau a teacher's certificate, Jonas a B.A. degree, Bulube a teacher's certificate, and Chief Ndabankulu a B.A. and teacher's certificate.

During the first session of the Assembly in 1964, Guzana advocated a change in the Transkei Constitution Act to enable the Chief Minister to appoint and dismiss his cabinet without first obtaining the Assembly's approval. Matanzima did not reject this suggestion, but declared that he would rather wait and see how the system worked.[2] Five years later, in 1969, the TNIP introduced a similar motion,[3] and the South African government accordingly amended the constitution and Ndamse was the first minister to be dismissed under the new provisions. At the time of the TNIP's request, Ndamse was still highly in favour and it could not have been requested simply to get rid of him, as has often been suggested. The change in procedure signified an official recognition that government by consensus had been superseded by a party system.

In some of the homelands the cabinet remains a body elected by the legislative assembly (see Chapter 3). In these cases each of the aspiring Chief Ministers submits a slate of names to the assemblies and in this way exercises some control over the incumbency of cabinet posts.

In Bophuthatswana, geographical distribution was important in the final selection of the first cabinet ministers. They were distributed as follows: Chiefs T. V. Makapan (Moretele), H. T. R. Maseloane (Madikwe) and J. B. Toto (Tlharo-Tlhaping), M. Setlogelo (Thaba Nchu) and T. M. Molatlhwa (Taung). Chief Minister Mangope is from the Lehurutshe constituency.

The first cabinet of the Ciskei after the 1973 general election was the first in the homelands to include no chiefs. Its members were A. M. Burns-Ncamashe – Education (Victoria East), R. B. Myataza – Justice (Hewu), N. Mkrola – Roads and Works (Herschel), L. F. Siyo – Internal Affairs (Mdantsane) and E. Z. Booi – Agriculture and Forestry (Glen Grey). Sebe himself is from Zwelitsha constituency. All are elected members of the Assembly. (Burns-Ncamashe, incidentally, has claims to the chieftainship of the Amagwali tribe.) Sebe nominated two chiefs as Speaker and Deputy Speaker, respectively Chiefs P. Z. Siwani (Zwelitsha) and Z. Njokweni (Peddie). The cabinet includes two businessmen, two agricultural officers, one university lecturer and one inspector of schools. On the other hand, Sebe's cabinet includes representatives of the major tribal clusters of the Ciskei: three Rarabes (Sebe, Burns-Ncamashe, and Siyo), one Fingo (Myataza), one Tembu (Booi) and one Sotho (Mkrola). In this way tribal balance and co-operation are promoted. The progressive image of Mabandla's shadow cabinet, which was made known before the election of cabinet members and of his CNP executive, made no difference to the election result. Sebe's own progressive but moderate image and solid organisational work provided a firm foundation for his victory.

In complete contrast with the Ciskei, the first Venda cabinet after the 1973 general election was the first in the homelands to include only chiefs and headmen. With their support, Mphephu succeeded in retaining the chief ministership, and beat his VIP opponent, Baldwin Mudau, by 42 votes to 18. He subsequently appointed to his cabinet Headman E. Nesengane (former inspector of schools) as Minister of Education, Headman F. N. Ravele as Minister of Justice, Chief Netshinbupse as Minister of the Interior, Chief A. M. Madzivhamdila as Minister of Agriculture and Forestry, and Chief J. R. Rambuda as Minister of Works. Thus the cabinet of Venda retained its traditionalist image.

The rural character of homeland parties and politics is emphasised by the very few elected members who reside in urban areas, or outside the homelands. Most elected members have an educational background and pursue a related profession or occupation. The following statistics give an indication of occupational distribution of elected members in several homelands. Occupations have been grouped together under the following categories: *Professional* (doctor, attorney, minister of religion, welfare worker, nurse); *Educational* (teacher, inspector of schools, university lecturer); *Clerical* (clerk, book-keeper, security officer, agricultural and dipping supervisor); *Businessman* (trader, builder, contractor); *Traditional leader* (chief, headman, counsellor); *Commercial employee* (salesman, public relations officer); *Farmer*; *Diverse* (housewife, labourer, pensioner).

In the Transkei general elections of 1963, 1968 and 1973 there had been 8, 11, and 0 election candidates respectively from outside the Transkei, of whom 2, 1, and 0 respectively were elected.

TABLE 7.I. OCCUPATIONAL DISTRIBUTION OF ELECTED
MEMBERS, TRANSKEI

Occupation	1963	1968	1973*
Professional	4	3	3
Educational	10	9	5
Clerical	3	5	4
Businessman	6	5	7
Traditional leader	13	10	13
Commercial employee	2	0	0
Farmer	7	12	9
Diverse	0	1	1

* Excluding Umzimkulu constituency where the election
was postponed because of the death of a candidate.

No particular trend in respect of occupational distribution over the past decade can be discerned, except that more teachers, farmers, and chiefs and headmen have been elected than in other self-governing territories in South Africa.

TABLE 7.II. OCCUPATIONAL DISTRIBUTION OF CANDIDATES AND ELECTED
MEMBERS, 1972, BOPHUTHATSWANA

Occupation	BNP	SP	TNP	Ind/Withdrawn	PP
Professional	1(1)	1	0	1	0
Educational	1(1)	0	0	0	0
Clerical	1(1)	1	1	0	0
Businessman	9(7)	6(3)	0	3	1
Traditional leader	3(2)	2	0	1	0
Commercial employee	0	0	0	0	0
Farmer	9(8)	1(1)	0	4	0
Diverse	0	0	1	0	0

Analysis of the occupations of candidates and elected members in the Bophuthatswana general election of 1972 shows the great measure of success of farmers and businessmen. Numbers in brackets refer to elected candidates. (See Table 7.II.)

The following table analyses the occupational distribution of candidates and elected members in the Ciskei general election of 1973. Businessmen, teachers and farmers dominate among candidates and elected members; within the Sebe faction as well as among other candidates.

TABLE 7.III. OCCUPATIONAL DISTRIBUTION OF CANDIDATES AND
ELECTED MEMBERS, 1973, CISKEI

| Occupation | Sebe group | | Other | |
	Candidates	Elected	Candidates	Elected
Professional	2	1	5	1
Educational	8	6	10	3
Clerical	2	1	2	0
Businessman	4	4	14	2
Traditional leader	1	0	2	0
Commercial employee	0	0	1	0
Farmer	1	1	6	1
Diverse	0	0	4	0

After the general election it was clear that Sebe had a majority of thirteen out of twenty elected members, and the thirty appointed chiefs held the balance for the election of the Chief Minister. Two months before the election it was reported that Sebe had the support of twelve chiefs, giving him a total of 25 out of 50 votes. Sebe obtained the one crucial vote for an absolute majority when N. Mkrola, elected member of Herschel, joined his ranks, and he subsequently defeated Mabandla for the chief ministership with 26 votes to 24.

In Lebowa, nine candidates were from White areas, and a further three from urban areas within Lebowa. The rest were from rural African areas. Fourteen candidates were the sons of chiefs and ten of them were elected.[4]

Parties were established after the election, and candidates could not be classified according to their party affiliations. Out of the sixty chiefs in the Legislative Assembly thirty-six supported the LPP. Chiefs and headmen were surprisingly unsuccessful in the election, whereas businessmen, farmers and clerks topped the polls. The comparative failure of chiefs can be ascribed to the fact that the numerous small chieftainships are poor support bases in the large, multi-member constituencies. In Sekhukhune

TABLE 7.IV. OCCUPATIONAL DISTRIBUTION OF CANDIDATES AND
ELECTED MEMBERS, 1973, LEBOWA

Occupation	No. of candidates	No. of elected members	
		LPP	LNP
Professional	5	5	0
Educational	4	1	1
Clerical	10	6	1
Businessman	36	13	2
Traditional leader	10	2	2
Commercial employee	3	1	0
Farmer	9	4	1
Diverse	3	0	0

all five chiefs and headmen were unsuccessful in the seven-member
constituency with its fifty-four chieftainships. Seven of the LPP
members mentioned in Table 7.IV crossed over from the LNP after
the election of the Chief Minister in May 1973.

The election in Venda of August 1973 was contested by the VIP
(led by Baldwin Mudau, a publicity officer in Johannesburg) a
number of independents, and a slate of candidates appointed by the
20 so-called "recognised leaders of the people" under the leadership
of Chief Minister Patric Mphephu and a number of chiefs.

The following table gives an indication of the occupational
distribution of candidates in this election, and of the elected members
in the legislative assembly.

TABLE 7.V. OCCUPATIONAL DISTRIBUTION OF CANDIDATES AND
ELECTED MEMBERS, 1973, VENDA

(Numbers in brackets refer to elected members)

Occupation	VIP*	Mphephu faction	Independent
Professional	0	2(1)	0
Educational	1	0	0
Clerical	5(4)	1	1
Businessman	11(7)	6(2)	2
Traditional leader	0	5(2)	2
Commercial employee	1(1)	0	0
Farmer	2(1)	4	1
Diverse	1	0	0

* Including two independent VIP candidates.

Only three VIP candidates, one Mphephu candidate and one
independent were from the Witwatersrand; the others all lived in
Northern Transvaal, mostly in Venda itself. In the Dzanani con-

stituency, the Mphephu candidates were elected in all five vacancies. This is also the home district of Chief Mphephu. In the Sibasa and Vuwani constituencies – with seven and six vacancies respectively – the VIP took all seats. In Sibasa two independent VIP candidates were elected and afterwards joined the VIP. Even the support of about 80 per cent of all chiefs and headmen and of the powerful and influential Zionist Christian Church was of no avail to the Mphephu faction, except in the Dzanani constituency where Mphephu's influence had been decisive.[5]

Businessmen, clerks and farmers were in the majority among candidates and elected members. In the VIP the bias was towards businessmen and clerks, whereas the traditional professions predominated in the Mphephu faction.

Chieftainship

Since the extension of White control over Africans in South Africa, chieftainship had often been systematically excluded from administrative work, and government-appointed headmen were used in their stead. Chieftainship received a stimulus when the Native Administration Act of 1927 made it possible for civil and criminal jurisdiction to be conferred upon chiefs and headmen. The introduction of the Bantu authorities rural local government system further strengthened the chieftainship. The number of officially recognised and appointed chiefs in the homelands increased rapidly. In the Transkei, in 1957 alone (the year when Bantu authorities were introduced), thirteen new chiefs were recognised. In 1955 there were thirty chiefs in the Transkei; in 1963 there were sixty, and at the end of 1973 there were ninety-one, including five paramount chiefs.

Recognising the importance of chiefs, contenders for chief ministerships in all homelands carefully tried to cultivate their support. In the Transkei in 1963, Poto and Matanzima described in their respective election manifestoes their past services to chieftainship. Matanzima reminded chiefs that their social and economic status had improved with the introduction of Bantu authorities and that it was he who had asked for the abolition of the Transkei General Council in favour of the Bantu authority system in 1955. As chairman of the Transkei Territorial Authority Matanzima could make the more substantial claims, and furthermore, as the favourite of the South African government, he had secured sufficient votes of chiefs to become the first Chief Minister. Spiritually, Matanzima was perhaps nearer than Poto to many of the less educated, more traditionalist chiefs, as is evident from his expressed belief that "my ancestors were on my side" during the election of the first Chief Minister and cabinet.[6]

A reputation of anti-chieftainship can be almost fatal to any homeland-based party or aspirant to the chief ministership. This factor probably contributed to the defeat of the SP in the Bophuthatswana Legislative Assembly: the party's opponents wrongly alleged that it was against chieftainship. This allegation was based on the opposition by the deputy leader of the SP shortly before the 1972 election to the constitutional stipulation that the Chief Minister of Bophuthatswana should be a chief: for this he was severely criticised by several members, including Mangope and former Minister Kgotleng.[7] Kgotleng contended that chiefs brought stability, and that the leaders of the African National Congress, the Industrial and Commercial Workers' Union and the South African Communist Party had deserted the people, whereas the chiefs were still there to lead them.

In the Ciskei, Sebe successfully warded off a similar threat in the election of a Chief Minister. He had enjoyed the support of the former Rarabe Paramount Chief, Velile Sandile, and his candidature was not supported by the latter's successor, Mxolisi Sandile. Shortly before the election of the new Chief Minister, Mxolisi said that Sebe was a commoner and that his election would cause the collapse of the chieftainship; but Sebe pointed out that he was related to the royal house of the Xhosas – a fact which undoubtedly worked in his favour.

In Lebowa, doubts were raised as to whether Phatudi would be able to handle chieftainship affairs if elected to the chief ministership: it was pointed out, in his defence, that he was the son of a chief.

The Mphephu faction in Venda, led by chiefs, contested the 1973 general election under the title of the "Recognised Leaders" of the Venda people and cast doubts on the intentions of the Venda Independence People's Party towards the chieftainship. The VIP, in turn, was at pains to declare its support for the chieftainship. In all homeland elections, individual candidates, parties and factions always explicitly declared support for the chieftainship.

The fact that after the 1963 election in the Transkei the majority of chiefs supported Matanzima, and the majority of elected members supported Poto, raised an interesting and hitherto unresolved question, whether chiefs and population had lost complete contact in respect of political preferences. During the life of the first Assembly a realignment of members took place and in 1968, just before the second general election, Matanzima had a majority of at least 23, but still not an elected majority. The 1968 election brought him an elected majority which was slightly reduced in 1973, and it appeared as if the chiefs and commoners were once again in broad agreement over political issues. The same phenomenon can be observed in other homelands as well. In Venda, after the first election of 1973, the majority of chiefs supported Mphephu and the majority of elected members Mudau. Although Mphephu was elected Chief Minister he rapidly lost support when several chiefs and headmen crossed the floor to Mudau during the first session of the Legislative Assembly. The different behaviour of Venda chiefs in 1974 from those in the Transkei in 1964 can in part be historically explained. In 1964 it was almost inconceivable for chiefs to contradict the South African government. This attitude accounted for some support from the chiefs for Matanzima who was regarded as pro-government in 1964. However, by 1974 several homeland leaders had increased their popular support by voicing independent opinions. A pro-government stand was no longer a sound basis for recruitment.

In Lebowa, Phatudi had an elected majority after the first election of 1973, and Matlala enjoyed the support of a majority of chiefs, but not sufficient to cancel Phatudi's elected majority. After Phatudi's election as Chief Minister, several chiefs crossed the floor to his party, and ultimately Matlala also followed suit. In the Ciskei, Sebe also had an elected majority after the 1973 election, and Mabandla a majority among the chiefs. When Sebe was elected Chief Minister, a few chiefs crossed the floor to join him. Only in Gazankulu and Bophuthatswana did the Chief Ministers enjoy majorities among elected members as well as chiefs after the first elections, and only in the Transkei in 1964 some chiefs walked over to the party with an elected minority. It appears from the foregoing that the chiefs tend to support the winning candidate. In the second place, where chieftainship has not been successfully established by parties as intermediate structures between parties and voters, chiefs are more easily swayed by the electoral preferences of their people.

Whereas tribalism can be an impediment to political participation it can also be a political mobilising force, adding another interest to those already determining political choice. The relatively strong tribal clusters into which tribes are grouped in the Transkei and Ciskei, and the tribal equilibrium of the Kwena and Tlokwa in Basotho Qwaqwa, create strong tribal political bases of action. On the other hand, the extreme tribal diffraction in KwaZulu, Lebowa and Bophuthatswana reduces the relative political influence of any one tribe or tribal cluster.

It is difficult to generalise in respect of the influence of tribalism on political behaviour. A particular chieftainship and tribal loyalty can exercise an influence contrary to the general trend within the tribal cluster to which the particular chief or tribe belongs. Or the measure of diffraction among the tribes within a cluster might have progressed to such an extent that no general trend is discerned, such as in Sekhukhuneland in Lebowa where candidates with different political loyalties were elected in the 1973 election. The apparent political homogeneity of the Tembu tribal cluster under the Tembu Paramount Chief in the Transkei was broken in the Umtata by-election in 1970 when, for the first time, a candidate of the DP was defeated in Tembuland. In the 1973 election two TNIP candidates were elected in Umtata, while DP candidates and independents with DP sympathies were elected in the other two Tembuland constituencies, Engcobo and Mqanduli. Similarly, the homogeneity of the DP under the tutelage of the Western Pondo Paramountcy in Western Pondoland in the Transkei was broken in 1973 when a TNIP candidate was elected in Port St. John's. The TNIP, again, in spite of the support of the Gcaleka Paramount Chief, lost a seat in Willowvale in Gcalekaland to a DP candidate, and another seat in Mt. Ayliff to an independent, in spite of the support for the TNIP of the Eastern Pondo Paramount Chief. In all these cases, strong chieftainships exist in the districts with political tendencies contrary to that of the tribal cluster which is represented by the paramount chief. Similar cases occurred in Bophuthatswana and Venda where, respectively, almost all candidates of the Seoposengwe Party and the Mphephu faction were defeated in 1973, except in those constituencies where Chief Pilane and Chief Mphephu reside. In the Ciskei, the Paramount Chief of the Rarabe, Mxolisi Sandile, supports the CNP led by Chief Mabandla, in spite of efforts by the seven senior Rarabe chiefs to dissuade him. Sebe and his CNIP, however, enjoy the solid support of the Rarabe Tribunal, which is an elected tribal advisory body to the Paramount Chief.

From the above-mentioned events it is clear that support of a paramount chief for a party does not ensure support of all subordinate chiefs and their people. Tradition requires that the paramount chief aggregates and represents the inclinations of his subordinate chiefs. He has in fact in modern times no power to exert his will on subordinate chiefs and headmen and their people. It is therefore possible for individual chiefs to influence voters against the prevailing inclinations of the tribal cluster. The influence of chiefs in modern politics should, on the other hand, not be overrated. There is sometimes no correlation between the political attitudes of seemingly influential chiefs and voting behaviour (see Chapter 9). This emphasises the relevance of non-traditional socio-economic and political variables in the determination of the pattern of political participation.

A few words are necessary on the factors which enable chieftainship to act as an intermediate structure between party and voters in rural areas. Although traditional leaders in the homelands have only subordinate and delegated administrative powers they are in closer physical proximity to the majority of the homelands' population than any local and central government institution. This fact, together with the religious, judicial and quasi-judicial duties and decision-making powers in domestic tribal matters attached to chieftainship, and traditional leaders' powers of land allocation, increased the administrative authority of traditional leaders above the level to which they had been placed in the administrative hierarchy. It is commonly recognised that contact with the West has disturbed the balance of power in African traditional communities. Changing conditions have diminished their traditional authority by whittling away its basis, especially in the economic and religious fields. While the chiefs lost economic power and prestige through their own deteriorating economic position and the achievement by tribesmen of equal or better economic positions through wage labour or other economic activities, there was a relative increase in their powers of land allocation, because the increasing population resulted in increasing demand for land. For the majority of rural tribesmen – including many migrant workers – the chief retains his prominent social position. Land, the kinship system, and other traditional social behavioural prescriptions are still important bases for economic and social security. The structure of traditional social norms and patterns of behaviour is still widely applied in tribal areas, and the chief, who is at the apex of this structure, still exercises a large influence.

Despite strict control over land allocation by homeland governments, the traditional leaders' power over land and its products (grass, wood, herbs, etc.) remains one of their most important coercive means. Traditional leaders may not arbitrarily dispossess landholders, but landholders may be driven away by making their lives unpleasant. Traditional leaders may also use their coercive powers to good effect. For example a certain Transkei chief, who had decided that all children in his area should attend school, announced that he would refuse permission to cut wood or thatching grass to all parents whose children were not at school.

Customary social behaviour helped to maintain a balanced society in circumstances which remained unaltered over long periods. These usages still have a socially stabilising influence, and thus ensure conformity with traditional values and social behaviour. The maintenance of such conformity retards the development of post-traditional needs and interests and thus facilitates the application of government decisions which do not interfere with tribal interests and values, but renders difficult the application of decisions not in this category.

The personal relationship of traditional leaders to their followers as a relevant factor in the enforcement of government decisions is also related to the recruitment of support for political parties. Government relies on chiefs to use their influence and traditional social structures to persuade their followers to accept innovative government decisions, especially in respect of agricultural improvement. Ironically, the duties of traditional leaders to help enforce government decisions and the backing they receive from the government is one of the main reasons why good relations with their people, that are essential for the formulation and carrying out of decisions, are deteriorating. This deterioration tends to strengthen the chiefs' support for ruling parties upon which they are increasingly dependent. Their ability to return favours bestowed by the party with increased recruitment for the party diminishes correspondingly.

Belief in magic and witchcraft or sorcery has diminished in modern times, but belief in the power of ancestors is still found among political leaders. Paramount Chief Sabata Dalindyebo of the Tembu, a member of the DP executive, said in the Legislative Assembly in 1964:

> Every morning early I get up and go and pay my respects to my great-grandfather and ask for everything I desire and I also ask for protection against my enemies. That is why in their attempts to deport me or kill me they have been unsuccessful, because I am in constant touch with my ancestors.

Certain other homeland leaders have also ascribed their success in elections to protection by their ancestors. There is no doubt that Christianity and modern life-styles are breaking down these beliefs. The most important consequence of the persisting belief in magic and witchcraft in traditional communities is that it permits a form of social sanction against anti-social behaviour.[8] Thus social stability and conformity are promoted. Not only does it assist the chief in exercising his function of maintaining locality order and integration, but it permits the relatively unrestricted carrying on of traditional values, attitudes, beliefs and patterns of behaviour. These parochial orientations also find expression in politics.

Tribal structures are employed by all homeland parties and factions to generate support. Coupled with the low level of urban

participation in homeland politics, this emphasises the rural character of homeland parties. Collective support is sought and obtained
by parties. Political choice is made to some extent within the framework of a structure of traditional social sanction. Politicisation of
social behaviour of individuals and their individual participation
are not obtained, and the parties thus fail to penetrate traditional
social structures and build their own grass-roots organisations.
Prevailing political parochialism is not diminished through party
action and the concomitant fragmentation remains. The political
participation of parochialist individuals is made possible through
the community structure which intervenes between them and the
party or candidate.

REFERENCES

1. Press statement by Mangope on 8.9.1972.
2. Transkei Legislative Assembly, *Hansard*, 1964, pp. 245–8.
3. Transkei Legislative Assembly, *Hansard*, 1969, p. 167.
4. W. J. Breytenbach, "Eerste verkiesing in Lebowa", *Bulletin*, Africa
   Institute, Pretoria, XI, 4 (1973), p. 151.
5. W. J. Breytenbach, "First election in Vendaland", *Bulletin*, Africa
   Institute, Pretoria, XI, 7 (1973), p. 279.
6. Transkei Legislative Assembly, *Hansard*, 1965, p. 261.
7. Bophuthatswana government, *Debates of the Bophuthatswana Legislative
   Assembly*, 1972, p. 130.
8. V. G. J. Sheddick, *The Southern Sotho*, London, 1953; M. Hunter,
   Reaction to Conquest, London, 1961, p. 317.

8

AFRICAN OBJECTIVES

Homeland Policies

The single most striking characteristic of the policies of homeland governments and their supporting parties is their uniformity over every problem. The approach of all homeland governments is utterly pragmatic, almost to the point of being devoid of any ideological content. Whereas there is agreement between homeland and Black consciousness leaders in several aspects, there is much ideological disagreement in relation to separate development. Understandably the homeland leaders are mostly concerned with material issues and contemporary problems confronting their people. They are largely supported by the respective opposition parties and no serious policy differences exist between governing and opposition parties, except perhaps in the Transkei where there are deep differences over the acceptance or rejection of separate development as a basis for future political development. The Black consciousness leaders utterly reject separate development and multi-racialism, and this rejection underlies the policy of the opposition DP in the Transkei. It is perhaps fitting to set forth African homeland leaders' views on separate development, which are also the framework for the functioning of their respective governments.

—Separate Development

All homeland leaders support such universal values as democracy and Christianity, and oppose communism and terrorism. Their pan-Africanist ideals and sympathy towards the Black consciousness movement are increasingly noticeable. Their acceptance of separate development is qualified and cautious, while a minority rejects it outright. At the time of the first transfer of self-governing powers to a homeland (the Transkei in 1963), the fruits of separate development were extremely unattractive to most Africans. The African separate voters' roll in South Africa had shortly before, in 1959, been abolished in exchange for the promise of future independent Bantustans; Africans could not directly participate in urban local government

144

in the White areas; several African political organisations had just been banned; local government in the rural African areas was based on traditional governmental structures; increasing employment was still to be made available for Africans through economic development of the African areas; African lower education and separate universities for Africans were considered by many to be inferior; Africans could obtain no rights on land in the White areas and no freehold title in many African areas; Whites were not permitted to invest in any way in the African areas; pass laws restricted Africans' movements in the White areas; and racially mixed sport and social gatherings were mostly forbidden. Theoretically there was no ceiling or restriction on the Africans' aspirations and activities in the African areas. But the failure of the ANC's passive resistance efforts, the turmoil of more violent African resistance in 1959–60 and the resulting banning of the ANC and PAC were still fresh in the memory.

It was at the beginning of the 1960s that the Transkei Territorial Authority under the leadership of Kaiser Matanzima asked for self-government for the Transkei, and Matanzima expressed his support for separate development, thereby testing the sincerity of the South African government's promises of unlimited development opportunities in the African areas. After he had accepted separate development, Matanzima emphasised African exclusivism in the Transkei as a reciprocal principle to White exclusivism in South Africa, and repeatedly stressed the necessity of the ultimate departure of Whites from the Transkei. This extreme exclusivism of Matanzima's early period in office was not shared by the homeland leaders who assumed office in the early 1970s. Matanzima's rigidity on separate development was maintained for almost a decade, but in August 1972, after his second visit abroad and increasing contact with other homeland leaders, he appeared to reject ethnicity as a basis for political development and seemed willing to allow Whites as Transkei citizens. Following Matanzima's lead, the majority of homeland leaders declared their support for a multi-racial federation in South Africa, the allowing of Whites as citizens in the homelands – albeit under certain conditions in the Transkei and Bophuthatswana— and the selection of South African sports teams on merit only and irrespective of racial origins.

The Lebowa Chief Minister, Cedric Phathudi, envisages Lebowa citizenship as consistent with retention of South African citizenship because, in his opinion, South Africa belongs to all races. The Transkei and Bophuthatswana Chief Ministers remain more locally oriented, and will only allow White citizens who bring their land into the homeland, under a new agreement with

South Africa over re-allocation of land. In the Transkei Matanzima has made it clear that all landless Whites will have to leave when their services become redundant. He also wants full citizenship rights accorded to all urban Africans outside the homelands; and Buthelezi "dreamed"[1] of full citizenship and participation of Africans in South Africa. Ntsanwisi called for full consultation of Africans and their full participation in decision-making.

Following the assumption of self-governing powers by several homelands in 1972 and 1973 and the resultant acceleration of political debate in South Africa, it became clear that the conception of the South African government and the homeland governments of separate development differed to some extent, especially over the objectives of the policy – or its "logical consequences", as the homeland leaders often call it.

The South African government's position is clear: the African homelands can achieve independence within the territories set aside in 1936, the consolidation of scattered areas being subject to consultation and a federation of non-independent homelands an impossibility. The African homeland leaders are not so clear, however, as to what they understand as being the logical conclusion to separate development, although they have repeatedly stated their disillusionment over the South African government's apparent unwillingness to carry the policy through to these particular conclusions. The sentiments of the Chief Minister of Lebowa – that separate development is not a final solution – are shared by other homeland leaders, who are all prepared to compromise with separate development on condition that it will be carried to its full consequences. Although not a stated objective, the post-separate development federation of Southern African states is possibly the "final solution" in the minds of the homeland leaders. "Post-separate development" is a concept which can be derived from the thoughts of homeland leaders, and refers to their envisaged federal state where constituent territories (which could include White South Africa) are equal units. This obviously implies Black majority rule and the end of separate development.

While operating under the framework of separate development, homeland leaders adhere to a separate-but-equal doctrine, explicitly expressed by Mangope. He especially emphasises equal opportunities in education, wages and land distribution. Matanzima and Phatudi also reject racial discrimination. For Matanzima, however, the post-separate development phase does not exclude some form of racial differentiation: he foresees the federation of Southern African states being completely non-racial in character, with the present homelands as constituent exclusive African, ethnic states. The fact the South African government is unwilling to grant more land to the homelands than the demarcated areas of 1936 is held by Matanzima, Mangope and Buthelezi to be a strong indicator that it is not prepared to carry its policy to its logical conclusion. For the homeland leaders, more land for African ownership is undoubtedly a major objective of separate development. Other homeland leaders, namely Sebe, Mabandla, Matlala, Ntsanwisi and Mphephu, also set great priority on land extensions.

To the homeland leaders self-government and the governmental powers that accompanied it brought some political self-respect and a power base for future interaction between Black and White in South Africa – although, in the eyes of many, these leaders are "government stooges". Underlying their participation in homeland self-government is the realisation that the White man will not easily surrender all his power in South Africa, including political power, and that opportunities offered within this power structure must be utilised for want of anything else.[2] Working patiently on the basis of self-government, homeland leaders can build a reputation for sound government, learn lessons in the wielding of governmental power, and amass credibility as political leaders within and outside the homelands – all with the ultimate purpose of exercising increased moral and political pressure on the South African government for increased powers, first in the homelands and then in the rest of South Africa.

With the growing disillusionment over the potentialities of separate development, some of the Africans' motives in accepting separate development became clearer. For the first time "positive" as well as "negative" aspects of separate development were articulated by a homeland leader, Mangope of Bophuthatswana. Mangope repeatedly rejected the following negative aspects during the Bophuthatswana election campaign from August to October 1972, and on various occasions later: insufficient transport facilities for the residents of Mabopane, an African city north of Pretoria, the inhabitants of which mainly work in Pretoria; the wage gap; racial discrimination; manifestations of the belief in White superiority, such as the prohibition on Africans to enter restaurants, and double standards in film censoring; differentiation in salaries and wages, although Africans must pass the same professional examinations as Whites and pay the same prices for consumer goods; job reservation; limited opportunities for homeland leaders in foreign affairs; and the uncompromising racial attitudes that are sometimes adopted by aspiring White politicians.

Certain positive aspects were also identified, and Mangope declared: "I would like more emphasis to be placed on development

rather than on separation, the development of man material."[3]
After the 1972 election campaign Mangope stressed that separate
development did not imply the perpetuation of provincial status
for Bophuthatswana; in other words, it held the promise of self-
determination and independence. One of the greatest advantages
of separate development is regarded as being the development of
industry and commerce within Bophuthatswana – even to the extent
that the Bophuthatswana government requested the South African
government to curb the activities of White traders just across the
border from Bophuthatswana.

Several other derivatives of separate development have been
mentioned by Transkei leaders from time to time as benefits, and
in the early stages, the Transkei government's dissatisfaction
over the "negative aspects" of the policy was more or less limited
to complaints over the restrictions on African labourers in White
areas. It is almost as if the TNIP had toed the line hoping for benefits until frustration set in, at which point dissatisfaction manifested
itself. The TNIP stood for separation of races on equal and
parallel lines, and rejected racial discrimination and White *baasskap*.
Even before the establishment of the TNIP, Kaiser Matanzima
said in October 1963 that separate development implied in the first
place the education of the Africans; secondly, the opening up of
trading to Transkeians; and thirdly, the building of a localised
government service. African education received the early attention
of the Transkei Department of Education after the granting of self-
government, and after thorough investigation new syllabuses were
introduced in 1966, closely following those of the Cape Provincial
Education Department and of the Department of Bantu Education;
the main change being that English was introduced earlier as the
medium of instruction, viz. at Standard III. Although the Department of Bantu Education syllabuses were mostly found suitable by
the Transkei government, the introduction of new ones marked a
successful break with Bantu Education, something which had been
looked forward to ever since its introduction in 1953 when it had
been the object of strong African, and especially ANC, opposition.
Thus the Transkei demonstrated that separate development could
be used to get rid of its most unpopular aspects within the homelands.

Mangope's view of the four "pillars of separate development"
is worth noting. The success of the policy, he said, would depend on
progress in these four fields: the reconsideration of the land issue
so that Africans could obtain more land; the need for Whites to
make "meaningful sacrifices for their policy" by spending more on
African education, social services, homeland development and

wages; "Black dignity" and the rejection of discrimination; and
the assumption of responsibility by the Africans, that is "the
way in which we as Black people make use of the opportunities
we now have . . ."[4]

It is clear that among the homeland leaders separate development does not have the status of a doctrine or philosophy. They
regard it as a practical opportunity for them to obtain what they
need. Both Mangope and Matanzima stated this clearly as their
reason for accepting separate development; Ntsanwisi declared
that he would pursue a policy of "dynamic and militant pragmatism",[5] grasping separate development as an opportunity for
consultation between White and Black; Sebe accepts separate development purely for practical purposes; Phatudi regards it merely
as a political platform; and Buthelezi thinks that it is the better
of two evils and the only way for Africans to participate in seeking
a solution for South Africa. Mangope also thinks it is second best
and declares that he prefers "social and economic equality . . . together with one-man-one-vote participation . . . in the central political system".[6] Among the opposition parties, Mudau, Matlala,
Mabandla and Pilane (respectively leaders of the VIP, LNP,
CNP and SP) accept separate development for practical purposes
and as a springboard; while Knowledge Guzana and his DP
reject it outright in favour of a multi-racial South Africa with provincial status for the homelands.

Although the DP was established on a "multi-racial" platform,
the party is not clear in its thinking on "multi-racialism". In 1972,
eight years after the party's establishment, its leader was informing
members of the national executive of the meaning of these concepts.
The view of Guzana, the party leader, is that non-racialism can be
regarded as enforced integration, without racial differences being
recognised for any purpose, whereas multi-racialism takes cognisance
of such differences for certain purposes. Under multi-racialism
voluntary separation will be allowed but not enforced, and it includes economic and political partnership, with neither race
dominating.

The DP has been criticised for accepting membership of the
Transkei legislative assembly while rejecting separate development,
the ideological basis for the legislative assemblies in the homelands.
However, the DP, like the TNIP, though perhaps for different reasons, accepted the assembly as a platform for propagating its policy.[7]

Immediately before the first Transkei general election in 1963,
when the chances of the Poto group (later the DP) of forming the
first government were still good, Poto declared that he realised it
would be difficult to implement multi-racialism within the frame-

work of separate development, and that it could only be implemented under full independence. This was confirmed at the time
by other candidates in the Poto group. Soon afterwards, the DP's
thinking on this question changed radically, and independence for
the Transkei and, as a recent consequence, the proposed federation
of Black states, were rejected entirely. This, said Guzana, was "a
constitutional mirage, non-existent and incapable of realisation".[8]
A plea for a provincial status for the African homelands within the
South African union was made by Poto and his successor, Guzana,
in January 1966, about two years after the DP was established.
They believed that it would be impossible for the homelands to
satisfy the people living within them economically, socially,
industrially, educationally and politically, and regarded ethnic
consciousness as altogether irreconcilable with the growing interdependence of the races and nations of the modern world. Homeland governments should therefore attend to local affairs only.

The party therefore favours full South African citizenship for all
people in the Republic. An independent Transkei, Guzana told a
meeting at Mqanduli in the Transkei, would relegate the Transkeians to the status of foreigners in the Republic; they would be
restricted to the Transkei where they would die of hunger. This fear
of isolation is generally evident in DP attitudes, especially in the
economic field. The TNIP, on the other hand, suspects that
the DP's multi-racialism will open the door to White economic
domination. While the DP is content to allow White traders and
landowners to remain in the Transkei towns, the TNIP is adamant
that these Whites should leave as soon as possible; and in fact
the greater part of many Transkei towns and many trading stations
in rural areas have been transferred to Black ownership under the
TNIP government.

The DP considers claims for independence and for additional
land for the Transkei, and the proposed federation of Bantustans,
as elaborations of separate development, and therefore opposes them
categorically. Some confusion was created in DP ranks by the Chief
Minister's declaration in 1972 that he would be prepared to grant
citizenship to Whites occupying the lands demanded by his government, if these lands were included in the Transkei. The situation
was aggravated by growing doubts among some DP members
about the feasibility of their multi-racial policy in present-day
South Africa. The former party leader, Poto, used his still considerable influence in favour of a continued rejection of separate development, and threatened to withdraw completely from politics if his
party decided to accept it. Some doubt still lingered, and to clarify
matters a special national conference was held by the DP on 16

September 1972. A motion by the leader was accepted "That the Democratic Party reaffirms its policy of multi-racialism and rejects a claim for Independence and short-sighted land claims which are implicit in the policy of separate development".[9] Independence for the Transkei will cause a major crisis in the DP, which will then lose all prospects of achieving its main objective of a fully integrated South Africa. In the event of independence the DP is nevertheless prepared to continue its participation in Transkeian governmental affairs, but it will continue to believe that the Transkei is part of a greater South Africa, and that a measure of rapprochement between South Africa and the Transkei will be possible afterwards.

—Land

The first legal prohibition on Africans acquiring land outside certain demarcated areas was imposed by the Native Land Act, 1913, which implemented the recommendation of the South African Native Affairs Commission of 1903–5, that African areas be reserved. In the nineteenth century certain land had already been reserved for exclusive occupation by Africans; for example, in the Cape Colony the annexation Acts relating to the Transkeian territories placed these territories outside the scope of common and statutory law on account of their inhabitants not being sufficiently civilised. In the Orange Free State Republic locations were awarded to African tribes which had assisted the Republic in the military field, and in the Transvaal Republic a Location Commission was set up in 1884 to allocate, keep in trust and administer reserves for Africans. In Natal, at the instigation of Sir Theophilus Shepstone, the Secretary for Native Affairs, the Natal Native Trust was created in 1865 to hold lands occupied by Africans in trust. Most of these measures were of a protective nature, intended to prevent the acquisition of African land by Whites, which would have been easy on account of their stronger economic position.

Before 1913 there were no legal restrictions on Africans acquiring land outside African areas. The 1913 Act enunciated the *status quo*, more than anything else, and the government realised that the reservation of more African land had to be implemented immediately. This was accomplished in an *ad hoc* way until the Natives (now Bantu) Trust and Land Act of 1936 released a further $7\frac{1}{4}$ million morgen to bring the total African area to about 20 million morgen. The acquisition of this additional land was a long-term process, and recent proposals by the South African government for consolidation of the homelands contain the final allocations in terms of the

1936 Act. Under these proposals only the two smallest homelands will consist of single territorial units (see Table 3.II, page 32).

Homeland leaders are openly opposed to the consolidation proposals and the South African government's intention of honouring the land quota of 1936. Without exception the leaders of homeland governments, and some opposition leaders, claimed more land for their homelands; Lebowa, Gazankulu, Bophuthatswana and the Ciskei also claiming certain White towns.

The governments of KwaZulu, Venda and Bophuthatswana complained that they had not been consulted over the consolidation proposals. Phatudi of Lebowa expressed the feelings of all homeland leaders when he declared that a single territory was preferred, and not four or five scattered areas. An aspect of the consolidation of land which causes great resentment is the implied removal of hundreds of thousands of Africans from tribal lands to newly acquired areas. A Land Commission appointed by the Lebowa Legislative Assembly in 1973 found great resistance among tribal Africans to removals.

The land question was considered as of such importance in Bophuthatswana that in 1973 a select committee was appointed, as well as a Land Board (in 1972), with both government and opposition members. The select committe recommended the inclusion of an additional 8 million ha., including eighteen White towns, in the Northern Cape Province and Western Transvaal; whereas the Land Board was given the permanent task of representing Tswana views on land to the South African government. Chief Minister Mangope stressed that separate development would fail if it did not succeed in giving "everybody or every group enough land to live on".[10] A select committee was also appointed by the Ciskei Legislative Assembly in 1973 to consider the position of landless people.

The most important contribution to the debate on land came towards the end of 1973 when, following Phatudi's lead, several Chief Ministers declared that they would provide certain guarantees to Whites who would be prepared to bring their land into the homelands. It was significant that a few White farmers accepted Phatudi's offer rather than relinquish ownership of the land, and even more significant was the South African government's apparent preparedness to consider such inclusion. This might well be the key to a possible solution to the stalemate over land.

The question over independence for the homelands is closely related to the land issue, and several homeland leaders consider it to be the ultimate test of the South African government's sincerity. Independence would also require settlement of land disputes (some

of which are ethnically founded) among the homeland governments. The Basotho of the Transkei, for instance, feel that they
should rather join Basotho Qwaqwa (which obtained self-government in 1974); and Lebowa and Bophuthatswana were unable
to agree on certain land occupied by large numbers of Tswanas
and Pedis. Similar disputes exist between Lebowa and Gazankulu.

Extensive land claims were made by Chief Kaiser Matanzima
during the first Transkei general election campaign in 1963. He
reminded his electors that the land between the Fish River (south
of East London) and the Kei River (the southern border of the
Transkei) belonged to them and that it had been taken away from
them by British imperialists. Three months later, in November
1963, he staked out land claims which he has since modified only
slightly – the districts of Queenstown, Indwe, Mount Currie, and
Elliot, and the White areas of Matatiele district – and added
that the Ciskei should solve the land questions between the Fish
and Kei Rivers. The South African Minister of Bantu Administration and Development, Mr. De Wet Nel, replied that the South
African government would not grant land to the Transkei beyond
the 1936 quota, and this remained the South African government's
point of view subsequently. In 1967 Matanzima almost seemed
to have laid the land issue to rest when he declared in a policy speech
in the Legislative Assembly that by the land between the Fish River
and Umzimkulu River (in Natal, slightly to the north of the
Transkei) he meant the existing African areas only and those to be
added in terms of the 1936 land laws; he excluded "White urban
complexes such as East London, Queenstown or Port Shepstone".[11]
However, starting with a motion in the legislative assembly by TNIP
member H. H. Nolutshungu in 1968, requests for the districts
of Elliot, Maclear, Mount Currie and the remaining White areas in
Matatiele, Port St. John's and Umzimkulu districts became almost
an annual event, to which was added in 1971 a request for control
over all Transkeian towns.[12] Territorial claims were extended over
an even larger area at the time of the 1972 session of the Legislative
Assembly, when the Chief Minister claimed at a meeting in Umtata
that the land between the Drakensberg on the Lesotho border and
the Umzimkulu River and between the Gamtoos River (west of
Port Elizabeth) and the district of Sterkstroom (north-west of the
Ciskei) belonged to the Xhosa, thus claiming an area several
times the size of the Transkei and including the Ciskei and the
seaports of Port Elizabeth and East London. He was supported
in the Legislative Assembly by Paramount Chief Botha Sigcau of the
Eastern Pondo who declared that the Umzimkulu River was the
Transkei's true north-eastern boundary (i.e. including certain

White areas of Natal and some African areas of KwaZulu), and that
Mount Currie district belonged to him as a descendant of
Faku.[13] (Faku was Paramount Chief of the Pondo in the mid-nine-
teenth century, and his territory stretched to the Umzimkulu River
in the north-east and well into the present districts of Mount
Currie and Matatiele to the north of the present Pondoland. On the
basis of these ancient boundaries of Pondoland, the Transkei Chief
Minister rejected a claim by Lesotho to the district of Matatiele.)
     Critics of Kaiser Matanzima point out that his land claims,
if acceded to, would greatly strengthen his power on a tribal basis
in the Legislative Assembly, as the disputed areas are to be popu-
lated mainly by tribesmen who favour him – namely Eastern Pondo
in Mount Currie, Basotho in Matatiele and Tembu and Emigrant
Tembu in Maclear and Elliot; and that his claims have become
more insistent and radical after the Glen Grey district had decided
by a majority vote of 84 per cent in October 1971 against joining
the Transkei. Inclusion of Glen Grey would have brought under
Matanzima's paramount chieftainship the loyalty of two of the
three Glen Grey chiefs – namely, Mtirara and Nhlonhlo, who control about 75 per cent of the district – while the number of Emigrant
Tembu in the Transkei, of whom Matanzima is paramount chief,
would almost have doubled, with a resulting increase of Emigrant
Tembu representatives in the Legislative Assembly. Another reason
for Matanzima's increasingly insistent pursuit of the land issue
could be the increased popularity of Chief Buthelezi of KwaZulu.
After Matanzima's claim for more land and power at his party's
conference of 1971, Buthelezi could point out with justification
"Chief Kaisers' stand was admirable, but I said the same things in
my inaugural speech at the opening of the Zulu Territorial Authority."[14] Matanzima's previous land claims were much more subdued,
less specific and without much popular support. Buthelezi could
therefore afford to ignore them. Increasing frustration, resulting
from the misconception that separate development could be used
as a tool for obtaining more land, no doubt also contributed to
Matanzima's increasing public statements.
     The transfer of the White districts of Mount Currie, Maclear,
Elliot, the remaining White portions of Port St. John's and Matatiele, and all Transkeian towns to the territory of the Transkei
is without question the Transkei government's main priority in its
negotiations with the South African government. The Transkei
Chief Minister maintained[15] that his government's claims were
reasonable – in that they included only a small portion of White
South Africa – and were based on historical fact. Until 1883 Mount
Currie, Elliot and Maclear formed an administrative part of the

Transkei; they were said to be inhabited by Pondomise, Bhele and Amazizi tribes (Maclear), Tembu tribesmen (Elliot), and Eastern Pondo (Mount Currie). Before land occupied by Africans was reserved for their exclusive use in 1913, Whites succeeded in acquiring freehold titles over these areas.

The Transkei government felt so strongly about the land question that it was prepared to make the achievement of independent status and even the maintenance of good relations with the South African government[16] depend on the satisfaction of its land demands. In an attempt to end the deadlock, Matanzima proposed at the TNIP conferences of 1972 and 1973 that the areas in question be released for purchase by Transkei citizens, and it was in August 1972 that he proposed the inclusion of these areas in the Transkei, together with their White owners. At the TNIP annual conference in 1973, Matanzima said: "We are determined . . . to pursue the claim on land until the Republican Government becomes aware of the unchristian attitude it has shown of arrogating to the White Community all South African land, leaving the bulk of the Black population with fragmented patches of stony and dry land on which to starve and rot." (The Transkei's situation in the best agricultural regions of Southern Africa detracted somewhat from this argument.)

In February 1972 Matanzima went so far as to call a secret meeting consisting of the Leader of the Opposition, all Transkei paramount chiefs, the front-benchers and chief whips of both political parties, and the Speaker of the Assembly in an attempt to obtain consensus of opinion on the land claims and thus strengthen his hand in negotiations with the South African government. The opposition refused to co-operate, and Matanzima unsuccessfully faced the South African Prime Minister alone a few days later. This did not deter him from declaring six months later that he would first put into the hands of Blacks all White spots remaining in the Transkei, then attempt to obtain the disputed districts, and finally seek amalgamation with the Ciskei.

The Transkei claims for more land are related to earlier African aspirations in South Africa. Economic advance for fuller citizenship was an important ANC policy objective in the 1930s, whereas today the idea of more land has great significance as a touchstone of economic viability for TNIP leaders, who associate economic viability with increased political power. TNIP leaders clearly regard the 1936 land legislation as a corollary of the Natives Representation Act, 1936, which placed the Africans on a separate voters' roll. They stress that the Africans were not party to these measures; that the measures were not intended to fix the boundaries of independent Black states; and that the 1936 land quota was compensation for the removal of the Africans from the common voters' roll in the *Cape Province only* (a removal which meant that "the rights of the Africans were taken away"[17]), whereas the quota of 7¼ million morgen was handed out to Africans in *all* the provinces of South Africa. Matanzima also denied that the Africans made improper use of their land; he pointed out that the average African farmer tilled about 2¼ morgen of land, which was insufficient for sustaining proper agricultural methods. More land was therefore a prerequisite for applying improved agricultural methods successfully.

During the Legislative Assembly's session of 1973 it became clear that the Transkei government's attitude over the land issue had hardened. Calling for complete control over all Transkei towns through elected African town councils, the TNIP chief whip, J. Ka-Tshunungwa (formerly a senior paid officer of the ANC) called Whites in these towns "blood-suckers" and hinted (contrary to the new TNIP policy of allowing White citizens – confirmed at the party conference three weeks earlier, on 22 March) that they should leave the Transkei. The Chief Minister also gave an assurance that they would continue negotiations for the transfer of land which was historically theirs, and added that people who wanted land which did not belong to them historically could take up arms and fight for it, thereby implying that Whites would have to fight for their unjustified claims. He later warned that the Black youth who were supporters of Black power movements would "take the land by force", and advised the Whites rather to "reason" with *him* over this land. Reacting to the South African offer to transfer all municipal land in the Transkei to the Transkei government as a final settlement, the Transkei Minister of Justice rejected it as meaningless and unacceptable. On an official visit to East London, accompanied by twenty-one members of the legislative assembly and two cabinet members, the Chief Minister stressed that the Blacks needed free ownership of the land, and that as long as they were denied it, they would have no power. He called for a division of South Africa on a proportional basis among the population groups, or alternatively, a multi-racial integrated South Africa where everybody shared equal rights. Unless the Blacks were satisfied, there would be a bloodbath in South Africa. (The latter remark probably strengthened segregationist attitudes as well as the doubts of many Whites about the Africans' desire for peaceful co-existence with Whites. It was in fact alleged that the threatening attitude of African leaders had resulted in prospective entrepreneurs losing interest in the homelands.)

In December 1973, when the Department of Bantu Administration and Development proposed the inclusion in the Transkei of the entire White area of Port St. John's, and several minor parts of Matatiele, Elliot and other adjoining "White" districts – the first sign of compromise. Matanzima remained adamant, however, and insisted that he would not relinquish any part of his land claims. Thus, the land situation in the Transkei remained unresolved, providing the homeland leaders with a unique opportunity for generating support among the Black population, who regard the refusal to transfer more land to African ownership as a manifestation of White oppression.

In KwaZulu the land question[18] received the attention of the first meeting of the Zulu Territorial Authority in January 1971. Several leading Zulus, including the acting Paramount Chief, Prince Israel, and the chairman of the Authority, Prince Clement Zulu, demanded to know how much land was due to Kwa-Zulu in terms of the 1936 Bantu Trust and Land Act. At that stage KwaZulu consisted of forty-eight blocks of land and 140 smaller "Black spots", inhabited by about $2\frac{1}{4}$ million people belonging to about 350 tribes. There were 59,000 ha. still due to KwaZulu. In June 1972, the South African government proposed to consolidate KwaZulu into six large blocks, two situated in Southern Natal and the others in Northern and Central Natal. These blocks included only two towns of any significance, Harding and Impendle, and would raise the total area of KwaZulu to 3,364,000 ha. More than 300,000 people would have had to be removed and resettled in consolidated areas. These proposals were revised after the Bantu Affairs Commission had toured Natal and heard White opinions on the original proposals. (This Commission is a statutory body, consisting mainly of members of the South African Parliament, with certain delegated executive powers.)

The new proposals, entailing consolidation of KwaZulu into ten blocks of land and the resettlement of about 133,000 Africans, were tabled by the South African Minister of Bantu Administration and Development in the South African parliament after the Kwa-Zulu government had complained bitterly about various aspects of the original proposals. A major complaint was that the Zulu people and their government had not been properly consulted: they refused to discuss the new proposals with the Deputy Minister of Bantu Administration and Development because he had come "to show us – not to consult with us",[19] but were prepared to negotiate with the South African government over this question in order to prevent a confrontation.[20]

A special session of the Legislative Assembly in January 1973 rejected the new proposals, and before that, on 21 July 1972, the executive council addressed a statement to the Commissioner-General for the Zulu and Swazi National Units, containing major objections to the proposals. First, the executive council could not accept that the land which had been reserved in 1936 would form the basis for the development of independent territories, because in 1936 no independent homelands had been envisaged. They respected the Nationalist government, Buthelezi said sarcastically, for its attempt to fulfil the promises made by the United Party government in 1936,[21] although these were unacceptable. In its statement the executive council said that it had expected all state lands and game reserves in the area, over and above the outstanding land from the 1936 quota, automatically to be transferred to Kwa-Zulu. The statement objected to the mistrust implicit in the allocation of all coastal land and the harbour of Richards Bay to White areas; and against the removal of so many more Africans than Whites. Later Buthelezi said they were not prepared to co-operate in the removal of people.[22] The executive council further objected to the fragmentation of KwaZulu, and the excision of certain towns including the resting place of King Shaka at Stanger. The executive council suggested that a referendum in Natal and KwaZulu be held so that people of all races could be consulted on the matter, but it thought that a joint commission of Whites and Zulus should rather have been appointed in the first place. The KwaZulu government is unique in its desire to share decisions on land allocation with the surrounding White population.

In Natal there was almost universal rejection of the consolidation proposals. The (White) Zululand Chamber of Commerce appointed a subcommittee to exert pressure in favour of the existing land division: it objected to the hardships which the removals would bring for both Zulus and Whites. A similar subcommittee was appointed by the (White) Natal Chamber of Commerce. Out of thirty-eight farmers' associations (all White) affiliated to the Natal Agricultural Union, only three supported the proposals, and as a result the Union itself rejected them, saying that without the approval of the KwaZulu government, farming on the borders of KwaZulu would be impossible. The Natal Indian Cane Growers' Association objected to the proposals on the grounds that it would cause many Indian landowners to lose their land. The Eshowe Town Council, as well as the Natal Parks Board, also rejected them because they would make it impossible for the Umfolosi and Hluh-luwe Game Reserves to be managed as ecological units. Belatedly, the Natal Provincial Council rejected the proposals in June 1973, and called for a referendum on the subject before the province was further carved up.

A stalemate was thus reached in KwaZulu, and in the process African objections to the South African land situation were voiced once again.

The staunchest supporters of separate development in the African homelands are the members of the Basotho Qwaqwa government of Witzieshoek. The fourth largest ethnic group in South Africa, the Basotho have the smallest territory: its people are spread widely over the White areas of the Orange Free State, Transvaal and, to a smaller extent, Natal and the Cape Province. There are also substantial numbers of Basotho in the Transkei, Ciskei and Bophuthatswana. According to the theory of separate development, self-government should be attained by national units, ideally belonging to the same ethnic group. This aspect of separate development gave rise to aspirations in Qwaqwa for the transfer of Basotho areas in the Transkei, Ciskei and Bophuthatswana to Qwaqwa. This tendency was to some extent strengthened by the covert feeling among Ciskei and Transkei Basotho that their language and culture were in danger of being swamped by the numerically superior Xhosa.

In the 1973 Transkei general election the lowest voter participation was recorded, significantly, in the Basotho areas, particularly Matatiele district.

The only reaction came from Matanzima who said that Transkei Basotho could move to Qwaqwa; their land would remain in the Transkei. It was thus made clear that for the area of one homeland to be increased through the addition of land belonging to another homeland was not a practical possibility.

—Independence

Underlying the granting of self-governing status to the homelands is the assumption that they will ultimately become independent. No time-table is set, and no specific conditions are imposed by the South African government before independence could be achieved. It is tacitly understood, however, that africanisation of the civil service in every homeland will be at an advanced stage before independence is granted.

The possibility of ultimate independence is accepted by the homeland-based parties and the homeland government leaders. While they accept the idea of homeland independence, there is a strong sense of being South African underlying the homeland leaders' attitudes. Their strong antipathy towards political fragmentation in South Africa is tempered by their firm grasp of South African political realities, and is expressed in their desire for a federation based on independent homelands, which can include White South

Africa. Understandably, unity within the homelands is an important immediate objective to lay a foundation for firm future political action. Homeland leaders are prepared to run the risk that well-developed homeland political systems can provide ethnic centrifugal forces detrimental to African unity in South Africa, and realise that they have no alternative.

In the Transkei one of the main differences between the TNIP and the DP is apparent in their respective attitudes towards independence for the Transkei. The TNIP accepts it as an ultimate objective and in 1968, after five years of self-government, made a request to the South African government that the Transkei be prepared for independence as soon as possible. The DP rejects it as the ultimate manifestation of separate development; it would be against the DP's multi-racial policy, divisive of South Africa, and economically detrimental to the interests of South Africa and particularly the Transkei, and it would deprive the Africans of their right to share in the wealth of South Africa as a whole. For the Transkei government any possible attempt by the South African government to revoke the self-governing status of the Transkei would be an act of aggression, and as a self-governing territory the Transkei remains "a separate national group within the framework of South Africa".[23]

Full independent status for the Transkei was requested by the Transkei government in a motion during the Legislative Assembly's 1972 session, on the condition that certain White areas be added to the Transkei, namely Elliot, Maclear, Mount Currie and the remaining White areas of the district of Matatiele, Umzimkulu, and Port St. John's. This request preceded by only a few months Matanzima's pleas for a federation of Southern African states under Black majority rule, which he made in the face of the South African Prime Minister's statement that the homelands could only obtain independence on the basis of the land set aside for the African population in 1936. Matanzima said in the Legislative Assembly in 1972 that separation of the races would be fictitious if the land question were not settled fairly, and it would be political suicide to call for independence without the disputed districts.

During the early years of self-government a faction within the TNIP pressed strongly for full independence. Its attempt to bring the matter of independence to a head led to the leaders of this faction, S. M. Sinaba and J. Z. Kobo, being expelled from the party.

The transfer of certain government departments to the Transkei government – as well as of certain land from the Republic to the Transkei – were considered by Kaiser Matanzima to be the Transkei Legislative Assembly's most important decisions during its first seven years.[24] The transfer of the Departments of Health (transferred on 1 April 1973), Posts and Telegraphs, Police, and Defence had often been requested, and was considered essential for continuous progress towards independence. Impatience over the slow rate of transfer of powers had grown, and the Chief Minister voiced a popular sentiment by asking: "If Lesotho, Botswana and Swaziland can control these Departments, why not the Transkei?"[25]

In March 1974 the TNIP annual congress adopted a motion in favour of independence for the Transkei within five years, even without the land claimed by the Transkei government, on condition that independence would not prejudice the land claims. On 25 March the Chief Minister introduced a similar motion in the Legislative Assembly.

The governments of KwaZulu, Gazankulu and Bophuthatswana supported the Transkei by also demanding more land and the satisfactory consolidation of existing areas as a prerequisite for independence. Gazankulu's Chief Minister added that any form of independence would have to be granted within the framework of a broader South Africa, and should not deprive Gazankulu inhabitants of their "inherent birthright which is reflected in their South African citizenship . . ."[26] KwaZulu and Bophuthatswana have made still further preconditions for their acceptance of independent status. KwaZulu requires economic viability, with which the transfer of the developing seaport of Richards Bay is associated, and internationally recognised boundaries. Bophuthatswana's additional conditions are related to those of KwaZulu: it demands international recognition of independence by bodies such as the United Nations and the Organisation of African Unity. Matanzima, Buthelezi and Ntsanwisi thought this demand by Mangope unrealistic, and refused to support it. Mangope also formulated another interesting condition, namely the payment of R240 million compensation by the South African government to the government of Bophuthatswana for previous underpayment of African labourers from the territory. He said in 1973 that this could be paid over a twelve-year period, which gave some indication to his time-table for independence. While he did not formulate this as a condition for independence, Buthelezi wanted assurances that the South African government would continue its budgetary aid after independence.

The governments of the Ciskei, Lebowa and Venda have made no particular conditions for independence.

—Amalgamation

Whereas federation of African homelands is a fairly new idea, the possible amalgamation of the Transkei and the Ciskei is a long-standing issue due to their close proximity and the predomi-

nance of Xhosa-speakers in both territories. Early attempts, in
1934 and again in 1939, by the Transkei General Council to obtain
amalgamation were resisted by the Ciskei, but in October 1966 the
then Chairman of the Ciskei Territorial Authority, Chief J. Mabandla (a Fingo), tabled a motion asking for a recess committee to
investigate all aspects of amalgamation with the Transkei. Territorial Authority members, especially the Rarabe members, resisted
the motion and the matter was not raised again. Two months later,
Chief Minister Matanzima of the Transkei made a plea for amalgamation on the grounds that it would be an extension of Transkei
borders – raising new fears among Ciskeians.

The Transkei government formally and unsuccessfully requested
the South African government in 1968 that the Transkei and Ciskei
be amalgamated into one "Xhosa State".[27] Mabandla, then the
Ciskei Chief Minister, declared in July 1971 that amalgamation of
the two territories would follow soon after the attainment of self-
government, but at about the same time he resisted attempts to
have the Glen Grey district of the Ciskei incorporated in the adjoining Transkei. A referendum in Glen Grey resulted in an over-
whelming vote against Transkei incorporation, namely 37,842
(83·7 per cent) against and 6,634 (14·7 per cent) in favour of incorporation. The possibility of amalgamation of the two territories
remained open, however, but became more remote soon after
Sebe's accession to the Ciskei chief ministership. Both governments
continued to pay lip-service to amalgamation, but vested interests
created by self-government became a serious obstacle.

While the Transkei and Ciskei cabinets made no progress beyond
the issuing of press statements, the cabinets of Lebowa and Venda
met several times in the second half of 1974 to discuss possible
amalgamation. At these discussions attention was also given to the
detailed implications of amalgamation, such as the possible phasing
out of the appointment of teachers and issuing of trading licences on
ethnic lines, and border disputes between the two homelands.

Amalgamation and federation are related ideas in the sense that
both represent forms of resistance to the ethnic fragmentation
which underlies self-government in the homelands, and both can be
regarded as attempts at greater African solidarity to improve the
African power base vis-à-vis the White government. The success of
amalgamation of non-independent homelands depends in the final
instance on the assent of the South African government. Non-
acceptance of independence (see Chapter 11) will lead to immediate
difficulties in achieving amalgamation of any two or more homelands. South African refusal to amalgamation attempts will however
undoubtedly strengthen feelings of solidarity.

—Economic Development

The political implications of economic development have always been stressed, and perhaps even overemphasised, by the Transkei government. For several years after the attainment of self-government, it considered economic self-sufficiency and independence – without ever clearly defining these concepts – as a prerequisite for political independence.[28] However, as the political climate warmed and the Transkei's economic development lagged behind the demands of population increase, the previous stand was reversed, and it is now accepted that political independence can precede economic independence. The quest for economic independence is in the first place an effort to diminish the Black man's economic dependence on White South Africa and to prove his economic capabilities. As a policy objective this was pushed into the background when the Transkei gave its support to the proposed federation of Black states, which implied that the constituent territories would be economically interdependent – so diminishing the political necessity for the Transkei's economic independence.

However economic development was considered an essential ingredient for political power, in the Transkei's relations *vis-à-vis* South Africa, or the other territories in a possible federation. Closely connected with conceptions of economic power are the repeated requests for additional land for the Transkei. More investment opportunities in land would increase African economic strength.[29]

Other homelands do not regard economic development as a prerequisite for political independence. The KwaZulu government sees it as an imperative for carrying out separate development and, like the Transkei government, regards it as closely connected with political power. Unlike the Transkei's insistence on more land for economic power, KwaZulu thinks that unity among Africans in the labour field will ensure them a large measure of control of the South African economy. Attainment of economic power, again, will mean that half the battle towards full freedom and human rights is won. The Bophuthatswana government is ambivalent towards economic affairs as a political determinant; while promoting exclusive African participation in commerce in Bophuthatswana – to the extent that it wants no White traders operating near its borders in the White area – it believes that a more equitable distribution of national wealth is necessary to achieve harmonious co-existence among racial and ethnic groups. The latter thought probably reflects the attitude of most Africans in South Africa, and the economic dispensation in South Africa is regarded by most homeland leaders as a key towards future political relations.

For a considerable time (until 1972) the South African government refused capital investment by Whites in the industrial and commercial development of the African homelands. Having no power over economic affairs, the Transkei government toed the line and was happy to assist the South African government in getting rid of most of the White traders in the Transkei in the belief that they were breaking a White stranglehold over the Transkei economy. The TNIP did not support the DP view that private White capital should be allowed in the Transkei.[30] The Transkei government preferred to depend on its Transkei Development and Reserve Fund, which it had created during the first session of the Legislative Assembly in 1964 with the object of financing economic development schemes and exploiting natural resources, and to create a reserve for lean years and disasters and emergency. The Transkei government maintained that investment by Whites would only lead to exploitation, unless the Transkei government could hold 51 per cent of the shares in any undertaking. In such enterprises three conditions should govern White investment: first, stipulations concerning the proportion of White to Black workers; secondly, the gradual withdrawal of White and simultaneous advancement of African workers; and thirdly, the eventual taking over of the entire enterprise by Africans.[31] At the same time, the Transkei government should, and would, take care not to inhibit the growth of African private investment and initiative through government business ventures. The Chief Minister assured possible investors in 1969 and again in 1973, that government participation would not lead to nationalisation. Since the South African government's announcement in 1972 that it would allow White entrepreneurs to establish industries in the homelands as agents of the Xhosa Development Corporation and Bantu Investment Corporation, the Transkei Chief Minister completely changed his view and invited White South African and overseas investors to the Transkei. He also welcomed the intention of leading banking institutions in South Africa to form a development bank for the homelands.

The more recently established homeland governments of Kwa-Zulu, Gazankulu, Lebowa, Ciskei and Bophuthatswana have favoured foreign and White investment in their respective homelands from the time they assumed office. They regard it as essential for economic development, and homeland leaders such as Buthelezi and Mangope make full use of overseas visits to discuss investment possibilities with possible investors. They encountered the fear among investors that investment in the homelands would be interpreted as support for separate development. However, homeland

leaders tend to see this problem as irrelevant to their overriding problem of poverty, and Buthelezi suggested that investors could
avert this problem by dealing directly with the homeland governments while merely notifying the South African government. Mangope also pledged guarantees against nationalisation and disrup-
tion by trade union activities. While seeing the necessity of
industrial development inside Gazankulu, Ntsanwisi also regards
South Africa as "one economic unit" with Gazankulu as an "unviable portion".[32] This did not detract from his efforts to attract
all the investment possible. Border industries in the White area
do not contribute to homeland development, and homeland
leaders therefore prefer industrial development inside the homelands.

A new and significant development in the economic field is the
homeland leaders' opposition to trade boycotts of South Africa.
Matanzima, Mangope and Sebe, for instance, warned the
Organisation of African Unity and Arab countries that an oil boycott of South Africa would only adversely affect the Africans.

Economic policies and priorities were better articulated in the
Transkei than in any of the other homelands. Although the
Transkei government has at its disposal the Transkei Development
and Reserve Fund, the Fund has contributed little to industrial
development, which has remained largely in the hands of the Xhosa
Development Corporation (XDC) – a statutory body established in
1965 under the Development Corporations for Bantu Homelands
Act, 1965, for the industrial and commercial development of the
Transkei and Ciskei. The activities of the XDC are co-ordinated
with the Transkei government's development programmes through
a Planning Committee established by the Chief Minister in 1970,
but meetings between the Directors of the XDC and the Transkei
cabinet are rare.

In what he called a new approach, the Chief Minister
announced in 1970 the following seven-point plan for the speedier
economic development of the Transkei:

(1) better planning and co-ordination of the efforts of the different development bodies in the Transkei;
(2) formulating plans to ensure greater agricultural production;
(3) planning a sound infrastructure for economic development;
(4) formulating plans and creating the political climate which
will attract private industries on an agency basis;
(5) exploiting the tourist potential of the Transkei and the arts
and crafts of the people;
(6) adjusting and adapting the educational system to faster
economic development;
(7) activating the people towards greater initiative and productivity.

Agriculture is recognised as the cornerstone of the economy, providing almost the entire resident population with employment. The Xhosa Development Corporation created 5,251 new jobs in the two-year period between 1970 and 1972, which earned the Chief Minister's praise, though many more jobs were needed. The Transkei Chief Minister considers the creation of new jobs as the greatest task in the Transkei's economic development, and efforts at primary and secondary education, agricultural and technical training are investments in the development of human potential; whereas new roads, bridges, water supplies and administrative buildings are needed for an economic infrastructure.

Among the homeland governments, the Lebowa government was the only one to request the South African government to establish a Department of Economic Affairs in order to co-ordinate and promote industrial and economic activities. Other homeland governments gave little attention to economic planning and were satisfied with stating broad objectives, such as the necessity for sound agricultural methods, and industrial development inside the homelands and not in the border industry areas. The KwaZulu government felt strongly about the necessity for micro-economic development as a prerequisite for macro-economic development. In 1973 the executive councillor for Community Affairs, Barney Dladla, visited the U.S.A. where he studied community development projects with a view to applying this approach to KwaZulu. The Ciskei government appointed the head of the Department of Town and Regional Planning of the University of Cape Town to undertake a socio-economic survey of the Ciskei for better development planning; and the Bophuthatswana government appointed economic planning committees to investigate various economic sectors and industries.

Homeland governments and opposition parties are generally dissatisfied with the work of the Bantu Investment Corporation, Xhosa Development Corporation and Bantu Mining Corporation. The fact that Africans cannot become members of, or be represented on, the boards of these corporations causes growing suspicion over their motives. Whereas these corporations are recognised as contributors to the economic development of the homelands, the homeland governments exert increasing pressure on the South African government for African shareholding and representation on their boards. Lebowa intends to establish its own development corporations, and Bophuthatswana established a Bophuthatswana Development Trust, into which the Chief Minister entered in 1974 in his private capacity.

—*Labour*

There is no subject on which the homeland leaders – government and opposition alike – are more unanimous than labour. The system of migratory labour, influx control, reference books, restriction on visits to urban areas and the use of police dogs in investigation of pass offences have been roundly denounced by almost all homeland governments. The Transkei government, however, conditionally accepted influx control as a regulation of "an orderly flow of labour to the industrial centres and . . . to ensure that people seeking work in the cities are assured that there will be work and suitable housing. . . ."[33] Rightly seeing the influx control system as closely connected with economic development in the Transkei, it requested that no Transkeians be repatriated from White urban areas to the Transkei unless there was employment and accommodation for them in the Transkei. The governments of KwaZulu and the Transkei also relate their land claims to influx control, and maintain that they need more land to accommodate the people repatriated from the urban areas. Buthelezi, referring to the foreign worker problem in Europe, also envisages the continued necessity of some control over people wanting to travel between the "states" of South Africa, or who are domiciled in one state and work in another, but such control must be without the "constraint and compulsion inherent in the pass system".[34]

Wage increases for African workers have almost continuously been called for by several homeland government leaders, notably Matanzima, Buthelezi, Sebe and Mangope. They rejected job reservation, and claimed equal pay for equal work. Matanzima maintained that the country-wide wage increases for African workers in 1973 were insufficient to close the wage gap, and Buthelezi pointed out that the difference between extreme poverty and extreme wealth could result in revolution. Mangope stressed that industrial training was the key to progress.

Over trade unions for Africans, the Transkei government adopted the attitude that trade unions fell outside its scope, while the KwaZulu government, on the other hand, asked the South African government to establish trade unions so that Africans could negotiate for better wages, and rejected the works committees established under the existing legislation. Barney Dladla, whose Community Affairs portfolio included responsibility for labour bureaux, threatened to instruct his department not to conclude labour contracts with certain firms, and so entered the field of labour negotiations on behalf of the KwaZulu government. He also proposed a "super-committee" to negotiate on behalf of the workers in the absence of trade unions.[35] On various occasions in 1973 Dladla successfully intervened in disputes between workers and management of firms in White areas.

Mangope, on the other hand, urged Tswanas to use the works committees, and his government appointed a labour liaison officer for border industries and those inside Bophuthatswana to assist in the settling of disputes. Mangope several times addressed White entrepreneurs and stressed the importance of economic partnership in South Africa as a determinant for "peaceful progress" and a basis for solving social and political problems. He regards proper wages and sound labour relations as keystones for economic partnership.

—Education

The medium of instruction in schools has top priority in the educational policy of all homelands. Under the Bantu Education Act, 1953, mother-tongue instruction was instituted for all primary school classes, and this was bitterly resented by the African population. English as a medium of instruction from standard III (the fifth school year) upwards is unanimously supported by all homeland parties and factions, and steps were taken in all homelands soon after becoming self-governing to implement this policy. Free and compulsory education is also regarded by all African leaders as particularly important and is accepted as an ideal. Towards the end of 1973 the Bantu Education Advisory Board of the Department of Bantu Education of South Africa started investigating means of introducing free and compulsory education for Africans in South Africa.

Dating from the days of resentment against Bantu Education, revision of syllabuses also received great prominence, although in the Transkei, where this had been carried through, it was found that the Bantu Education syllabuses were the most suitable. A former Transkei Minister of Education, C. M. C. Ndamse, agreed that it was not the content that was inferior under Bantu Education so much as the facilities, equipment and teachers.

University education is given special prominence by the Transkei and Bophuthatswana governments. In 1972 both governments asked for their own territorial universities, and in both cases it was argued that independence for the Ciskei and Lebowa would cut off the Transkei and Bophuthatswana from their universities (Fort Hare and the University of the North are situated respectively in the Ciskei and Lebowa). Bophuthatswana also contended that its own university would contribute towards the development and planning of the territory; whereas the Transkei complained that Fort Hare could not cope with the Transkei's annual output of 880 matriculation students. In both territories the opposition parties opposed the establishment of universities and maintained that existing facilities were adequate.

—African Unity

The willingness of homeland leaders to co-operate within the structures of separate development implies a measure of acceptance of the ethnicity which is inherent in the establishment of separate homeland governments. In spite of professed support for African unity in South Africa, the more articulate homeland leaders, Mangope, Matanzima and Buthelezi, have also given clear evidence of the persisting vitality of ethnicity. Ethnic pride is evident in the KwaZulu government's intention to erect monuments to Zulu kings and national heroes, and its planning of "national" celebrations, such as Shaka's Day.

Shortly after assuming office as Chief Executive Officer of the Zuly Territorial Authority in 1970, Buthelezi used terms such as "human dignity of the Zulu people", "Zulu state", "Zulu pride" and, referring to the Zulu, "this national consciousness" in an article in *The World*.[36] In 1973, after opposition parties had been established in KwaZulu, the Buthelezi government still maintained that political parties would be divisive of the Zulu nation, and regarded Zulu unity as a prerequisite for any moves it might make towards the achievement of African unity in South Africa.

The Bophuthatswana government's initial opposition to a federation stemmed from its essentially Tswana orientation. The opposition Seoposengwe Party, on the other hand, professed support for African unity and maintained that the South African government only wanted to divide the African population into ethnic groups for its own advantage. Although Mangope in 1973 also briefly supported the federation, he later returned to a narrower ethnic viewpoint and voiced preference for a federation with neighbouring Botswana. Mangope's commitment to Bophuthatswana is clear from the following notes he used when addressing the inaugural meeting of the Bophuthatswana National Party in August 1972:

(1) There must be *FAITH* and *TRUST* in and loyalty to Bophuthatswana and her peoples. . . .
(2) We must strive for national unity and evolve a policy whereby every Tswana will have a share in his government and feel that he belongs to it and Bophuthatswana.
(3) We must strive for a fair and equal treatment of all sections, areas and/or constituencies of Bophuthatswana and an unbiased realization of the rights and privileges of every section of the community.

(4) We must strive for the preservation of the Tswana culture. . . .
(5) We must strive for economic independence . . . to build a
    prosperous and economically sound Bophuthatswana. . . .

Little change has occurred in the Transkei National Independence Party policy over African identity and nationalism.
For several years Matanzima did little to remove the conception
that he had exchanged African nationalism for a narrower ethnic
nationalism: his actions tended rather to strengthen it. In 1968,
for instance, the TNIP election manifesto declared: "The TNIP
stands for Transkei nationalism and Transkei independence!"
– and Chief Jeremiah Moshesh, a Sotho-speaking member of
Matanzima's cabinet, was allowed to complain in the Legislative
Assembly that the Sotho language was receiving discriminatory
treatment in the Transkei government service, and to declare,
during the same session: "We [the Basotho] are not a tribe, but a
nation. To prove to you that I am proud of my language, I will
carry on the debate in my own language. . . ."[37] Early in his first
term of office as Chief Minister, Matanzima told a meeting at Rhodes
University, Grahamstown, that nationalism was vital to a nation,
that he believed in Xhosa nationalism because he was born in it,
and that his heritage as a Tembu required him to promote the
happiness, peace and prosperity of the Xhosa national unit of whom
the Tembu formed a part. While these remarks could be narrowly
interpreted, they could also be more broadly relevant to African
nationalism. A few years later Matanzima warned chiefs who had
influenced their people to vote for the DP's multi-racial policy,
that they might lose the allegiance of their subjects because they
were "trying to work against the strong forces of nationalism . . .".[38]
Nationalism was here contrasted with multi-racialism (co-operation with the Whites), and it was implied that nationalism was
stronger than tribalism. Matanzima's use of the word "Bantu"
in every session of the Legislative Assembly strengthened suspicion
over his ethnic affinities, but on the other hand, he used the words
"African" and "Black" more often when referring specifically to
his own people. Recently, as Black consciousness became more
manifest in South Africa, he publicly declared that he was "still" a
Black nationalist,[39] and on another occasion[40] he called on Africans
to rid themselves of tribal ties and to develop instead a national
consciousness.

Transkeians in general have always been aware of the Chief
Minister's sentiments as an africanist, and many believed that
during his 1972 visit to the United States "something has happened" to activate his sentiments. His utterances on his re-

turn surprised even his closest associates, and there is some doubt as
to whether he and his party have the organisational power to contain the forces of racialism which might be unleashed through a
haphazard propagation of Black solidarity, based on Black identity,
for political purposes. An almost similar situation prevailed during
the 1950s when the ANC's civil disobedience campaigns disrupted into bloody riots, while the national executive remained
powerless to control its followers. It is widely believed that
Kaiser Matanzima accepted separate development because it
offered an opportunity for the Africans to achieve exclusive control over their own destiny and progress. It is common knowledge
that his entry into governmental affairs only followed the
announcement in 1953 that the White official members of the
district councils and the United Transkeian Territories General
Council would be withdrawn. For almost two decades afterwards
Matanzima remained circumspect in his utterances on African
nationalism.

The concepts of "Black consciousness" and "africanism" are
unknown among certain sections of the homeland populations, but
pride in the African cultural heritage and increasing self-confidence
in social intercourse with Whites became conspicuous after the
achievement of self-government. In the early 1970s Black consciousness became firmly established among certain sections of the homeland populations, because it was seen either as a logical corollary
to the racial separation emphasised by separate development, or as a
means for raising up the African population materially and psychologically. There is also a feeling that Black solidarity can only
become a means of general improvement after a basic level of development has been achieved through the utilisation of all the opportunities offered by separate development. In the homelands there is
a general, and quite definite, feeling that the slogan "Black is beautiful" does not imply that "White is ugly". Homeland politicians –
perhaps under the influence of the ideal for African unity – have
little manifest concern for anxious minority groups, such as the
Basotho in the Transkei and Ciskei, Ndebele in Lebowa, Swazi
in KwaZulu and Pedi in Bophuthatswana.

The most articulate homeland leader in favour of Black (as
opposed to "African") solidarity is Gatsha Buthelezi, who maintains that Black consciousness is a weapon which can be used to
fight Black inferiority complexes caused by White domination.
Buthelezi recognises the danger of racism which is raised by Black
consciousness and warns against it. Ethnic differences, however,
are not incompatible with Black consciousness, he says; the Blacks
are "brothers in spite of them".[41] Realising that his exhortation

for Black unity and improvement may raise fears among Whites,
Buthelezi proposed at the Progressive Party Conference in Durban
in 1973 that a Bill of Rights be drawn up in which minority rights –
among others, those of the Whites – would be safeguarded. Implied
in the proposal is Buthelezi's aspiration towards Black domination
of South Africa.

It is also Buthelezi, more than any other homeland leader, who
has tried to win the confidence of Indians and Coloureds in the country, by stressing their common problems the solution of which calls
for unity and mutual help. Opposed to Buthelezi's viewpoint is that
of George Matanzima, Transkei Minister of Justice, who maintains
that unity with Coloureds and Indians must be achieved later;
at this stage it will only "complicate the issue".[42] A step in this
direction was the Transkei government's decision in April 1974
to grant Transkeian citizenship to Coloureds born in the Transkei.

In Bophuthatswana, Mangope declared himself "totally against
the concept of Black solidarity where it implies the grouping together of Blacks purely because their skins are black as against
Whites purely because their skins are white". To him that was an
"intolerable racist attitude".[43] Nevertheless, Mangope has several
viewpoints coinciding with those of the Black consciousness movement – e.g. in respect of the ability of the Black people to improve
themselves through community effort, his refusal to acknowledge
the superiority of Whites, and the common nature of the Black
man's problems in various parts of South Africa.

No official propaganda has ever gone out from the offices of
the TNIP supporting Black consciousness or Black power. However,
certain manifestations of Black consciousness are evident in the
party, such as Kaiser Matanzima's announcement in 1973 that a
raised clenched fist would thenceforth be his party's sign, his reminder to followers on returning from the U.S.A. in August 1972
that "Black is beautiful" (subsequently repeated in Umtata by his
wife); and the loud acclaim for his Black power salute and cry of
"Unity" when he left the Legislative Assembly at the close of the
1971 session.

In the Transkei the DP suddenly found itself outmanoeuvred
by the TNIP on Black consciousness and African unity. It hesitated
to declare its policy on Black consciousness which, it feared, was
only another manifestation of racialism and therefore did not fit
the party's broad framework of multi-racialism. Although opposed
to a racialistic approach, its policy manifestoes and statements
have always emphasised *African* needs and problems, and have
never explained how, if it came into power, it would deal with a
multi-racial society.

It is evident that Black consciousness and African unity are the greatest political issues to appear on the homelands' political scene in the 1970s. The consequences for relations with the South African government for Africans in White urban areas, the homelands themselves, and even for relations with neighbouring African states are enormous. Political participation in homeland politics can increase phenomenally and unless the expectations aroused are satisfied the prospects for peaceful political change in South African can be fatally damaged. The homeland leaders realise that the only hope for the achievement of their objectives lies in the political mobilisation of the African masses. In African unity and Black consciousness they found an appropriate emotive issue for those people not impressed by the bread and butter politics of the homelands.

Issues in Homeland Elections

Bophuthatswana and the Transkei have been selected for a description of issues in their respective general elections. In both cases correlation of election issues with previous policy statements shows great consistency. In these two territories as well as in other homelands election issues tend to be largely homeland oriented, while attention is also paid to issues which affect urban voters in White areas.

— Transkei

The issues of the Transkei general election of 1963 remained almost unchanged in the elections of 1968 and 1973. The 1963 election was dominated by the opposing viewpoints of Matanzima and Poto. Matanzima propagated a Black Transkei with its own civil service, and ultimate independence, exclusive African rights to land ownership, the franchise and participation in economic development, with chiefs and elected members in a single-chamber parliament. Poto, on the other hand, stressed the establishment of an upper house of chiefs and an elected lower house, equal pay for all Africans throughout South Africa, and continued presence of Whites in the Transkei where they could have full citizenship rights. Underlying these differences was Matanzima's acceptance, and Poto's rejection of separate development, and the concomitant acceptance and rejection respectively of a future independent Transkei as a separate state. Widely divergent policy statements were made by the 180 candidates who were not bound together by party discipline. Their attention was focused mainly on general advancement of the Transkei population, education, and higher wages, while only a very few candidates were concerned with the ideological implications of separate development.

The various election manifestoes issued by the Transkei National Independence Party, Democratic Party, and Transkei People's Freedom Party in 1968 reflected the most important aspects of their respective policies. A fair degree of consensus existed between the parties in respect of educational policy; improved health services; opposition to terrorism and communism; relaxation or even abolition of measures restricting the access of Transkeian labourers to the Republic; the preservation of chieftainship; universal suffrage; a friendly policy towards Whites in the Transkei; safeguarding of minority groups (tribes) in the Transkei; and improved agricultural, mining, and industrial development. The voters were required to choose between the parties on the grounds of differences related mainly to the acceptance or not by the parties of ultimate independence for exclusively Black territories. For the TNIP this included the formal acceptance of the policy of the governing party in the Republic of South Africa, viz. separate political development of the various African territories and White South Africa with the goal of ultimately achieving independence, the gradual withdrawal of Transkeian Whites, a Transkei national anthem (*Nkosi Sikeleli I'Afrika*) and flag, increased administrative and governmental responsibility, more land, and friendly relations with the Republican government and the governments of the other self-governing or independent homelands. At the same time the TNIP wanted to conserve and foster tribal law and custom – perhaps as a political strategem more than anything else because its chief support came from more traditionally oriented people.

The Democratic Party, on the other hand, stressed its goal of a multi-racial South Africa of which the Transkei should form an integral part in all respects. It therefore rejected independence as a goal, the withdrawal of Whites from the Transkei, a separate flag and anthem, more land, and increased governmental and administrative powers. As a corollary it regarded as irrelevant a policy propagating friendly relations with neighbouring White South Africa and independent homelands. The DP also propagated the adaptation of traditional culture to Western culture, the strengthening of family life, and better welfare services.

The Transkei People's Freedom Party differed from the DP mainly in respect of its aspiration towards immediate independence, and the resulting diplomatic ties with friendly countries. Its difference with the TNIP was in respect of its acceptance of the Transkei as a multi-racial territory and its impatience in respect of independence. It further stressed, rather vaguely, modernisation and development, and the participation of youth in public affairs.

Manifestoes were scarce in the 1973 election. All TNIP candidates issued the same manifesto in all constituencies. Each candidate, however, had his own photo and the name of his constituency on his pamphlet. Matanzima also issued a policy statement in printed, leaflet format. The DP issued no general manifestoes, and its leader, Guzana, only released a policy statement to the press. Some individual independent and DP candidates issued manifestoes, however.

The TNIP candidates' collective manifesto is a good summary of African aspirations in South Africa in general, even though it contains some references to Transkeian situations. The following is the complete text of this concise manifesto:

(1) I/We pledge myself/ourselves to give full support to the Cabinet in its efforts to develop the economy of the Transkei.

We shall activate the Transkeian citizens in farming, building of roads and bridges, building of clinics, building of schools with Government subsidy, provision of water supplies for domestic and agricultural use, Compulsory Education, Commercial undertakings, Irrigation schemes.

(2) I/We pledge assistance to the Transkeian Government in its claim for additional land comprising the Districts of Elliot, Maclear, Matatiele Farms, Mount Currie and Port St. Johns.

(3) I/We shall struggle, in support of the Government, to remove from the Statute Book all discriminatory laws which are a source of inhumanity, e.g. Pass Laws, Influx Control regulations, discrimination in wages and salaries, restrictions on movement of stock.

(4) I/We shall assist the Government to activate the establishment of industries in the Transkei so as to provide work for Transkeian citizens and augment the Revenue of the country.

(5) I/We shall fight for the establishment of Farmers Co-Operatives, Land Bank, Trading Companies to step up the economy of the country.

(6) I/We stand for complete independence and the federation of the black states. Complete equality amongst all races is our objective.

UNITY IS STRENGTH

Matanzima's manifesto endorsed in more general terms these objectives, as well as his belief that separate development will "demonstrate to the world that Black and White in South Africa can live together". He also envisaged the "building of a civilised society based on African traditions and customs". In speeches Matanzima referred to equal wages, the proposed African federation, land claims, increased localisation of the civil service, his opposition to oppression of any population group; and also mentioned the possibility of an independent Transkei within five years.

Guzana's statement to the press reiterated his party's rejection of separate development and the regional development of the Transkei as an integrated part of South Africa. This will entail industrial decentralisation towards underdeveloped areas such as the Transkei and permission for people of all racial groups to invest capital in the Transkei and participate in its government. Guzana also favoured the abolition of discriminating legislation, such as influx control measures, the migrant labour system, and the reservation of amenities for certain racial groups only, as well as improved educational facilities, rural land ownership in tribal areas, and fixing of minimum wages. Individual DP candidates went into more detail and promised that they would promote trade unions, and the establishment of a civil service association and of clinics and agricultural schools, market halls, improved wages, compulsory education, and improved social welfare benefits.

The printed proceedings of the Transkei Legislative Assembly afford members of the Assembly an opportunity to prove to their constituents and followers their efforts for the promotion of their parties' policies, or of the local or general welfare. Similarly the TNIP has tabled questions in the Assembly in order to highlight certain important points of policy; while the DP has tried to question publicly certain government actions. The TNIP awoke fairly late to the fact that motions and questions could be employed for policy purposes. Only eight questions have been tabled by the TNIP members during the sessions from 1964 to 1970; as against the 526 by the DP and seven by the TPFP – the latter being represented for only three years (1966–8). During 1971 and 1972 the TNIP tabled 54 questions and the DP 141. The number of motions tabled varied considerably for all parties, namely between a total of 32 for 1972 and 103 for 1965. The proportion of motions tabled by the TNIP remained low, and never rose above approximately 20 per cent of the total during the years 1964 to 1967. However, in the 1968 session, preceding the second general election, it suddenly rose to almost half of the number tabled by the DP and just over 25 per cent of the total number of motions tabled – the TPFP having tabled about 17 per cent of the total number of motions. There was another sharp increase in the TNIP's proportion of the total number of motions in 1971 and 1972, the years of increased difference of opinion between the Transkei government and the South African government on the land issue and, arising from this, on independence for the Transkei.

The Democratic Party motions concentrated mostly on practical matters which resulted from their difference with government policy in the Transkei and South Africa, or on matters which they regarded as of particular local importance. Education, public works, labour matters, political and civil rights, social welfare, health services, and agriculture received by far the most attention from the DP. The TNIP's motions on matters of a practical nature have been supplemented by those on relations with the South African government, such as land claims, constitutional matters, labour relations, and chieftainship affairs. In this way the Transkei government attempted to publicise its negotiations with the South African government, while at the same time gaining support for the TNIP and increasing public pressure on the South African government. A strong tendency persists in the TNIP to take up needs of a purely local nature with cabinet members without referring these requests to the Legislative Assembly. This course of action is available to the DP as well but it seldom if ever uses it.

—Bophuthatswana

In his election campaign, preceding the Bophuthatswana general election of October 1972, Chief Minister Mangope devoted his speeches mainly to expositions of his party's policy and to attacks on the Seoposengwe Party. In propagating his policy, separate development received particular attention, especially its positive aspects (e.g. equal wages, no job reservation in African areas, self-government, and exclusive business rights in African areas for Africans), while the negative aspects were roundly denounced (e.g. discrimination and ideas of White superiority). Most attention was reserved, however, for economic aspects of policy such as agricultural development (conservation, proper land use, credit assistance, refresher courses, improved markets), industrial development in the border areas and within Bophuthatswana, increased mining development, the payment of indirect taxes to the Bophuthatswana government, technical training for development, adequate land as a basis for independence, compensation for the poor wages paid to Tswanas in the past, and generally a higher standard of living. Complete independence as an objective was called for, and co-operation with other governments was promised, but not a federation of states. Non-Tswanas would be allowed to remain in Bophuthatswana with full and equal rights if they assumed citizenship. In the educational field a Tswana university was called for, as well as more schools, and a changed medium of instruction. Mangope also committed his party to the fight against terrorism and doubted the right of "freedom fighters" to decide what was best for the African population of South Africa.

Complementary to the general statements of policy, Mangope made a relatively small number of pertinent promises in his speeches, e.g. that higher wages for Tswanas in urban areas would be requested by his government, a strong Tswana nation would be built with the support of urban and rural people; conferences and congresses would be arranged so that people could express their needs; a township council for Mabopane would be established, and Ga-Rankuwa's council would receive increased powers; freedom of speech and the right to differ and debate was guaranteed; and non-Tswanas would not be expelled from Ga-Rankuwa.

Most of the issues in the Seoposengwe Party's campaign were grievances, such as the dissatisfaction resulting from resettlement of people, for example at Machaviestad and Mabopane; and the imposing of Bophuthatswana citizenship on, and Tswana-isation of, non-Tswanas living in Bophuthatswana, required by the Bophuthatswana government. The BNP was accused of intimidating voters, and of spreading a false rumour that the SP intended to give Bophuthatswana to the Xhosas and Zulus. Irregularities in respect of the general election were alleged even before the election took place. The SP also maintained that Mangope actually created division in Bophuthatswana when, as deputy chairman of the Territorial Authority in 1966, he disagreed with Pilane over the self-government issue; and that the BNP was in favour of tribalism by including chiefs in the Legislative Assembly, whereas the SP favoured election of all members. The SP accused the Bophuthatswana government of not doing enough for economic development of the territory; and for not recognising the needs of the people in respect of land, wages, influx control, and the sharing of income from mining profits.

Policy manifestoes were issued by the BNP and SP shortly before the Bophuthatswana general election of 4 October 1972. Candidates supporting these parties distributed leaflets for the promotion of their candidature, and the Tswana National Party's sole candidate also issued a leaflet. An independent candidate, M. N. Tsoke, who later went under the banner of his own and now defunct Progressive Party, issued posters in support of his candidature.

Both the BNP and the SP accepted separate development explicitly in their manifestoes. The BNP accepted only the "positive aspects", meaning "separate but equal development in all spheres of life"; and the SP accepted it "*only* for the implied promise of handing back to us our homeland" and for its promise of granting "sovereign independence". The BNP further stressed its purpose to "build a strong and secure Bophuthatswana Nationalism".

In a much more detailed and extensive manifesto than that of the SP, the BNP devoted much attention to economic policy. In respect of agriculture it promised exploitation of the land to achieve maximum productivity; for the farmers credit facilities, technical assistance, training and marketing facilities; establishment of co-operatives as a means for obtaining credit and reasonable prices for the agricultural producer; the establishment and improvement of various irrigation schemes; the improvement of livestock; investigation of consumer marketing so as to ensure the highest possible benefit to the farmer; improvement of cattle sale services; the establishment of milk schemes for improved milk production; "clamouring" for more land; and the establishment of a land board which will investigate land requirements and represent the Bophuthatswana government in respect of land deliberations. The economic policy of the Seoposengwe Party propagated that the Bophuthatswana government should have the final say "as to whom to approach for the exploitation of . . . minerals, and the siting of . . . industries or growth points". Foreign entrepreneurs should be allowed but curbed so as to continue fostering Tswana entrepreneurship; and the Bantu Investment Corporation should be allowed to operate until a "Batswana Development Corporation" could be established. On the land issue, the SP claimed back the land which historically belonged to the Tswanas. The demarcation of a boundary should be done in consultation with all parties concerned.

In respect of commerce and industry, the BNP promised the following: establishment of border industries ("since they ease the unemployment problem") and industries within Bophuthatswana; representation for better wages for Tswanas inside and outside Bophuthatswana; establishment of a National Industrial Corporation Fund to assist Bophuthatswana entrepreneurs; rectifying various grievances concerning the Bantu Investment Corporation; appointment of a Bophuthatswana licensing board, and reservation of trading licences for citizens only; encouraging the activities of the Bantu Mining Corporation; payment of taxes by mining and industrial concerns in Bophuthatswana to the Bophuthatswana government; and giving preference to citizens in the allocation of mining sub-contracts.

On educational matters the BNP promised the implementation of compulsory education as soon as possible; easing of the teacher shortage; loans to tribal and community authorities for educational purposes; the use of the BIC beer profits for school buildings; the establishment of a university and technical high school; improvement of teachers' salaries and conditions of service. The SP promised to raise educational standards in primary and secondary schools, introduce technical training facilities, and free and compulsory education, with a view to the ultimate establishment of a university.

Under the heading "social welfare" the BNP promised increased old-age pensions, old-age homes, recreational facilities for the disabled, clinics and maternity depots; training facilities for nurses, appointment of "our own" doctors and district surgeons; employment of as many social workers as possible; the construction of a "stadium of world standards"; the erection of a capital for Bophuthatswana; building of community halls; encouragement to the establishing of holiday resorts; and putting up of police stations and "other institutions meant for the safety and well-being of citizens . . . where necessary". The SP manifesto mentioned nothing in respect of social welfare.

For the public service, the BNP promised localisation, better salaries and housing, appointment of married women, and consideration of previous experience and salary when making new appointments. The SP also promised localisation of the public service, and a greater measure of decentralisation to local authorities, school boards, licensing boards, health boards, urban councils, and agricultural boards. The Tswana National Party promised, briefly, industrial and agricultural development, increased pensions, better educational facilities and a university, and the investigation of certain particular complaints in respect of irrigation schemes and resettlement of people. The BNP manifesto listed its promises and objectives in a comparatively detailed way so that careful reading is necessary. On the other hand the SP manifesto contains rather general statements of preferences and beliefs, makes much more casual reading, and is much shorter than the BNP manifesto. The manifesto of the TNP contained nine points, some of them meaningless (e.g. "8. In all Urban areas.")

There were no major differences between the various parties in respect of material objectives or ideology. The main differences remained of a personal nature between Mangope and Pilane, and included certain educational priorities (should a university be established immediately or later) and two issues not mentioned in the election manifestoes, namely the Tswana-isation of members of other ethnic groups, and the federation question.

Education, influx control, wages, job reservation, land, independence, economic development, agricultural development, and racial discrimination formed the core of the issues in the Transkei as well as Bophuthatswana. This was the case, in fact, in all the homeland elections of 1972 and 1973. Local variations on these themes were found, and in Lebowa Phatudi and Ramusi stressed to a far greater extent the eradication of discriminatory practices than any other homeland leader; in Bophuthatswana Mangope stressed the need for a Tswana university, which other homelands rated much lower; in the Ciskei, Sebe, and in Bophuthatswana, Mangope pointed out strongly that economic development inside the territory was preferred to economic development in the (White) border areas, whereas in the Transkei border area development has never been an issue. Some issues were unique to particular territories: in the Transkei, but in no other territory, the acceptance of separate development was fiercely debated; in Bophuthatswana and the Ciskei, national unity – unity of different tribal and ethnic groups in the respective territories – received particular attention of politicians; in Bophuthatswana the position of a large number of non-Tswanas living in the neighbourhood of Pretoria caused much bitterness between the parties; in Lebowa, the alleged allocation of development resources to people in certain areas only gave rise to much debate; and in Venda the very establishment of political parties was hotly debated.

Policy of BPC and Saso

The policy of the BPC is not well articulated or publicised, and the organisation discourages research into its activities. Consequently little is known about its policies and priorities. It regards the government-created institutions for Indian, Coloured and African representation as misleading, and chooses to work outside the framework of separate development.

At its first annual conference in July 1972, the BPC defined its objectives in the fields of education, labour, economics, politics and theology, and decided to promote and establish Black business on a co-operative basis for the advancement of the Black community (and not for the benefit of particular individuals); to promote Black trade unions and unity among them; to formulate and carry out a Black education policy; to reorient the "theological system" towards the aspirations of Blacks; to promote Black consciousness and Black communalism; and to "redirect" the political thinking of the Black people in order to involve them in national and local affairs through the machinery of the BPC.

The BPC opposes foreign investment in South Africa, and maintains that foreign firms discriminate against Blacks and indulge in racism. It believes that the wealth of the country rightly belongs to the Blacks, who need no subsidies from foreign firms. The national executive accordingly sent a letter to thirty-one foreign firms in South Africa requesting them to eradicate racism and exploitation.

Saso policy can be deduced from the minutes and decisions of the annual general meetings and, to a lesser extent, from Saso publications such as the *Saso Newsletter* and occasional fact papers. Policy statements by individual leaders are rare. Broadly, Saso's long-term aim can be summarised as a striving towards a non-racial South Africa (where the Black man will dominate through his numerical superiority); and in the short term it strives for a position of strength for political bargaining with the Whites, employing Black consciousness as the consolidating force. Meanwhile, Saso regards the Whites as irrelevant in the Black attempts for self-realisation.

In this inward movement a particular terminology is evolving. Terms such as "conscientisation", "relevance", "psychological liberation", "sensitisation" and "involvement" are in constant use, especially in connection with Black attempts at self-improvement. The term "Black" refers to Africans, Coloureds and Indians, but excludes the people of all three races who do not identify themselves with the "Black struggle". A Black can be a White who identifies himself psychologically and otherwise with the Blacks. On the other hand, however, Saso warns Blacks against personal contact with Whites.

—Separate Development

Saso rejects the point of departure of several homeland government leaders, namely that they will take what they are given and use it to get what they want. It considers that the White government knows very well what the African wants and has so designed the governmental system that it can prevent the Africans from getting what they want. The Bantustans are accordingly called "dummy platforms" and "phoney telephones".

The *Saso Newsletter* characterises separate development – and particularly the creation of Bantustans – as oppressive, designed to cheat the Africans, and detrimental to their interests over land ownership, industrial and mining development, labour exploitation and politics. It sees the creation of ethnic-based homelands as a divisive measure devised to retard the Africans' advance towards "emancipation".

Saso's utter rejection of separate development became increasingly obvious. In a Saso fact paper, entitled *Separate Development and Black*

Solidarity, issued in 1971, the anonymous author complained that the "philosophy" of separate development often did not correspond with practice, and maintained that separate development should allow the Black people's aspirations towards their own identity to take their course. He mentioned the "indigenisation" of Black universities as a disagreeable aspect of separate development.

Saso's rejection of separate development and the governmental machinery for the homelands was followed by a rejection of all homeland leaders. At the 1972 meeting it was clear that Saso regards homeland governments as racist, oppressive institutions which only *appear* to act in the interests of the Blacks, and the homeland leaders as misleading the Blacks through militant speeches which create expectations which cannot be realised. At the same time the homeland leaders act as ambassadors for White South Africa, a role which is eagerly promoted by the White press. The meeting therefore decided to call upon the homeland leaders to withdraw from the system: all the homeland leaders rejected the letters subsequently written to them by the Saso executive.[45]

—Political Involvement

Although it is a students' organisation committed to Black consciousness, Saso is thoroughly committed politically. The Saso Planning Commission exhorted branches to keep in mind as guidelines for action Saso's commitment to "self-reliance" and "liberalisation", and its role as a "trade union for students". Its political involvement is concisely explained in another, undated fact paper (*The Politics of Protest for Black Students*). Political activities, it says, must record dissatisfaction and express opinions on the political needs of students; obtain a hearing for students; instil political awareness, confidence and education; develop ways of determining long-term change; arouse Black consciousness and Black solidarity; lessen dependence on Whites and develop a self-help attitude. Several problems are foreseen by the paper: confrontation with the "establishment", lack of solidarity, apathy, fear, economic insecurity and dependence on White support; whereas it regards educated leadership and the creation of the right political climate among Blacks as a *sine qua non* for effective protest. Possible means of protest, according to the paper, are community development projects, encouragement of Black solidarity and the co-ordination of all Black activities, opposition to conceptualisations of Black as "different", the development of Black theology as a theology of protest, the use of boycotts, meetings and published statements.

The importance of the press as a medium for realising these objectives was recognised at the General Students' Council in July 1972.

Saso's Commission on Publications stated that the press in South Africa did not represent Black interests and that it "miscommunicated" the Blacks. An independent Black press was therefore necessary to communicate objectively with the Black community. To achieve this, the Commission recommended a Black Press Commission, as well as several interim measures such as the encouragement of certain independent journals and the exertion of pressure on White-controlled African newspapers to change their editorial policies. These recommendations yielded virtually no result. The African newspapers felt, for instance, that they served the requirements of the African reading public adequately and saw no reason for changes in editorial policy.

—Economic Development and Labour

Industrial decentralisation towards the borders of the homelands is seen by some Saso members as an attempt by the South African government to weaken the solidarity of Black workers by distributing them into all parts of the country. The homelands are also regarded as economically unviable, and the retention of mineral rights by the South African government is criticised; the Bantu Investment Corporation, for its part, is accused of exploiting African businessmen. Foreign investment is rejected because it helps stabilise the South African government. Increased wages and other benefits for Africans by foreign firms are also rejected as mere conscience-salving and as a contribution towards the building of a middle class which will resist change.[46]

The Community Development Commission of Saso recommended in 1972 the establishment of trade unions by the permanent organiser of Saso; also that he negotiate with employers to employ students expelled from Black universities. The General Students' Council of July 1972 decided that a Black workers' council should be established to act as a co-ordinating body for Black workers, to obtain solidarity and unity among Black workers, to "conscientise" students in their role and duties towards Black workers, and to organise "clinics" for leadership and in-service training for Black workers.

In order to forge ties between students and workers and to create understanding for the working conditions of Black workers a scheme called "Edu-ploy" – education by employment – was launched in 1971. Under this scheme, students will be put in employment to experience working conditions that will enable Saso to advise workers on their problems. A pilot scheme in December 1971 and January 1972 failed on account of poor preparations.[47]

—Education and Culture

Saso regards the present educational facilities for Blacks in South Africa as irrelevant to the needs and aspirations of the Blacks. They merely serve the "political philosophy" of the country, and are aimed at subjugating the Blacks, awakening self-hate among them and creating a gulf between intellectuals and the people. The Commission defines education as not only developing knowledge and skills, but also a promoter of what is treasured in culture and history, while it must also make Blacks aware of their responsibility towards their "oppressive situation". It recommends making education more acceptable to Blacks, infiltrating school boards and committees, establishing parents' committees and Saso branches at schools, approaching individual teachers and teachers' associations, investigating ways and means of providing free school and university education, and simplifying Black theology so as to spread it among the Blacks.

Saso concerns itself not only with formal education; it also undertakes literacy programmes as part of its community development projects. It regards illiteracy and the high drop-out from African schools as an effect of White racism which forces Africans to leave school and seek work. By improving literacy, Saso means to improve the social, economic and political condition of Blacks, believing that literacy will permit wider communication, "conscientisation and sensitisation", and will aid the liberation of Blacks from White-imposed "slavery, oppression and subjugation". Its intention is to stamp out illiteracy within ten years without the aid of White or multi-racial organisations.[48] Saso's bitterness and cynicism, and its tendency to blame Whites for Black problems, is nowhere so clear as in the case of education.

After the third general meeting in July 1972 one of Saso's priorities was the establishment of a free university for Blacks, regardless of whether or not its degrees would be recognised by other universities. This decision followed one of the most serious confrontations between Saso and university authorities in South Africa, sparked off by a speech on graduation day at the University of the North. Abraham Tiro, a graduate student, criticised the university authorities on several counts, including the low level of student and Black staff involvement in the affairs of the university. Generally, students complained of the Western cultural orientation of curricula, especially in the social sciences, and the scant attention to Black culture.[49] Tiro was expelled, but this was followed by massive boycotts of lectures at all Black universities, encouraged by the so-called "Alice Declaration" issued by Saso leaders at Alice (Fort Hare). When students were expelled during these confrontations,

Saso offered several bursaries for study at the University of South Africa.

Saso rejects separate universities and Black education in general in South Africa as irrelevant to the needs of the Black community, and out of keeping with the cultural and historical ethos of Black people. A charter was drawn up[50] for a Black university. It was decided that Black education should promote Black unity, initiative, self-reliance, enquiry and creativity, and political, social and economic change. A university must serve to improve knowledge and skills, and the cultural and intellectual level of the community, achieve social integration, promote the "soul of Black folk" by finding foundations of "spiritual awareness and a religious redirection", and inculcate new universalistic values to replace the old ones of backwardness, dependence and immobility. University curricula must enable the student to use and control his environment. Emphasis must be on social science related to Africa, with particular reference to the content and direction of the Black experience. Pride and confidence in Blackness, traditions and indigenous ways of life must be instilled, and élitism and intellectual arrogance discouraged.

At the 1972 General Students' Council the Commission on Education submitted a "Black Students' Manifesto", rejecting the existing system of Bantu Education in South Africa and confirming the political objectives of Black education.

Saso's Culture Commission recommended in 1972 that Black poetry should be encouraged to help develop Black culture; Black music should be canalised through an academy for music in order to relate it to the struggle for emancipation; and Black liberation songs should be written. It also recommended the establishment of a Saso drama council and the writing of dramas with political content to illustrate the Blacks' political way of life; the staging of a Black passion play with a Black Jesus in order to "conscientise" those who have adopted White theology; the holding of Black film and art festivals to introduce Black artists to the public.

Black culture, as conceived by Saso, is essentially a culture for liberation – politically motivated and related to the Blacks' position in South Africa.

—Black Consciousness

The underlying principle of all Saso's activities, and its main immediate objective, is Black solidarity and consciousness. In promoting Black consciousness, the youth is regarded as of particular importance since it is the "live wire of any community". Parents must be encouraged to give their children Black names and to teach them relevant folklore and games. Picnics, youth camps and community development projects must be organised for children at school in order to promote Black solidarity. Contacts with teachers must be sought in order to orient children towards Black consciousness and the rejection of White values. The same objectives must be pursued through drama and debating societies for youth who have left school. Students must be encouraged to read Black literature, sell Saso pamphlets and get involved in community development projects.[51]

Various leadership seminars have in fact been held by Saso – e.g. at Edendale, Alice and Turfloop – at which the dynamics of student leadership, community development, "action training" and daily campus problems were discussed.

The "Saso Policy Manifesto" establishes Saso as an organisation upholding Black consciousness, and striving for the psychological and physical liberation of Blacks. "Black people" are those who are discriminated against by law or tradition in South Africa, in the political, social and economic fields. The manifesto explains Saso's attitude towards Whites. They must be excluded from all Black attempts at realising their aspirations, and personal contact with them must be discouraged. Saso believes that White and Black will remain together in South Africa, and does not want its attitude to be construed as anti-White, but as a positive way of attaining a normal situation. Integration, Saso maintains, is not a process of assimilation to White values and society, but a voluntary, automatic process of proportionate contribution towards a joint culture by all groups. White attempts at integration are regarded as aimed at absorbing Blacks into White society; Blacks must define their own values.

—International Policy

Saso has made contact with ten students' organisations abroad, five of them in Africa, and at the general meeting of July 1972 it was decided also to seek closer ties with students' organisations in Latin America and Asia. Another decision recommended the establishment of a Pan-African Students' Union one of whose objectives would be greater unity and co-operation between students in Africa, and the promotion of relevant and meaningful education in Africa. In 1973 Saso became a member of the Southern Africa Students' Union and took a leading part in expelling the non-racial (but predominantly White) National Union of South African Students from the inaugural conference at Roma, Lesotho.

REFERENCES

1. *Rand Daily Mail*, 7.8.1973.
2. Cf. speech by Jonas in Transkei Legislative Assembly, *Hansard*, 1971, pp. 94–5.
3. Bophuthatswana Government, *Debates of the Bophuthatswana Legislative Assembly*, First Session, First Assembly, 21.3.1972–27.4.1972, p. 43.
4. *Daily News*, 26.1.1973.
5. *Daily Dispatch*, 20.11.1973.
6. *Daily News*, 26.1.1973.
7. Cf. K. M. N. Guzana in Transkei, *Hansard*, 1972, p. 130; and Victor Poto in Transkei, *Hansard*, 1964, p. 12.
8. *Daily Dispatch*, 29.3.1973.
9. Hand-written minutes of the DP conference of 16.9.1972.
10. Bophuthatswana Government, *Debates of the Bophuthatswana Legislative Assembly*, 1972, p. 281.
11. Transkei, *Hansard*, 1967, p. 93.
12. Transkei, *Hansard*, 1968, p. 66; 1970, p. 89; 1971, p. 67; 1972, pp. 119 and 462.
13. Transkei, *Hansard*, 1972, pp. 125–8.
14. *Daily Dispatch*, 15.4.1971.
15. Matanzima's speech at TNIP conference, Umtata, 12.4.1971.
16. See Matanzima's speeches at TNIP conferences at Umtata on 12.4.1971 and 11.4.1972.
17. Matanzima as reported in *Daily Dispatch*, 26.8.1963. Also: *The Star*, 9.2.1972.
18. In this connection see J. L. W. De Clerq, *KwaZulu en Konsolidasie*, University of Zululand, May 1973.
19. *Rand Daily Mail*, 28.4.1973.
20. Transcription of interview with Buthelezi by J. Langner, SABC news representative, 25.1.1973.
21. Undated transcription of interview with Buthelezi by J. Langner.
22. *Rand Daily Mail*, 30.4.1973.
23. Transkei, *Hansard*, 1966, p. 75. Also: *Daily Dispatch*, 16.10.1967.
24. Matanzima's speech to TNIP conference, Umtata, 12.4.1971.
25. Ibid.
26. Report of speech by Ntsanwisi in *The Star*, 12.4.1972.
27. Transkei, *Hansard*, 1968, p. 271.
28. For instance: Transkei, *Hansard*, 1966, p. 93.
29. Statements of Matanzima at Pilanesberg reported in *Rand Daily Mail*, 29.1.1973; and at East London, reported in *Rand Daily Mail*, 7.5.1973.
30. Transkei, *Hansard*, 1967, p. 300.
31. Transkei, *Hansard*, 1964, p. 171.
32. *The Star*, 30.7.1971.
33. Transkei, *Hansard*, 1967, p. 95. Also Transkei, *Hansard*, 1970, p. 230.
34. *Daily Dispatch*, 7.8.1973.
35. Policy speech in KwaZulu Legislative Assembly, 1973.
36. *The World*, 28.12.1970.
37. Transkei, *Hansard*, 1966. p. 113.

38. *Daily Dispatch*, 2.11.1968.
39. *The Star*, 15.8.1972.
40. At the opening of the new residence of Chief T. Pilane, leader of the Seoposengwe Party, reported in *Rand Daily Mail*, 29.1.1973.
41. *Natal Mercury*, 21.3.1973.
42. *Daily News*, 12.3.1973.
43. Press release, dated 8.9.1972.
44. "I write what I like", *Saso Newsletter*, Sept./Oct. 1972, pp. 19–20.
45. Saso, Minutes of 3rd General Students' Council, 1972, Decision No. 21/72.
46. M. P. Gwala, "Priorities in culture for creativity and Black development", paper delivered at Saso's 3rd General Students' Council, 1972; "I write what I like", *Saso Newsletter*, Sept./Oct. 1972, p. 19; *Saso 1972*, p. 8.
47. Executive report to Saso's 3rd General Students' Council, 1972.
48. Saso fact paper, "Literacy project", n.d.
49. Saso fact paper, "Black universities in South Africa", n.d.
50. By a "National Formation School", in December 1972.
51. Saso, Report of Community Development Commission to 3rd General Students' Council, 1972.

9

ELECTIONS

Electoral Framework

The first general election in a self-governing homeland took place in the Transkei in 1963; the second also in the Transkei in 1968; and in 1972 and 1973 several general elections were held in newly self-governing homelands: in Bophuthatswana in October 1972, in the Ciskei in January 1973, in Lebowa in April 1973, in Venda in August 1973, and in Gazankulu in October 1973. The third Transkei general election was held in October 1973.

The electoral procedure is basically similar in all homelands, the only major differences being in respect of the registration of voters. (See also Chapter 3.) In the Transkei and Ciskei, voters are registered before the nomination of candidates, and the number of vacancies in each electoral division (constituency) is determined by the number of registered voters in that constituency. A voters' list is compiled in the Transkei, but not in the Ciskei. In all other homelands, registration of voters continues until the day of the election, and the number of vacancies is determined arbitrarily (such as in Bophuthatswana, where each constituency is allotted two members irrespective of the number of voters) or based on the population size and number of chiefdoms in the constituency (such as in Lebowa). In all the homelands the South African Department of Information distributed leaflets, put up posters, and gave film-shows and talks – the latter mainly in rural areas where many voters are illiterate – to instruct the people in voting procedure.

In every homeland, voters indicate their choice by making a mark against the name of their preferred candidate(s). Illiterate voters are assisted by officials in the presence of two witnesses, one of whom is nominated by the voter. No voter is allowed to bring into the polling station any documents indicating the names of candidates he prefers; illiterate voters must "select by word of mouth" the candidates of their choice. Voters receive in their reference books an endorsement to the effect that they are registered as voters. The names of Transkeian voters must also appear on the electoral list on election day. In homelands without voters' lists, the endorsement in the reference book is sufficient proof of registration. On receipt of a ballot, the voter's name is deleted (in the Transkei) and a mark affixed in his reference book (in all homelands) to the effect that he has voted.

Voters who are outside the homeland on election day may cast their votes at polling stations which are established at every magistrate's and Bantu Affairs Commissioner's office in South Africa. In some homelands, elections were held on one day only (e.g. Transkei and Lebowa), in others on two consecutive days (e.g. Ciskei and Venda), while Transkei voters outside the Transkei had three weeks in which they could cast their votes. Due to printing problems, however, ballot papers reached urban polling stations two weeks late. The size of the administrative task of arranging a homeland election is reflected in the fact that in the Transkei election of 1973, 1,500 polling stations were established in South Africa and South West Africa.

In Bophuthatswana every citizen over the age of eighteen is entitled to vote. A citizen of Bophuthatswana (and the same applies to all homelands, except the Transkei) must be born in or domiciled in the territory, speak a Bantu language related to that of the territory's population, or be related to a member of the territory's population. There are disqualifications, such as guilt of treason, murder, terrorism or corrupt practices, mental disorder and being listed as a communist. Members of the Legislative Assembly must be over twenty-one years of age.

A voter is entitled to vote in a particular constituency if he is domiciled within the constituency, or was born in it but is now domiciled outside it. Furthermore, he may choose a constituency for himself if he was born and is domiciled outside it. This provision was inserted for the benefit of Africans in White areas who were either born there or had no close ties with any part of the homeland after a long period of absence.

The cost of elections without voters' lists is comparatively low, but this has disadvantages. Parties and candidates cannot predict the number of voters in any given area, and the exact size of the electorate in electoral divisions remains unknown. Knowledge of population statistics, and information given by chiefs' representatives in White urban areas, have enabled parties and candidates to form an impression of the size of the electorate in many urban areas. There is also no way to determine the percentage of participation in elections – and thus the efficiency of campaigning. From the point of view of the government officials, there is some difficulty in identifying homeland voters in view of the extremely broad citizenship categories/norms laid down by the Bantu Homelands

Citizenship Act of 1970, referred to above. There was some uncertainty among officials, for instance, as to whether they should
regard Shangaan-speaking people living in Lebowa as voters of
Lebowa, or whether Pedi-speaking people in Bophuthatswana
had to be registered as Bophuthatswana voters.

Universal franchise was introduced in the Transkei in 1963, and
all Transkei citizens over the age of twenty-one years, or eighteen
years in the case of taxpayers, are eligible to vote. Transkei citizens
are those Africans born in the Transkei, or domiciled there for at
least five years, or who speak a dialect of Cape Nguni but were not
born in the Transkei and who owe no allegiance to another homeland, as well as Sotho-speaking Africans who are descendants of a
Transkei tribe. For the 1963 election the Transkei was divided into
nine electoral divisions, which coincided with the nine regional
authorities which form the upper level of a two-tier local government system. The number of elected members per electoral division
was allocated according to the number of voters registered in
each region or division. The absence of parties, and the fairly large
number of members to be elected in several divisions, contributed
to an exceptionally large number of candidates being nominated
in several constituencies. In addition to paying visits to voters outside the Transkei, candidates had to canvass large areas within the
territory, often difficult terrain without modern communications.

The problems caused by these exceptionally large constituencies
were realised, and the system was changed, with the consent of
both parties, in preparation for the 1968 election. The Transkei's
twenty-six administrative districts are now regarded as twenty-six
constituencies and the number of elected members per constituency
is allocated to the number of voters *pro rata*. Fewer candidates
participated in the Transkei election of 1968 than in 1963, and as a
result of the increased number of constituencies, the number of
candidates contesting each constituency was much smaller. Confusion among voters was less, and candidates could canvass more
efficiently. Also, in 1968 for the first time two main parties contested
the general election, together with the small TPFP and a number of
independents, thus reducing the alternatives open to the voters.

Campaigns

Campaign techniques are similar in all homelands. The main
feature is invariably a dialogue between the leaders of the two main
parties or factions, conducted at public meetings and through press
statements. Election campaigns are conducted almost exclusively
with the help of voluntary workers; and the help, or at least the
sanction, of chiefs and headmen is diligently sought by all. The

press and radio play a relatively small role because of the relatively widespread illiteracy in rural areas and because African parties have no control over these media. Planning, co-ordination and control over election campaigns are corollaries of party strength. Where no parties or strongly controlled factions (e.g. in Gazankulu and Lebowa in 1973) exist before an election, individual candidates or small slates of candidates act independently; and where party discipline has degenerated, as in the DP of the Transkei, party followers in some areas assist "rebel" candidates who were not approved by the party executive.

In all homelands, Chief Ministers (and in some cases the members of the cabinet as well – see Chapter 3) are elected by the legislative assemblies. When the results of general elections are known, the canvassing among *ex-officio* and elected members begins in all earnest for support in the vital election of the Chief Minister. In the Ciskei, the incumbent Chief Minister, Chief Mabandla, made important policy adjustments shortly before the election of Chief Minister; he claimed large portions of South Africa for the Ciskei and declared support for an African federation in South Africa. He was narrowly defeated by Sebe who had the support of the majority of elected members. In the Transkei, in 1963, the belief that Matanzima had the support of the South African government swung the majority of chiefs in his favour, and he defeated Poto who had an elected majority. In Venda the incumbent Chief Minister, Chief Patric Mphephu, accompanied the Venda chiefs on a visit to the Manyeleti game reserve and returned only on the day of the election of the Chief Minister. He was elected over-whelmingly but soon afterwards several chiefs crossed the floor to the opposition, who had an elected majority, and thus substantially reduced Mphephu's majority in the Assembly. In other homelands, canvassing was equally intensive. In several territories a realignment of loyalties occurred immediately after the election of Chief Ministers (see below).

The same pattern for canvassing is followed in all homelands. Parties or slates of candidates are formed to co-ordinate campaigns. In the second phase, individual candidates, slates of candidates and parties canvass vital support among voters in urban and rural areas. This phase concludes with the general election. Nominated members, in all cases appointed before the election, are then subject to canvassing by the parties and factions who emerged from the general elections as possible contenders for power. This phase is only concluded with the election of a Chief Minister, and the long-term exertion of influence for the re-alignment of loyalties then begins.

—Bophuthatswana

During the two months preceding the Bophuthatswana election of October 1972, the BNP leader, Chief Mangope, addressed at least thirty major meetings in an area stretching from the Northern Cape Province to the urban areas of the Witwatersrand – no mean achievement for an incumbent Chief Minister. He devoted several speeches entirely to attacks on his opposition, the Seoposengwe Party. On the whole, he covered a wide range of topics: agricultural development and policy, separate development and discrimination, economic policy and potential of the territory, the activities of the six government departments of Bophuthatswana, a general description of BNP policy and its achievements, terrorism, relationships with other ethnic groups, Tswana unity and nationalism, thoughts on the need for hard work and dedication, and the right to freedom of speech. Little was said on local problems and needs, which might have been relevant to the particular audience, except in Temba, Mabopane and Ga-Rankuwa, all of them centres of SP support.

The sheer volume of words used by Mangope to attack the SP gives an indication of the intensity of the election campaign. Most of these attacks followed speeches by SP leaders and took the form of an analysis of their statements, rather than of the published manifesto of the SP. The petty nature of the debate indicates that the main differences between them concern tactics, not points of principle. Thus Mangope pointed out various contradictions in SP statements and wanted to know why the SP participated in a Bophuthatswana election, had only Tswanas as members and had a leader who preached Tswana unity during his term of office as chairman of the Territorial Authority (1961–8), yet professed to favour a single African nation and Prime Minister in South Africa; again, while he propagated one African nation and prime minister in the urban areas of Soweto, Pilane and some other SP candidates declared themselves in favour of a Kgatla front when addressing audiences in Kgatla areas (Pilane is a Kgatla chief). Mangope made skilled use of Pilane's previous utterances to give an impression of instability. He pointed out that as chairman of the Territorial Authority, Pilane never gave his opinions on the land question, salaries, African solidarity, agricultural credit and the resettlement of rural Africans; also, that Pilane agreed with the Bophuthatswana constitutional committee's recommendation of 1972 that two-thirds of the members of the Legislative Assembly should be chiefs. Yet, Pilane suddenly appeared as a champion for more land, resettled groups, African solidarity, and a popularly elected assembly. On the land question, he suggested that the SP's lack of policy was behind its call for a national convention on land. He pointed out that the SP was against chieftainship, yet had a chief as leader; that it wanted to use Bophuthatswana to further the objectives of Black solidarity; and that it made wild promises over tractors, land and free and compulsory education. The style of the SP was also attacked: it was using the National African Chamber of Commerce as a political party; it concentrated on personalities and not on policies; Pilane was dictated to by the newspapers; and the SP, although professedly in favour of separate development, was against its spirit, and wanted to share "rights" with other groups, even with Whites. He challenged Pilane to prove his allegations that cabinet members were uneducated and his claims to high educational standards in the SP.

Mangope said surprisingly little of the BNP leaders' achievements during their three years incumbency before the general election. A few points were claimed to their credit, however, such as the attainment of self-government in 1972, the proposed development of Heystekrand as the new capital, the building of several tribal offices and schools, agricultural improvement, the establishment of a township council for Ga-Rankuwa, and the establishment of various government boards for specific purposes.

Mangope adopted in his election speeches a clearly moral or philosophical tone at times. He emphasised, for example, an attitude of self-reliance, dedication, hard work, self-confidence and determination as a prerequisite for independence: the people should realise that there was nothing they could not do themselves. Freedom of speech and the right to differ and debate he regarded as "basic". It was perhaps for this reason especially that he took offence at the SP for alleged personal attacks, and said that the voters should rather be told what the different parties intended to do for them. Mangope's thoughts on the purpose of an election and on representation are idealistic: people should vote so that they can share in the government; an elected representative should not be self-centred but responsible to his voters. He should report to them on proceedings in the assembly, and bring forward their problems and difficulties. Thus they could strengthen the government in order that it can obtain certain improvements for them, such as better wages. The Chief Minister himself should fear his people, who could remove him; he owed them homage, just as they owed homage to God who created them.

The Seoposengwe Party maintained that the three months available for an election campaign were insufficient and that as a result it could not nominate candidates in all constituencies; nine months would have been preferable. In the event, the SP appeared at least as well organised as the BNP in support of its various candidates.

In the belief that the majority of its supporters were in the White urban areas of the Transvaal, and because of the brief time span available, the SP concentrated its campaign there. This ultimately proved a tactical mistake, as relatively few urban voters participated. According to Pilane, the SP held only four major meetings in rural areas in Bophuthatswana. However, the SP's superior organisation in the urban areas became evident when, often with the help of young people, it frequently disrupted BNP meetings amidst the chanting of "*Tsholetsa Seoposenge*" ("Lift up Seoposengwe").

The BNP leadership addressed more meetings than the SP in the rural areas of Bophuthatswana. The BNP had no branches with which to support the election campaign, and most of the organisational work was done from the party's secretariat with general secretary Mogotsi as the main functionary. In practice Mangope and Mogotsi did all the planning and co-ordinating, with the BNP's executive endorsing their decisions. Members of the executive were, however, very active in their own areas. The BNP relied to some extent on the support of chiefs for basic organisational work, but the main local organising rested on the shoulders of the candidates and local organisers. For the purposes of the election, honorary organisers were appointed in each constituency and in urban areas. These organisers had met only once early in the campaign to discuss common problems, and thereafter approached Mogotsi with particular problems. There was no institutionalised party control over their activities.

BNP officials feel that their party did not have the support of the press. Afrikaans newspapers sympathetic to Mangope because of his (qualified) pro-separate development stand, rarely publish news on local African affairs and did not assist in the election campaign, whereas the English and African press appeared to favour the SP at the time of the election. Only the news services of the SABC reflected the BNP policy statements, and that on a very limited scale.

Several rallies were addressed by leaders of both parties, particularly by Pilane, Mamogale and Lesolang for the SP and by all members of the Bophuthatswana cabinet for the BNP. Rallies of both parties were attended mainly by Tswanas and about 400 to 500 people usually turned up. In rural areas meetings were usually attended by only about 25 to 60 people. Usually meetings began with prayer, followed by opening remarks by some local dignitary, and introduction of the speakers by another local dignitary, a welcoming speech, and then the main speeches, concluded by a vote of thanks, time for questions and a benediction. Sometimes the speeches were interspersed with music or an oration to the main speaker. Candidates usually shared the platform with, and were introduced by, one or more leading persons in their party. The BNP used its co-ordinating apparatus to enlist its more able candidates in aid of weaker ones in neighbouring constituencies.

Meetings were arranged by the local party supporters and organisers, who received the assistance (in urban areas) of Bophu-thatswana government representative advisory board members and chiefs' representatives. In rural areas the chiefs were supposed to give permission for meetings of all political parties, but both the SP and the BNP sometimes accused them of being unco-operative. The SP also believed that some school principals, while putting their school buildings at the disposal of the BNP for meetings, were afraid to do so for the SP. Chiefs' urban representatives performed another important function: in the absence of a voters' list, they were able to supply relatively precise information on the number of voters from the various constituencies, as well as the political inclinations of voters, within their areas. Since most chiefs supported the BNP, and furthermore since most members of the Bophuthatswana government urban representatives' advisory boards in the Transvaal and Orange Free State were BNP suppor-ters, it can be concluded that this information was utilised mainly by the BNP.

The two candidates of the Tswana National Party, Modise and Tswai, were comparatively quiet, and addressed no public meetings, preferring to concentrate on private visits to possible supporters, and addressing small groups. Modise also followed BNP speakers and handed out leaflets at their meetings.

All parties concentrated their canvassing efforts on White urban areas and on the homeland itself. Voters in White rural areas, although constituting a substantial number (perhaps as many as in the White urban areas), were almost forgotten by all parties. Tswana labourers on White farms in the vicinity of Lichtenburg, however, were the objects of intensive canvassing by both parties, and the BNP won the constituency by a fairly narrow margin.

— *Transkei*

The 1963 general election was remarkable for the personal cam-paigns conducted by the two contenders for the chief ministership, Poto and Matanzima. Both sought the support of the nominated chiefs, and later of the 45 elected members, and in the absence of political parties, they also canvassed among the 180 candidates. They travelled extensively throughout the Transkei and sent agents to various urban areas outside the Transkei. Some candidates allied themselves with the cause of either Poto or Matanzima, lending the campaign an aura of a party contest. Slates of candidates were formed in most constituencies, mostly by candidates favouring Poto. Slate-forming proved beneficial and promoted effective campaigning. Election manifestoes were issued by about a quarter of the candidates, only nine of whom availed themselves of an offer by the East London *Daily Dispatch* to publish their manifestoes the day before the election. Meetings were addressed by all candidates, and the support of opinion leaders such as teachers, traders, chiefs, headmen, and old people were avidly sought. Political discussion involving these opinion leaders formed a quiet but important part of the election campaign, although its exact influence is hard to assess.[1]

In the Gcaleka by-election in November 1964, the first after the 1963 election, the parties for the first time employed their machinery to assist their candidates. The DP candidate, M. Dumalisile, was assisted at meetings by the most prominent DP men – Poto, Majeke, Tutor Ndamase, Jafta, Mpondo, Luwaca, Raziya and Dr. Bala. Special committees for canvassing were appointed by the DP and TNIP in the by-elections in Umzimkulu and Fingo in 1965, while cabinet ministers and leading opposition members assisted the candidates. After the 1968 election, the TNIP divided the Transkei into regions among members of the cabinet for purposes of assisting party candidates. The techniques used in the 1968 and 1973 general election campaigns remained much as in 1963, with meetings, rallies, political discussions, canvassing among opinion leaders, leaflet distribution and visits to constituencies and voters in urban areas.

The 1973 election campaign started exceptionally early. C. M. C. Ndamse, a prospective TNIP candidate for Mount Ayliff, held a series of meetings in the constituency as well as in Cape Town during May 1973. In the event he was not nominated by the TNIP as a candidate, and contested the election as an independent. Also in May, Kaiser Matanzima held preparatory meetings in "The Mission" administrative area of Butterworth district, where the DP was considered to be strong. Guzana also started his campaign in May with meetings in Willowvale, Kentani and Mqanduli.

The TNIP outdid the DP in the intensiveness of its campaigning. Whereas the DP's campaign was restricted almost entirely to the Transkei itself, with one rally at East London, the TNIP sent members of the cabinet to the Western Cape, the Witwatersrand, the Vaal complex, Bloemfontein and Zwelitsha at the end of September. The visit of Ministers George Matanzima and J. Moshesh to the

Transvaal was partly frustrated by mine officials who refused to permit political meetings on mine premises, following the shootings at Carletonville where several Africans had been killed shortly before.

The number of meetings addressed by Kaiser Matanzima and Guzana did not approach the phenomenal effort of Chief Minister Mangope of Bophuthatswana: the party leaders did not address more than two rallies each month between May and October. Matanzima, however, spent a fortnight in the Mt. Ayliff constituency in September, where the TNIP made a special effort to beat the independent, C. M. C. Ndamse. Kaiser Matanzima personally addressed at least eight meetings there and was once accompanied by Paramount Chief Botha Sigcau, in whose area the constituency falls.

Ndamse's campaign was equally intensive, and he visited several White urban areas where absent voters were employed. Instead of addressing general meetings for all Transkeian voters in a particular urban area, Ndamse obtained the names and places of work of absent voters from labour registers in the Transkei and then concentrated his urban visits on these voters alone. He was the only candidate to follow this approach and, according to him, it proved highly successful.

The political significance of voter registration was not fully realised by the TNIP, and even less by the DP. According to the TNIP constitution it is the duty of branch committees to see that favourably disposed voters are registered. During the 1967 session of the Legislative Assembly the Minister of Education encouraged supporters of all parties to register as voters. The party also sent a circular to its supporters in urban areas entitled "To those who have not yet registered themselves as Transkei voters". Apart from the assistance received from parties, the registration of voters was in the hands of Transkei government officials who relied mainly on the assistance of chiefs and headmen.

In 1963, voter registration would not have been successful in Tembuland if the Paramount Chief – who was later a member of the DP national executive – had not told his people to register, after some conjecture that he would oppose registration and after his people's refusal to register unless told by him to do so. The Paramount Chief subsequently visited Cape Town and Transvaal exhorting them to register so that "the Tembus will have the strongest possible voice in the new Transkei government".[2] Other chiefs also directly participated in the registration drive by visits to urban areas or through emissaries and their urban representatives.

The increase of only 71,944 in the number of voters between 1963 and 1973 shows that the official drive for registration had lost momentum, and that the TNIP's efforts had little effect.

Voting Behaviour

How is one to account for the large measure of absenteeism at polling stations? Among rural people there is a suspicion which springs from partial ignorance of voting procedure and from being too closely identified with one or the other policy or political party; among the urban people, on the other hand, there is scepticism over homeland politics, fear of losing residential rights in urban areas as well as previous unhappy political experience. This trend is especially clear in White areas, where voting in all homeland elections has been extremely low. Next to the appeal of alternative policies and political leaders, the influence of chiefs and headmen over rural voters is the single greatest factor in the elections; the results are determined largely by voters resident in the homelands. Thus, rural attitudes, aspirations and needs, with their inherent conservatism, inevitably receive much attention in homeland elections. Because many homeland residents have relatives in White urban areas and from time to time visit them as migrant workers, the problems of life in those areas are well known among them – a factor which politicians need to take into account. The potential strength of the urban voters is also an ever-present reality, and homeland politicians must accommodate them in their policy formulations. Hitherto, these urban voters showed little interest in homeland elections – which could account for the increasing concentration by homeland politics and policy declarations on such broad themes as the African federation issue, African unity in South Africa, wage increases – and homeland leaders' participation in international debates, e.g. the oil embargo and trade boycotts of South Africa. There is no indication as yet that this new universalistic trend interested more urban voters in homeland politics.

Table 9.I. on page 201 indicates the rate of participation in homeland elections.

The highest vote was recorded in the Ciskei, where voters had been registered very successfully. The only factor which distinguishes the Ciskei from other homelands is the strong political competition among large tribal groups — the Rarabes, Fingos, Tembus and Basotho. The Ciskei campaign did not differ at all from campaigns in other homelands: the same techniques were used, and the issues were generally the same. The Sebe faction (later the Ciskei National Independence Party) conducted a closely controlled campaign, and the Mabandla faction (later the Ciskei National Party) a very unco-ordinated campaign.

TABLE 9.I. VOTERS IN HOMELAND ELECTIONS

Homeland*	Total population, 1970 (within and outside homeland	Registered voters	Participating voters
Transkei (1973)	2,997,000	952,369	323,092
Bophuthatswana (1972)	1,680,000	—	213,843
Ciskei (1973)	915,000	480,801	343,292
Lebowa (1973)	2,097,000	—	189,344
Venda (1973)	360,000	—	69,325
Gazankulu (1973)	650,000	—	39,254

* Year of the election in brackets.

After the Ciskei election, Sebe's victory was almost – but not quite – wiped out by Mabandla's slight lead among the *ex-officio* members, and he was only narrowly elected Chief Minister. In Lebowa Phatudi's electoral victory was also almost cancelled by support for Matlala among the *ex-officio* members. In Gazankulu no parties contested the election and Ntsanwisi was elected Chief Minister unanimously. In Venda the Venda Independence People's Party won 13 out of 18 seats but its leader, Baldwin Mudau, was defeated by 42 votes to 18 by Chief Patric Mphephu in the election for the chief ministership when Mudau failed to obtain the support of *ex-officio* members. In the Transkei and Bophuthatswana the victorious parties also had the support of the majority of *ex-officio* members (except in the Transkei in 1963) and elected their leaders as Chief Minister. In 1963 in the Transkei the Matanzima faction lost the general election but had sufficient support among *ex-officio* members to win the election for Chief Minister.

In the Transkei, Lebowa and Ciskei the victorious parties in the election for the chief ministership afterwards gained substantial support from opposition members who crossed the floor. In Venda and Bophuthatswana, however, large majorities were soon reduced by government members crossing the floor to the opposition. In both cases it was mostly chiefs who crossed the floor: in Bophuthatswana after dissatisfaction over the dictatorial methods attributed to the Chief Minister, and in Venda after grass-roots pressure by the people who mostly voted for the Venda Independence People's Party, which was forced into opposition by the *ex-officio* members.

Party discipline undoubtedly reduced the number of candidates in general elections, as was proved in three successive Transkei general elections. Concomitantly, it also channelled and restricted voters' choices to two, and sometimes three main alternatives. Poor nomination structures in the two Transkei parties caused an increase in the successful independent candidates and indicated some willingness among voters to act independently of party discipline where their wishes at grass-roots level had been ignored.

—Bophuthatswana

The absence of a voters' list, and the fact that a Tswana domiciled and born in an urban area could indicate the constituency of his choice on election day, made canvassing difficult. Candidates could not compete with each other for any fixed number of votes. Voters who had a choice of constituencies tended to select a neighbouring constituency – e.g. voters in Pretoria selected mainly Odi (Ga-Rankuwa) and Moretele (Hammanskraal). It was generally thought that the SP gained more votes than the BNP in White urban areas, whereas it lost heavily in tribal areas, except where it had the support of a few powerful chiefs – e.g. Pilane in Mankwe and Molete in Ditsobotla.[3]

Voters were generally well informed on the voting procedure, although many turned up after the closing of polling stations. Many voters in White urban as well as rural areas were confused about the role of political parties. In urban areas a longer campaign would have given people more time to consider the merits of the various parties and establish their *bona fides*. It must be remembered that the BNP as well as the SP were completely new and unknown to most people. In the rural areas, people are not well versed with the functions of political parties as such, which have often been confused with their leaders; difficulty was experienced with voters who wanted to vote for "Mangope" or "Pilane", instead of a particular candidate.

Without a voters' list, the percentage of participating voters could not be calculated precisely. According to 1970 census reports there were approximately 817,300 potential voters in 1972, of whom about 500,000 lived in White urban areas. Of the total number of votes cast, about 60 per cent were from rural areas. Some observers estimated the percentage poll in some White urban areas as no more than 15 per cent, while in some tribal areas almost all potential voters participated. The low percentages in urban areas can partly be ascribed to the voters' fear that they would be "endorsed out" of the urban area if they identified too closely with a homeland; besides, many urban inhabitants are uninterested in homeland politics. Some voters, however, were under the impression that a stamp in their reference books to the effect that they had voted would be a confirmation of their residential rights in the urban area.

Altogether 213,843 voters participated in the election, which is probably less than 40 per cent if one takes into account that four constituencies were unopposed.

Each voter had to vote for two candidates in each of the two-member constituencies. Votes (*not voters*) were distributed as follows:

TABLE 9.II. DISTRIBUTION OF VOTES, BOPHUTHATSWANA GENERAL ELECTION, 1972

	Votes	Candidates	Elected members
Bophuthatswana National Party	262,485	16	12
Seoposengwe Party	141,536	11	4
Tswana National Party	6,015	2	0
Progressive Party	3,485	1	0
Independents	11,472	9	0
Spoiled ballot papers	2,693	—	—

In addition the BNP had the support of eight members who were elected unopposed. The SP captured only Mankwe, the home constituency of Chief Pilane, and Odi, which includes Ga-Rankuwa and Mabopane, the largest urban area within Bophuthatswana. Only four of the 48 nominated members supported the SP after the election, with the result that the BNP had a very large majority in the Legislative Assembly. After Mangope had left the BNP in November 1974 and established the Bophuthatswana Democratic Party, the number of the combined opposition in the Assembly – i.e. the SP and the BNP – rose to 23.

—Transkei

In a rural, parochial society the traditional leaders have great influence. In the Transkei this has been decisive in elections and is at the root of the controversy between the DP and the TNIP over an upper house of chiefs in the Legislative Assembly. In her work on the 1963 general election Carter found[4] that organisational work by candidates who formed slates contributed to their electoral success in the Fingo, Dalindyebo and Emigrant Tembuland regions, whereas no correlation between slate-forming and electoral success was evident in the other regions. In Dalindyebo and Emigrant Tembuland the successful slates had the explicit support of Paramount Chief Dalindyebo and Chief Kaiser Matanzima. In Nyanda region all candidates supported Paramount Chief Victor Poto who deemed it unnecessary to express support for any particular candidate, with the result that no single slate of candidates was elected.

In regions with a number of small chiefdoms such as Emboland and Maluti the chiefs had little discernible influence. Carter also contended that the weakness of the paramount chieftainships of the Eastern Pondo and the Gcaleka was responsible for their lack of influence over voting behaviour. While this is partly true, these paramount chiefs made no significant attempt to influence voters, and Botha Sigcau, Paramount Chief of the Eastern Pondo, even forbade Matanzima and Poto to address voters and candidates in his region before the election.

Carter's work contains extremely interesting information on the voting preferences of urban voters in the 1963 election.[5] Returns from particular polling stations are now officially regarded as confidential and are therefore inaccessible, even to cabinet members. Carter found that the urban voters, in those urban areas where a significant number voted in any particular constituency, preferred only approximately half the candidates who were eventually elected. It was also clear that urban voters were unfamiliar with candidates and tended to vote for candidates with familiar surnames or for those whose names appeared first on the ballot paper. Recently, when political parties realised that their own estimates of urban voter support could be mistaken, they became interested in knowing the voting returns from urban polling stations – but of course could not do so.

Voter ignorance increases the importance of organised canvassing and the influence of traditional leaders. The present opposition leader Guzana referred to it during the first session of the Legislative Assembly in 1964,[6] and interviews with returning officers at polling stations in various parts of the Transkei in the elections of 1963, 1968 and 1973 confirmed that ignorance was rife. In spite of the information campaign on voting procedure, many voters still had no inkling as to what they should do when they reached the polling stations. Explanations by polling officers were naturally given in extreme haste. Many voters also did not know the candidates, and preferences were formed on the spot, sometimes assisted by slips of paper with the names of slates of candidates, handed to voters at some stage before the election or on election day. In the 1968 general election it was reported that some voters still did not know of the existence of political parties. However, consciousness of the activities of the Transkei government penetrated to all sections of society, and experience at the polling stations during the 1963 election and at by-elections in almost half the constituences prepared voters for more meaningful participation. Thus, in the 1964 by-election in Gcaleka voters were confronted for the first time with party candidates, and learnt that they could not vote for both Poto or

Matanzima. Leaders of both parties tried to interpret the results of the 1964 (Gcaleka) and 1965 (Fingo and Umzimkuli) by-elections as proof of support for their particular viewpoint on separate development. That this was not the sole determinant was moved by three African journalists who interviewed 500 voters at random in Fingo and Umzinkulu in 1965 and found that their choices were determined by various factors: instructions given by chiefs or headmen; one of the candidates visiting the area and therefore being known to them; the Chief Minister Poto holding a meeting and telling them to vote for his candidate; encouragement from certain respected local people to vote for a particular candidate; or the simple fact that they fancied a candidate's name.[7] On the other hand, the division of the Transkei into 26 constituencies enabled the smaller chiefs to exercise a more direct influence on voting. This was probably realised by the Transkei government whose majority in the first Legislative Assembly (1963–8) was largely due to the support of the majority of chiefs in the Assembly.

An analysis of the political loyalties of chiefs and elected members after the 1968 election, which was closely contested at a time when the organsing power of the DP and TNIP was more equal than at any other stage, shows that the influence of chiefs should not be over-estimated. After the 1968 election the chiefs and elected members supported different parties in 11 out of the 26 constituencies. The Butterworth constituency was regarded as a safe DP seat, but was captured unopposed in 1968 when the DP candidate turned up late at the nomination court. The chief in this constituency at the time supported the DP, but crossed over to the TNIP after the Butterworth constituency had been captured by the TNIP in 1974. In several constituencies there are elected members who are on opposing sides to the chiefs in the constituency. Chiefs who are not members of the legislative assembly have not been considered.

The influence of chiefs on voting is supplemented by the influence of headmen. Thus, according to an official present at the counting of votes, ballot boxes from administrative areas (subdivisions of districts/constituencies) where the headmen support a certain party, have an almost 100 per cent return for that particular party, while ballot boxes from neighbouring administrative areas, whose headmen have different political loyalties, showed an almost 100 per cent return for the other party.

As administrative functionaries the recommendations of chiefs and headmen are sought in respect of a variety of matters, such as the allocation of lands (which carries much power as agriculture is the main economic activity in the Transkei), application for old

TABLE 9.III. DIFFERENT POLITICAL ALLEGIANCE OF CHIEFS AND
ELECTED MEMBERS, TRANSKEI

Constituency		TNIP		DP		Independents	
		Chiefs	Elected	Chiefs	Elected	Chiefs	Elected
Flagstaff	1968	3					1
	1973	3	1*				
Mt. Fletcher	1968	3	1	1			
	1973	3		1			1
Mt. Frere	1968		2	2			
	1973		2	2			
Mqanduli	1968	6			2		
	1973	6			2		
Willowvale	1968	2	1*		1		
	1973	2			2		
Engcobo	1968	2		1	3		
	1973	2		1			3
Ngqeleni	1968	1		1	2		
	1973	1		1	2		
Qumbu	1968	4			2*		
	1973	4			2*		
Tsolo	1968	1	2	1			
	1973	1	1	1			1
Umtata	1968	1	1	1	1		
	1973	1	2	1			
Bizana	1968	5	2				
	1973	5	1				1
Elliotdale	1968	1	1				
	1973	1					1
Port St. Johns	1968	0		0	1	0	
	1973	0	1	0		0	

* Includes one chief or chieftainess.

age and other social welfare pensions, educational matters, and
agricultural improvement. They are also recognised arbiters in
disputes between local people, and many chiefs have limited civil
and criminal jurisdiction. Chiefs and headmen have been accused
of abusing their powers and of intimidating their followers to
influence their voting behaviour. There is little doubt that these
practices exist, and in a debate in the Legislative Assembly, members
of the DP and the TNIP referred to it.[8]
Kaiser Matanzima's aspiration for a paramount chieftainship of the

Emigrant Tembu created an opportunity for his opponents to instill the fear in the Fingo and Western Pondo regions that a victory for Matanzima would enable him to assume office as paramount chief over the people of these areas as well. These rumours caused some voters to oppose the TNIP. Rumours can be an important factor where communications are poor; they can be spread quite extensively concerning a candidate, without his knowledge, and are difficult to counter. Thus, in the Umtata by-election of 1970 an independent candidate, C. M. W. Sangoni, found too late that even people in his own administrative area believed a rumour that he had withdrawn his candidature. The DP accused the TNIP during the by-elections in Nyanda and Dalinyebo in 1967 of distributing leaflets which gave the impression that the TNIP candidates had the support of the respective paramount chiefs of the Tembu and Western Pondo – both leading DP personalities.

Chiefs have been accused by the general secretary of the DP that they convened meetings of headmen, civil servants and teachers where these officials were then told to support the TNIP. Accusations of intimidation of another nature were levelled by the TNIP against White traders. It was alleged that these traders feared that they would have to leave the Transkei under TNIP rule, and therefore tried to influence voters in favour of DP candidates in the Fingo by-election of 1965. Some of them allegedly threatened to withhold credit from people who supported the TNIP, while others provided refreshments to DP supporters on election day, and still another reportedly said he would dismiss his employees if they supported the TNIP.

Next to chiefs, teachers have perhaps the greatest influence as a professional group on political attitudes. A fairly strong anti-TNIP attitude exists among Transkei teachers, and a communications breakdown between the Transkei Teachers' Association and the Transkei government followed allegations of malpractices among teachers by the Transkei Minister of Education in 1971. After polling officers had mostly been appointed for the 1973 election the cabinet directed that only female teachers be appointed, an order which could be accommodated only partly at that stage. No reasons for this directive were given, and it can only be speculated that the cabinet feared that male teachers would influence voters against the TNIP in their capacity as polling officers. Significantly, before the election, supporters of Ndamse, who opposed the TNIP as an independent in Mt. Ayliff, were hopeful of his success because they counted on support for him by the teachers and the chief in the constituency.

Without parties the allegiance of elected members of the first Transkei Legislative Assembly was difficult to determine, but it has generally been estimated that the Poto faction won three out of every four seats. According to Carter's information the result of the first election for Chief Minister in December 1963 was as follows:[9]

	Chiefs	Elected Members
Matanzima	42	12
Poto	16	33
Spoilt papers	2	

A reaignment of loyalties took place soon after the result of the election for Chief Minister was made known, and in 1966 the TNIP could boast with a majority of 23 in the Assembly. The TNIP suffered a set-back in the Gcaleka by-election of 1964 when it lost to the DP. In the 1968 election the TNIP reversed the previous position and won 28 seats against the DP's 14, and 3 independents, of whom two rejoined the DP and one rejoined the TNIP. With the support of about 57 chiefs, the TNIP's overall majority in the TLA was 63 in 1968. After the addition of one chief as *ex-officio* member, the gaining of one seat in the Tsomo by-election in 1971, and the loss of one by-election to an independent in Flagstaff in 1969, the TNIP's overall majority before the 1973 election was 64.

Participation in the three successive Transkei general elections was as follows:

TABLE 9.IV. VOTER PARTICIPATION IN TRANSKEI
GENERAL ELECTIONS, 1963–73

	1963	1968	1973
Registered voters	880,425	907,778	952,369
Participating voters	601,204	451,916	323,092
Number of candidates	180	146	96[10]

Approximately 75 per cent of all registered Transkeian voters live in the territory. If it is taken into account that according to the 1970 census, 1,271,000 Transkeians out of a total of 2,997,000 live outside the territory it becomes clear that only a fraction of the eligible voters outside the territory actually registered as voters.

The enthusiasm for the 1968 election was less than in 1963. The percentage of voters participating declined from about 68 per cent to 50 per cent. The latter figure could have been higher as three members were returned unopposed. In 1963 601,204 voters voted as against the 451,916 (excluding spoilt papers) of 1968, and in 1973 only 33.9 per cent voters participated in 21 out of the 26 constituencies. Although the TNIP won a clear majority of seats in 1968 it did not obtain an absolute majority of votes. It won about 44 per cent of the votes; the DP about 36 per cent, independents about 18 per cent and the TPFP about 2.4 per cent. In eight constituencies the TNIP won with comparatively narrow margins of between 3,362 (Willowvale) and 787 (Bizana); the other six constituencies being Flagstaff, Kentani, Idutywa, Lusikisiki, Matatiele, and Tabankulu.

In 1973 the TNIP for the first time obtained a majority of votes as well as a majority of elected members. No less than 55.2 per cent of all votes went to the TNIP, whereas the DP obtained only 26.9 per cent and the independent candidates 17.9 per cent of the votes. In spite of the TNIP's increased number of votes, it lost several seats, namely one seat in each of the constituencies of Bizana, Mt. Ayliff, Tsolo, Elliotdale and Mt. Fletcher to independents, and one seat in the constituency of Willowvale to the DP. The TNIP also gained one seat in each of the constituencies of Port St. Johns and Umtata from the DP. The DP lost three seats in Engcobo to independents. The TNIP won St. Mark's (two seats), Xalanga (one seat) and Flagstaff (one seat) unopposed, and the DP won Libode (one seat) unopposed. The number of unopposed members is therefore two more than in the 1968 election, and does not account for the massive decrease in participating voters.

A feature of the election was the high number of seats lost to independent candidates, namely eight (five TNIP losses and three DP losses). Altogether 23 independent candidates participated, against the 26 of the DP and the 38 of the TNIP. In most cases the independents were aspiring candidates under either the TNIP or the DP who, after their rejection by the parties concerned, opposed the official party candidates as independents. The three independent candidates elected in Engcobo later rejoined the DP. In the election in Engcobo even the TNIP candidates obtained more votes than the official DP candidates.

Close victories of less than a thousand votes were scored in a number of constituencies, namely Bizana, Elliotdale, Mt. Fletcher, Nqamakwe and Ngqeleni. In Ngqeleni, won by the DP, the difference between the DP and TNIP candidates was only 240 votes. In Lusikisiki, the TNIP beat its nearest opponent, an independent, by 12,485 votes. After the election, two constituencies were held jointly by the TNIP and independents, namely Bizana and Tsolo; and one constituency jointly by the DP and an independent, namely Mt. Fletcher.

The complete defeat of the DP in Umtata, previously jointly

held by the DP and the TNIP, was engineered by the DP candidates themselves. S. Mgqweto, an official DP candidate, joined forces with an independent (and former DP aspirant candidate), F. S. Twala, against the other official DP candidate, P. B. Feke. The rebel, Twala, obtained 4,583 votes, and the DP lost the constituency with 1,391 votes.

A record number of chiefs, namely seven, stood as candidates in the 1973 election; five for the TNIP and two for the DP. Only Chieftainess Nozizwe Sigcau of the TNIP was defeated (in the Willowvale constituency).

The Transkei electoral law requires that voters vote for as many candidates as the number of vacancies in the constituencies. It is therefore possible that the wishes of voters are not correctly recorded in constituencies where a participating party nominates less candidates than the number of vacancies. In the 1973 election, for example, the DP nominated only one candidate in each of the constituencies of Tabankulu, Tsolo and Kentani, each with two vacancies, and two in Engcobo with three vacancies. Voters who supported the DP candidate in each constituency therefore had to record votes for at least one other candidate who had not been nominated by the DP. In no case did it change the result of the election, however, in view of the large TNIP and independent majorities, but the number of votes recorded by TNIP and independent candidates in the election in general was thus increased by its opponents.

REFERENCES

1. G. M. Carter, *et al*, *South Africa's Transkei: The Politics of Domestic Colonialism*, Heinemann, London, 1967, chapter 7.
2. *Daily Dispatch*, 1.8.1963. Also see *Daily Dispatch*, 1.7.1963, 9.7.1963, 13.7.1963.
3. W. J. Breytenbach, "First Election in Vendaland", *Bulletin*, XI, 7 (1973), pp. 390–2, Africa Institute, Pretoria.
4. Carter, op. cit., chapter 7. Also see *Daily Dispatch*, 30.9.1963, 5.11.1963, 8.10.1963, 1.10.1963, 16.11.1963, 28.11.1963, 29.11.1963, 2.12.1963.
5. Carter, op. cit., chapter 7.
6. Transkei, *Hansard*, 1964, p. 200.
7. *Daily Dispatch*, 30.8.1965.
8. Transkei, *Hansard*, 1967, pp. 391–2.
9. Carter, op. cit., p. 148.
10. This number includes 5 unopposed members as well as 4 candidates who had originally been nominated in Umzimkulu constituency, where the election was postponed as a result of the death of one of the candidates before election day.

10

POLICY FORMULATION AND
DECISION-MAKING

Two related aspects are dealt with in this chapter: first, how policy is formulated by the organisations under discussion and, second, the nature of the decisions which they initiate. Other relevant processes have already been dealt with, viz. elections, policy statements, interrelationships between parties and voluntary associations, and formal organisational aspects.

In the Transkei, confrontation between the DP and TNIP over a period of ten years enables us to draw certain conclusions in respect of their approach to the parliamentary situation, and it will be shown how the DP – in opposition – used the Legislative Assembly to create an impression of attempted participation in government. The parliamentary organisation of parties will also be referred to. Motions submitted by the parties have been analysed, rather than legislation, because, in terms of the homeland governments' powers, motions may cover a much wider range of subjects and are more illustrative of policy in operation. Only the Transkei has a sufficiently long history for a meaningful analysis of motions. Brief reference will be made to decisions other than motions.

Policy Formulation

Most of the African political organisations give their members the opportunity to participate in the policy formulation process by stipulating constitutionally that policy can be laid down by the national congress only. The policy decisions by these annual congresses are taken on the initiative of branches who submit motions for consideration of the congresses. Decisions thus taken are deemed to become policy in the Black People's Convention, South African Students' Organisation, Ciskei National Independence Party, Ciskei National Party, Seoposengwe Party, Lebowa People's Party, and Venda Independence People's Party. In respect of all these organisations the national congress is also the highest governing body, with some constitutional delegation of power to the executive committees of Saso and CNIP, and also to the leader of the CNIP. The Bophuthatswana National Party is the only exception to the rule through its provision that only the party leader can determine the party's policy. At the first party congress, held on 24 February 1973, the delegates were required to endorse the policy as formulated by the leader, Chief Minister Mangope.

Personal observation, rumour and personal visits by politicians to different localities are relatively important in the political communication process. The so-called African press is mostly apolitical, whereas the so-called White press is concerned mainly with the interaction among White political parties. Underdevelopment in rural areas, and prevalent suspicion, apathy, or lack of interest in politics in urban areas, are detrimental to a free interchange of political ideas. As a result, policy formulation is left to a large extent in the hands of national political leaders.

African parties in the homelands act mainly as support bases for the homeland governments and are used to endorse policy decisions made at the highest level, and to recruit support at times of election. The relationship between ruling and opposition parties is such that the activities and decisions of the latter are mostly irrelevant to government and administration, whereas governing parties can indeed point to their participation in the decision-making process. However, the conversion of policies formulated at grass-roots level into government decisions is a rare occurrence in all homeland parties, communication in these parties being mostly from top to bottom. It is therefore not surprising that differences over policy played a relatively small role in the internal party disputes and re-alignment of party loyalties, as demonstrated in another chapter. Rather, concern over personal support bases and disagreement over political tactics lay at the root of these divisions. There is broad consensus in all homelands among parties over certain policy aspects such as education, economic development, wages, influx control, improved social benefits, and the federation idea. These matters automatically culminate in government decisions – i.e. without much argument. Homeland party leaders are invariably the most important policy formulators, they are the most important integrative forces within the parties, and they are the most important link between the parties and the legislative assemblies. Decisions of party congresses are not well publicised, and those of parliamentary caucuses not at all. It is therefore difficult to relate the activities of the policy-making structures with the policy statements of party leaders and (in the case of governing parties) with government decisions. Generally the input (and feedback) function of congresses has a marginal effect on party affairs, including policy.

None of the homeland-based parties provides services to local communities or to party followers, with one or two exceptions where private initiative plays a decisive role. It is characteristic of Saso, however, that its entire effort is directed at the direct involvement of members and branches in community service. It is therefore easier to identify decisions with grass-roots organisation in Saso than in the homeland parties where the party leadership is often the only visible link between party and government decisions.

The centralisation of policy formulation in homeland parties is best illustrated through detailed reference to the Transkei's experience. There is widespread uncertainty (but no concern) at all levels of the TNIP as to which party institutions are responsible for policy formulation. The party's constitution contains no explicit provision in this respect, but determines that the "decision arrived at by the Conference, the National Executive Committee on behalf of the Party, is binding to all members . . .". The TNIP's "Programme of Principles" can only be altered by a "national conference of the Party". The status of this document is not quite clear – not being part of the constitution, although prospective members are required to subscribe to the policy of separate development as set out in this programme. In practice, however, the programme provides a broad framework for party policy, closely enough defined not to allow much scope for elaboration and rationalisation.

Ordinary members of the TNIP and members of branch executive committees are under the impression that decisions by the annual congress in respect of policy are binding on the party leadership, and that they can be revoked only by a congress decision. A vague notion exists that the national executive has some sort of final power of review. At higher levels in the party, however, greater weight is attached to the powers of the national executive. What actually happens is that branch executives submit draft motions to the annual congress, where the motions are discussed briefly (though sometimes not at all) and then referred to the national executive without a vote being taken. At the congress, which lasts two days, there is usually insufficient time for a proper discussion of motions. The national executive has the power to reject any motion which coincides with an already established point of policy, or which it considers contrary to party policy. The party executive thus has the final say in policy formulation. The TNIP's parliamentary caucus further discusses motions adopted at the congress – which is always just before the opening of the annual session of the Legislative Assembly. The caucus may reject motions it considers unsuitable. The division of powers of policy formulation between the caucus and the national executive is not defined; their powers of review largely overlap, with the national executive members giving the lead in the caucus.

Motions are not formally submitted to Transkei government departments, though members of the Legislative Assembly and cabinet take up matters raised at the annual congress with the departments concerned. There is no procedure for following up motions at the next annual congress or evaluating the success of previously approved motions.

The impression of continuity in party policy is given by several annual recurrent themes, such as requests for more land, an exclusively African Transkei, the necessity for economic development and aversion to pass laws. However, there is no detailed long-term planning over any one of these matters and it appears as if the preferences and experiences of cabinet members sometimes dictate policy formulation. Thus alleged discourtesy towards leading TNIP members by White staff of the Departments of Posts and Telegraphs and of the Police (both controlled by the South African government) sparked requests for Transkei control over these Departments.

Within the national executive the cabinet members are the most powerful, and the cabinet can indeed be regarded as the most important agency for policy formulation, follow-up and execution, and selection of leading persons within the party. Most important within this inner core of the TNIP is the leader, Kaiser Matanzima, who commands the absolute loyalty and trust of the entire leadership. As a result of his strong power basis within the party, his force of personality and intellectual ability, Matanzima is able to obtain his own way without opposition within the congress, the caucus and the cabinet. He was opposed seriously only once – by C. M. C. Ndamse, a former university lecturer, who could only do so as a result of the substantial support he had enjoyed among intellectuals within the party.

Matanzima's power within the TNIP is best illustrated by his announcement of far-reaching policy changes in August 1972 without consulting the national executive, cabinet, caucus or national congress. Returning from a visit to the U.S.A., he announced his willingness to allow Whites to become citizens of the Transkei under certain conditions, and his support for a federation of self-governing homelands in South Africa.

Essentially a pragmatist, Matanzima knew he would be able to carry his own congress with him while creating confusion in the DP's ranks. Matanzima's changed policy is in keeping with his objectives as a self-declared African nationalist: Whites will only be allowed to become Transkeian citizens with the inclusion of their land in an enlarged Transkei, and the Africans will still be the majority population group; whereas a Black federation would immeasurably strengthen the bargaining power of the South African Black population *vis-à-vis* the South African government. As a political broker, Matanzima is able to interpret correctly his people's sometimes poorly expressed inclinations in clear-cut political objectives. Matanzima know the emotional reaction of his people towards many aspects of their life in South Africa, and sometimes chooses his phraseology accordingly. Thus, at the 1972 annual congress of the TNIP, referring to his land claims, he said "The land we claim . . . was unilaterally and cynically raped by the Union Government"; and on economic development, "We have as much right to land and financial expenditure as he [a White person] has. It is the Black sweat which has given him a comfortable home while the Black man is living in filthy locations. It is the Black man that has contributed principally through his cheap labour to the wealth of the White men in South Africa." Expressing universal African values, Matanzima is able to maintain his undisputed position as the most important policy formulator in the Transkei, and as one of the most prominent articulators of African needs and aspirations in South Africa.

Several important external factors influenced Transkei government policy in recent years. The first was the South African government's own interpretation of its policy of separate development, which was not always understood in the Transkei. As seen by the Transkeians, there are several inconsistencies between the theory and practice of separate development. They include South Africa's firm adherance to the 1936 land delimitation; its refusal to approve a Black federation of non-independent Black territories; its dialogue with Black Africa and resultant "White" treatment of visiting foreign African statesmen and officials; and the paternalistic attitudes of White officials and politicians towards homeland leaders. Frustration and angry reaction have followed, and certain policy aspects have been stated with increasing urgency and aggressiveness, giving the impression of a looming confrontation, and helping to establish the style for similar demands to be made by other homeland leaders.

Matanzima's leading role in South Africa's African politics was increasingly challenged by new-comers on the scene, particularly Gatsha Buthelezi, Hudson Ntsanwisi and Lucas Mangope. The Transkeian leaders were forced to adopt a more universalistic note. The formerly firm conviction that an independent African Transkei would come to pass were shaken, the Transkei being increasingly visualised as part of a larger state, and a slight concession was made in favour of non-racialism. Consultations with other homeland leaders followed, and the common nature of many problems experienced by homeland populations (also those in White areas) was stressed. The homeland leaders demonstrated that they were aware of African priorities and needs.

Two trips abroad tended to broaden Matanzima's vision – a fact he acknowledged himself, but – contrary to opinions held by many people – these visits have not changed his views. In certain White South African political circles there is a vague but firm belief that there is a concerted attempt at instilling universalistic values by "the Americans" in South African society, and that this would be detrimental to the carrying out of separate development. When Matanzima, on returning from the U.S.A., announced the policy changes just mentioned in connection with a Black federation and White citizens in the Transkei, brain-washing by "the Americans" was immediately suspected in these circles. However, the changes are in accordance with the objectives of African nationalism, although less parochially stated. They cannot be regarded as substantial changes in personal outlook, although they are important changes in terms of party policy and political tactics. After his visit to Great Britain, Matanzima declared on 11 April 1972 at his party's annual congress: "My visit to Great Britain was an eye-opener. I was highly impressed by the nationalism of the British people who are divided up into four tribes, viz. English, Welsh, Scots and the Irish. Their conservatism is fascinating as evidenced in their recognition of the Crown as a unifying factor in the British Empire. . . . Never before has the unity of our people [i.e. the Transkei population] become a *sine qua non* in their struggle for the attainment of human rights enjoyed by all people in the free world." On his return from the U.S.A. in August 1972, he said that his visit had inspired him with a spirit of nationalism, and to reject second-class citizenship. Visits abroad by Buthelezi, Sebe, Phatudi, Ntsanwisi and Mangope had the same effect of broadening pre-existing convictions.

In the DP the power of considering "policy statement and adjustment in the light of a changing and developing community" is conferred upon the national executive committee by the constitution of the party. However, considering the irregular meetings of the national executive and the dissension over leadership issues, innovative thoughts on party policy are highly unlikely. Nothing new has in fact emanated from the DP since its first policy declarations of 1964.

Motions adopted at the DP's annual congresses are not *ipso facto* regarded as party policy, and are subject to reconsideration by the national executive and parliamentary caucus. The caucus decides which congress motions are suitable – and in the party's interest – to form the basis for motions tabled in the Legislative Assembly. The caucus also considers motions received directly from constituencies. The DP's informal structure makes the party machinery almost powerless in policy formulation, and places this responsibility on the formally appointed leaders whose position, because of continuous leadership disputes, has remained very tenuous. In spite of these difficulties the leader, Guzana, has proved in practice the most important factor in maintaining a consistent party policy, interpreting and elucidating policy and maintaining autonomous thinking when the TNIP seemed to be trespassing over the traditional DP field of multi-racialism.

Senior civil servants in the civil services of the homelands are mostly White officials who have been seconded by the South African government, which is also their paymaster. Where homeland preferences clash with South African policy, these public servants are in a difficult position in the sense that they are for practical purposes serving two masters, although they are homeland officials. In respect of sensitive matters the homeland governments make little use of these top public servants for policy formulation purposes.

Localisation of the public service in homelands is undertaken from the lower levels upwards. Middle-level positions requiring professional training (law, engineering, agriculture, medicine) are to a large extent filled by Whites. In other positions Africans have been promoted to higher levels, including secretarial posts.

Senior African homeland public servants who make a definite contribution to policy formulation are the government representatives appointed by the homeland governments in White urban areas. They are usually people who have achieved public prominence and are in the position to observe at first hand the problems and grievances of Africans in White areas. Two or three such representatives are appointed by each government for those areas where the largest concentration of people from the particular homeland is found. In their regular reports to their governments they convey these problems as well as current political feeling. Greater concern over the citizens outside the homelands followed the appointment of these officials.

Decision-making

In the Transkei the members of the opposition tabled more questions and motions in the Legislative Assembly than the government members, and although the annual sessions lacked the time to discuss all the motions tabled at any session, the Democratic Party maintained

TABLE 10. I. SUBJECT OF MOTIONS, PER PARTY, TRANSKEI

		1964	1965	1966	1967	1968	1969	1970	1971	1972	1973
1. Public service	DP	0	8	2	3	1	0	1	2	1	1
	TNIP	1	5	0	1	1	0	0	1	0	3
	TPFP	—	—	0	0	1	—	—	—	—	—
2. Health facilities	DP	2	2	7	1	5	5	5	4	0	1
	TNIP	0	0	1	1	1	0	0	1	0	0
	TPFP	—	—	0	0	1	—	—	—	—	—
3. Constitutional matters[a]	DP	1	3	3	3	1	2	0	1	2	1
	TNIP	2	0	2	0	4	2	0	3	2	0
	TPFP	—	—	1	2	3	—	—	—	—	—
4. Cultural matters[b]	DP	0	3	2	0	1	1	0	0	0	0
	TNIP	0	1	0	0	0	0	0	0	0	0
	TPFP	—	—	0	1	0	—	—	—	—	—
5. Chieftainship affairs	DP	2	7	1	2	1	2	3	0	1	0
	TNIP	0	2	1	1	0	2	1	1	4	3
	TPFP	—	—	0	0	1	—	—	—	—	—
6. Educational matters	DP	9	9	2	2	3	7	4	3	2	6
	TNIP	0	1	0	0	1	0	0	0	2	1
	TPFP	—	—	0	0	1	—	—	—	—	—
7. Local government	DP	0	2	0	1	1	0	1	0	0	0
	TNIP	0	0	0	0	0	1	0	1	0	3
	TPFP	—	—	0	0	1	—	—	—	—	—
8. Economic development	DP	1	4	2	2	1	1	1	0	1	3
	TNIP	0	0	0	0	1	0	0	0	0	2
	TPFP	—	—	0	0	1	—	—	—	—	—

9. Political and civil rights[e]	DP	6	6	2	4	4	5	2	2	2	1
	TNIP	0	0	0	0	0	1	1	1	2	0
10. Agricultural methods and assistance	DP	3	5	3	3	3	3	6	3	1	1
	TNIP	0	0	0	0	0	1	1	0	0	3
11. Transkeian land and towns	DP	0	0	0	1	0	0	0	0	0	0
	TNIP	0	1	0	0	2	1	2	3	0	2
12. Public works and facilities including transport	DP	0	7	5	6	2	2	6	6	2	3
	TNIP	1	3	0	0	0	0	0	6	0	7
13. Labour matters[d]	DP	2	9	2	1	3	2	7	2	5	1
	TNIP	5	0	0	0	1	1	2	3	0	3
14. Social matters[e]	DP	3	6	6	2	2	4	2	2	1	1
	TNIP	0	1	1	0	0	0	0	1	0	0
15. Administrative matters	DP	2	12	2	3	2	2	3	4	1	1
	TNIP	0	0	0	0	1	1	0	0	0	0
16. Particular issues[f]	DP	2	5	3	3	1	1	0	0	0	0
	TNIP	1	1	0	0	0	0	0	1	2	3
17. TLA procedure	DP	0	0	0	0	0	0	0	0	0	0
	TNIP	2	0	1	0	1	1	0	0	1	0
Total		46	103	41	43	54	48	48	53	32	50

(a) Including constitutional review, relations with S.A. government, independence, election symbols.
(b) Including official languages, radio services.
(c) Including "political" prisoners, bannings, passports.
(d) Including industrial conciliation, influx control, wage determination, apprenticeship.
(e) Including social pensions and grants, voluntary associations.
(f) Including censure of particular minister, re-appointment of officials.

its steady flood of motions and questions. At the 1969 session the Chief Minister suggested that the opposition should take their requests directly to the government departments concerned for consideration by the ministers. By that time it was well known that the relatively small number of motions and questions tabled by TNIP members could in part be ascribed to the fact that they directly approached the appropriate cabinet members.

TABLE 10.II. SUBJECT OF QUESTIONS, PER PARTY, TRANSKEI

	General policy and administration			Local administration and importance			Of personal concern		
	DP	TNIP	TPFP	DP	TNIP	TPFP	DP	TNIP	TPFP
1964	40	0	—	5	0	—	3	1	—
1965	61	0	—	13	0	—	16	0	—
1966	78	1	0	24	0	0	17	0	0
1967	38	2	2	33	2	2	22	1	1
1968	40	0	1	21	0	1	20	0	0
1969	30	0	—	17	0	—	17	0	—
1970	20	1	—	4	0	—	7	0	—
1971	37	12	—	18	2	—	23	2	—
1972	30	15	—	12	11	—	21	12	—
1973	16	11	—	14	12	—	5	5	—

Motions and questions are used by the DP to demonstrate to its followers its activities in the Legislative Assembly, while the TNIP uses them mainly to spotlight action of the Transkei government, and since 1971, also to express dissatisfaction with aspects of the South African government's policy, for example (in 1971) questions about the absence of Africans on the Fort Hare University Council, lack of control over Transkei towns by the Transkei government, the repatriation of Transkei citizens from White areas, and the absence of Africans on the village management board of Elliotdale, which has been zoned Black. In 1972, questions by the TNIP showed that it was not the Transkei government that granted loans to traders, that Africans could not become shareholders in the Xhosa Development Corporation, that Africans could not count on Transkei government assistance in the acquisition of land in Transkeian towns because it had no control over these towns, and that the granting of loans to African traders also fell outside the Transkei government's scope. In 1971 TNIP members tabled questions showing that Whites received no preferential treatment in the granting of livestock import permits, and that the spread of tuberculosis was not the fault of the Transkei Department of Agriculture. In 1972 it was pointed out in a similar way that a particular administrative area could not be agriculturally rehabilitated because the inhabitants had damaged the machinery, that agricultural students at Tsolo School of Agriculture who had made no progress were sent home because it cost the government money to keep them there, and that a new school for girls was planned for Umtata.

From Table 10.III it is clear that the TNIP only started submitting motions in earnest at the session of 1968, and questions in 1971. Motions by the DP concentrated largely on practical matters, as well as political issues which flowed from their opposition to separate development. While the TNIP submitted a number of practical motions, it submitted about an equal number of motions concerning the relationship between the Transkei and South

TABLE 10.III. MOTIONS AND QUESTIONS SUBMITTED BY CHIEFS[a] AND ELECTED MEMBERS, TRANSKEI

	DP			TNIP			Total
	Chiefs	MTLA	Total	Chiefs	MTLA	Total	
1964 Motions	3	34	37	2	7	9	46
Questions	6	42	48	0	1	1	49
1965 Motions	11	77	88	5	10	15	103
Questions	14	76	90	0	0	0	90
1966 Motions	3	33[b]	36	1	4	5	41
Questions	12	107	119	0	1	1	120
1967 Motions	1	39[c]	40	0	3	3	43
Questions	11	87[d]	98	1	4	5	103
1968 Motions	7	33[e]	40	1	13	13	54
Questions	5	78[f]	83	0	0	0	83
1969 Motions	4	33	37	2	9	11	48
Questions	8	56	64	0	0	0	64
1970 Motions	7	34	41	3	4	7	48
Questions	1	30	31	0	1	0	32
1971 Motions	10	22	32	2	19	21	53
Questions	3	75	78	6	10	16	94
1972 Motions	3	16	19	0	13	13	32
Questions	1	62	63	23	15	38	101
1973 Motions	3	17	20	8	22	30	50
Questions	4	31	35	11	17	28	63

(a) Members of cabinet are in all cases included among MTLA.
(b) Including one motion by TPFP.
(c) Including three motions by TPFP.
(d) Including five questions by TPFP.
(e) Including nine motions by TPFP.
(f) Including two questions by TPFP.

African governments, particularly over land issues, the constitution of the Transkei, labour problems, and chieftainship (see Table 10.I). Thus the TNIP publicises its dealings with the South African government, thereby also increasing pressure on it.

An increasing number of questions were tabled by the DP in respect of (i) matters of local concern – i.e. requiring information or explanations in respect of matters concerning a particular district or administrative area, or a region, tribal or regional authority, or a particular school, road, bridge, or dam; and (ii) matters of individual concern – i.e. information about, or explanations in respect of government actions concerning qualifications of particular government servants, suspension of a particular government servant, procedure followed in respect of the granting of a particular licence or piece of land, conditions of service of a particular government servant or group of government servants, suspension from office of a particular chief, and the number and names of persons banned under the provisions of Proclamation No. R.400 of 1960.

Chiefs, who are *ex-officio* members of the Legislative Assembly, need not obey the caucus of any party. It is clear from Table 10.III that they do. Their general absence from participation in motions and questions can also be an indication of a general inability to participate constructively. There is also a marked tendency by most chiefs to abstain from participation in debates. As a result the few elected TNIP members had a particularly heavy work load during the first Assembly of 1963–8. This trend continued after 1968 when the TNIP had a majority of elected members.

The fact that the number of DP members in the Assembly was depleted through the defeat of most of its candidates in the 1968 general election caused a noticeable decrease in the average number of motions and questions tabled by DP members during each session:

TABLE 10.IV. AVERAGE NUMBER OF MOTIONS AND QUESTIONS SUBMITTED PER SESSION, PER PARTY, TRANSKEI

	Motions		Questions	
	DP	TNIP	DP	TNIP
1964–8	48·1	9·0	87·6	1·4
1969–73	29·8	16·4	54·2	16·4

The fact that the TNIP'S number of elected members almost doubled after the general election of 1968 made only a slight difference in its performance during the sessions of 1969 and 1970 (see Table 10.III). Its sudden increased submission of motions and questions in 1971, 1972 and 1973 can be ascribed to a change in tactics by the TNIP caucus in respect of publicising its policy and highlighting the difficulties of the Transkei government's relationship with the South African government.

Questions and motions by DP chiefs have mostly been the work of Chiefs D. D. P. Ndamase and S. Majeke – both *ex-officio*, and then elected members since 1973 and 1968 respectively. The large increase in questions by TNIP chiefs in 1972 (see Table 10.III) was due mainly to two chiefs: Chieftainess Nozizwe Sigacu (10) and Chief Mteto Matanzima (4). The TNIP mostly opposed DP motions, but a number of motions have been adopted unanimously over a number of years – e.g. in respect of influx control and chieftainship affairs.

Although a shadow cabinet was appointed by the DP in the Transkei Legislative Assembly, its existence and the names of its members are not commonly known even to prominent DP supporters. Many TNIP members of the Legislative Assembly also do not know the names of the shadow cabinet. Although the existence of a shadow cabinet was confirmed during research by the leader of the DP, and the names of members given, it rests on an informal basis, like the entire structure of the DP. Subject to change, it has at no stage included the DP rebels from Tembuland, referred to in previous chapters. The members of the shadow cabinet are also chairmen of study committees of the DP caucus whose duty it is to do research on and study each government department with a view to debates in the Assembly.

Three select committees of the Assembly are appointed annually. Members are proposed by the Chief Minister and approved by the Assembly. Apart from members of the cabinet, who serve on the Committee on Standing Rules and Internal Arrangements, and the Business Committee, only four chiefs have been committee members between 1964 and 1972. Ministers are not members of the Committee on Public Accounts. The Committee on Public Accounts and the Committee on Standing Rules and Internal Arrangements have five members each, and have always had two DP members each, while the Business Committee with six members has had only one DP member annually. The turnover of committee membership is low, and when changes occurred – sometimes every two years – only one member has been replaced. The biggest change ever was in the Committee on Public Accounts in 1971 when three members were replaced.

The establishment of caucuses and appointment of shadow cabinets by the leader of the opposition became common in all self-governing homelands, where opposing parties developed.

In all homelands the party caucuses were sufficiently strong to maintain discipline among members – necessary for keeping the governing party in power. In one instance only was a governing party defeated (although it did not bring about the fall of the government). The Ciskei National Independence Party was, within its first month of being in power, defeated by the Ciskei National Party by 25 votes to 22 on the question whether *jabulani* (beer brewed by the Xhosa Development Corporation) should be allowed for sale in the Ciskei. The CNP was against the introduction of *jabulani* on the grounds that the XDC were enriching Whites whose interests it allegedly was serving, and that *jabulani* was "destroying the nation".[1] After this shaky start, the CNIP gained in strength, and proceeded with a working majority of 27 against 23.

During election campaigns political parties and election slates and factions lay claim to benefits which they consider to be the result of their efforts. Thus, a TNIP pamphlet mentioned the following "achievements" of the party: increased africanisation of the civil service and police; increased capital expenditure by the Transkei government, which improved the "buying power of our people"; a substantial increase in the turnover of commercial banks in the Transkei; improved educational facilities; building and maintenance of roads and the resulting increased employment opportunities; increased employment of unskilled labour in the Transkei; increased pension beneficiaries; increased trading opportunities for Africans; curbing of subversive activities and maintenance of law and order; agricultural progress – viz. the construction of the Lubisi Dam and irrigation scheme; establishment of fibre, tea and coffee plantations and a meat factory; improved production of wool; increased afforestation; more employment opportunities for Transkeians through negotiations with the South African government.[2]

The Transkei government has always been careful to point out examples where its actions brought relief or satisfaction of particular needs. In drought-stricken areas of the Transkei, in 1971, assistance was given through the offering of employment on building projects and roads; labourers were paid from a specially created drought fund. Salary increases for all government servants, chiefs, headmen, and teachers in 1973 were $2\frac{1}{2}$ per cent higher than increases at the same time in the South African civil service and were hailed as a step towards the closing of the wage gap in South Africa. In the 1973 budget speech, which preceded the 1973 general election by six months, the Chief Minister pointed out progress under his government during the past ten years.

In Venda, during the first general election of August 1973, the

Mphephu faction pointed out the achievements of the Venda government under the leadership of Mphephu: for example, the attention that was being given to training more teachers, the commencement of a five-year plan for development of educational facilities, the provision of free training facilities for farmers, the building of a number of dams, the improvement of livestock, the expansion of a sisal project, and the taking of control by the Venda government of fish breeding and forestry.

L. L. Sebe, who became Chief Minister after the 1973 general election in the Ciskei, held two portfolios under former Chief Minister Mabandla, namely Education and later Agriculture and Forestry. In his election campaign, Sebe pointed out various achievements during his term of office, such as an improved teacher-pupil ratio, better educational facilities and service conditions for teachers. For the benefit of the homeland inhabitants the Bophuthatswana National Party claimed that various improvements were due to the efforts of its leaders, such as the larger measure of self-determination, the establishment of six government departments, and the appointment of a public service commission, improved agricultural services and educational facilities, the proposed development of a new capital town, the establishment of various town councils, the building of tribal offices, and more opportunities for Tswanas to enter the commercial field.

The KwaZulu government, on the other hand, is anxious to make it clear that it has little power, being at the first stage of constitutional development. One of the main problems of the KwaZulu government, and indeed of all homeland governments, is shortage of funds, and thus a restriction on the allocation of budgetary resources. Most income is received by way of a grant from the South African government and almost everything is earmarked for essential public works, educational facilities, salaries, etc. Very few resources are available for allocation as a result of political or policy preferences. Another major, but relatively fixed, source of income is the general tax payable by Zulus. This was augmented by a special tax imposed during the session of 1973.

In spite of its limited scope regarding the allocation of resources, the KwaZulu government, unlike the Basotho Qwaqwa government (which at the time of research was also in the first phase of constitutional development) gained massive popular support through its public identification with the masses' political and economic needs, and its objections against South African discriminatory practices.

The homeland governments have been able to bring some satisfaction to their people by contributing to the socio-economic development of the territories and by changing or removing certain important areas of friction which existed under South African rule, such as pass offences, aspects of Bantu Education, and local government through Bantu authorities.

The homeland citizens in the White areas of South Africa realise that the homeland governments have no jurisdiction outside the homelands and can do nothing directly to relieve their particular problems, such as housing shortages, influx control and transport problems, arrests for pass offences, job reservation, and low wages. Several homeland leaders nevertheless were at pains to point out that they were acting on behalf of the urban Africans in negotiations with the South African government. Buthelezi called the urban Africans "part of our electorate";[3] Matanzima, during visits to the urban areas, always stressed his negotiations with the South African government on urban problems; Dladla interceded on behalf of Zulu workers in wage disputes during 1973 and 1974; Mangope pleaded with employers for higher wages and managerial training; Sebe claimed that he had challenged influx control regulations and that certain restrictions on Ciskeians were removed as a result; and the Lebowa People's Party congress of December 1974 paid special attention to the problems of Africans in White urban areas.

The Bophuthatswana government in 1973 appointed an industrial relations officer to assist Tswana employees in the border industries. In the White urban areas, all homeland governments appointed urban representatives with sufficient status to deal with problems resulting from housing complaints, contravention of labour laws and influx control measures, or unemployment. These representatives have direct access to the highest South African government officials and have been able to solve numerous complaints. They have no jurisdiction, however, concerning the application of measures in respect of wage determination, and labour disputes. They are also empowered to arbitrate in disputes between citizens of their territory living in the urban areas, and are required to assist urban inhabitants who wish to settle in the homelands, especially prospective entrepreneurs; and they render assistance in respect of educational and cultural matters such as school committees and councils and youth organisations. The activities of these urban representatives have only a marginal effect on the circumstances of the urban inhabitants, to whom, understandably, the homeland governments have not yet proved their relevance and beneficial influence in material terms. This explains to some extent the poor participation in homeland elections by urban voters. Close study shows that there is a relationship between the actions of homeland leaders and changes in the African policy of the South African government. This relationship is not equally clear to the rank and file Africans in the urban areas, who therefore do not react to it.

—Saso

Saso's objective is to assist Black communities to determine and realise their own needs, not to provide continuously for the needs of these communities. It has no intention of becoming a welfare organisation. Apart from assisting the Black community, the various projects are regarded as a means of involving members in the physical development of the Black community. The projects are supposed to plant a sense of self-reliance in students and communities alike, and this is regarded as a prerequisite for self-emancipation.[4] At the same time the students become acquainted with aspects of leadership of their people.

Saso projects include:

(i) The Black workers' project for co-ordinating the needs and aspirations of Black workers, and establishing Black trade unions where necessary.

(ii) The Education by Employment project which obtained vacation employment for students, whereby their relationship with Black workers could be strengthened.

(iii) Numerous student protests in connection with the management of Black universities – about 14 major protests between 1968 and 1974.

(iv) A free university scheme which obtained grants for Black students and organised lectures related to Black studies.

(v) Literacy programmes were extended to all Saso branches for promotion of literacy and adult education.

(vi) Community development projects included construction of approximately three dams, a number of school buildings and a community centre by Saso members and local communities in various homelands. Two health and preventive medicine projects were also initiated but not concluded.

(vii) The Promotion of Black Educational Advancement project sought to collect R100,000 as a trust fund for educational grants, and financing a voluntary students' service for community development projects.

(viii) A Black Press Commission was set up in 1972 to promote the publication of Black newspapers and magazines.

(ix) Saso's Cultural Commission has the task of promoting all forms of Black art.

The most conspicuous and successful among Saso's projects have been the students' protests, some community development projects, and its cultural activities. All other projects experienced serious difficulties from the start.

Several problems hampered the execution of projects, and in some cases prevented it. Objectives could sometimes not be achieved as a result of poor planning, whereas student reaction to calls for participation in projects has been generally disappointing due to poor understanding of projects and lack of interest. Saso's prescriptive approach to community programmes – i.e. of identifying the needs and prescribing a programme for meeting the needs – sometimes caused resistance in the communities who then abandoned them as soon as Saso workers left the scene. Financial problems are perhaps the most serious and have led to the abandonment of certain programmes; they made it impossible to visit remote rural areas, which was considered essential for the conscientisation programme.[7] From the reports of branches and affiliated centres in 1972 it was clear that poor planning, obscure objectives, procrastination and lack of finance and material were mainly responsible for poor performance in the execution of community projects.

REFERENCES

1. *Daily Dispatch*, 15.6.1973.
2. Appendix to TNIP election manifesto, 1968.
3. *Weekend World*, 17.3.1974.
4. Saso, Executive report to the 3rd General Students' Council, 1972.
5. Ibid.

I I

SOUTH AFRICAN ORIENTATION

The rejection of the ethnic fragmentation of South Africa into home-lands by BPC and Saso and other urban-based and Black conscious-ness oriented organisations has been made explicitly clear in pre-ceding chapters. It was also pointed out in Chapter 8 that homeland leaders only conditionally accept separate development as a basis for political participation and, moreover, that they have visions of a greater South Africa which would include not only its present terri-tory, but also neighbouring states within the framework of a federation.

The propagation of the federation idea underlines the homeland leaders' rejection of the ideology of separate development. The proposed federation with its Black majority rule is their vision of the ultimate end of separate development. It will at least partially consist of units created by and under separate development, but as they see it, one of the main objectives of the White South African government, namely White rule in the White areas, would not have been achieved. It is therefore possible to refer to the federal idea of the homeland leaders as a post-separate development phase. "Post-separate development" emphasises their South African orientation, and explains their continuing concern over the problems of Africans in White areas.

It would have been easy to wash their hands of these urban com-munities on the grounds that they were powerless in White areas, and try to exert indirect pressure on the South African government through international agencies. However, it is clear that they re-gard the presence of almost a third of the African population in White areas as an imperative for their direct involvement in South Africa, and not the homelands only.

African Federation

The first of the homeland leaders to propagate federation was S. T. Bokwe, a general dealer near Alice in the Ciskei, and leader of the tiny Bantu Nationalist Conservative Party. In 1966 Pilane,

229

then chairman of the Tswana Territorial Authority and later leader of the Seoposengwe Party in Bophuthatswana, called for the formation of one African nation under the leadership of Kaiser Matanzima. However, when Bokwe founded the BNCP in December 1968 one of its objectives was to unite the Africans "on a federal basis into one nation". Contrarily, Bokwe maintained that the amalgamation of the Ciskei and Transkei would not be economically viable, and would constitute a sell-out of the birthright of the Rarabe tribe to the Transkeians.

Next to take up the federal idea was Chief Minister M. M. Matlala of Lebowa who declared in July 1971 that separate development would not be worth having if it implied the permanent division of the Africans. Matlala failed to sustain his call with a further initiative, and it was taken from him a year later by Matanzima.

Homeland leaders consider their objective of a Black federation to be in accordance with the South African government's policy of separate development, and to support this view, frequent reference is made to the late H. F. Verwoerd's prospect of a commonwealth of Southern African nations, which might be formed after the Bantustans had become independent. Although Verwoerd never elaborated these views, there are indications that he favoured an economic community, and it can be assumed that he never envisaged a federation of Black states which would force a political confrontation with the White South African government, nor a federation of Black and White states in which the Black majority ruled.

Following Verwoerd's train of thought, Matanzima declared in his first policy speech in the Transkei Legislative Assembly that "the different parts of South Africa are inter-dependent, and our future is tied up with that of greater South Africa. It can be foreseen that eventually South Africa will embrace a number of fully Bantu-governed states linked with the white Republic of South Africa in a co-operative association – a South African Commonweath of Nations."[1] Nothing contained in the "Programme of Principles of the Transkeian National Independence Party", issued in 1964, and the "Manifesto of the Transkei National Independence Party, 1968 Election" conveyed a contrary thought. These documents spoke of friendly relations and co-operation with neighbouring White and Black states, including other independent Bantustans.

In August 1972, on the day of his return from a visit to the United States, Matanzima suddenly gave new meaning to these objectives when he proposed the formation of a federation of African states in South Africa. He had now succeeded, as never before, in capturing the imagination of the entire African population of South Africa.

Those Africans who were in various stages of disenchantment over what they suspected of being the ethnically orientated politics of the homelands were particularly impressed. Matanzima, while still standing on his rather parochial Transkei platform, suddenly became a South African politician. He was praised by the *Weekend World* as coming "into line with the real thinking of the Black man in South Africa",[2] although there were some misgivings within his party that his views might represent a reversal of TNIP policy.

It is significant that Matanzima's emergence from parochial politics coincided with the emergence of Black consciousness in South Africa, and with the increasing prominence on the South African scene of other homeland leaders such as Buthelezi and Mangope. Competing for prominence at first, they later joined forces in an attempt to work out a joint approach to common problems.

The TNIP's formal acceptance of the federation idea was unanimous.[3] Apart from fears of a possible reversal in policy, there was also unease in the party for other reasons. For example, the Bhaca of Umzimkulu district, bordering on Natal, were not much interested in closer ties with KwaZulu, a sentiment expressed at the installation of a new Bhaca chief in 1972. Furthermore, because during the rule of Chief Faku until the second half of the nineteenth century the KwaZulu territory between the Umtamvuna and Umzimkulu Rivers had belonged to the Eastern Pondo, there is a possible dispute with KwaZulu over this area, and Eastern Pondo support for closer ties with KwaZulu could be qualified. Both the Bhaca and Eastern Pondo areas are TNIP strongholds. During March 1973, the secret Sons of the Transkei, which had hitherto supported the TNIP, expressed strong opposition to federation with KwaZulu in a pamphlet distributed in Umtata. This pamphlet accused Matanzima of a sell-out, spoke of secret talks between him and Chief Buthelezi, and hinted at Xhosa and Eastern Pondo opposition. However, in September 1973 the Eastern Pondo Paramount Chief, Botha Sigcau, came out in favour of a Black federation.

When Matanzima expressed his ideas on a South African federation, Gatsha Buthelezi of KwaZulu was ready to support them as a step towards Black unity in South Africa. In fact, Buthelezi had raised the possibility of a federation in South Africa before Matanzima. He declared in 1971 that he was prepared to lead an independent KwaZulu into a federation of South African states "if that was in the best interests of the Zulu people".[4] Buthelezi's immediate support for Matanzima's ideas greatly contributed towards the successful propagation of the federation idea that followed – especially as he expressed this support at a stage (towards the end of 1972) when leaders such as Mangope of Bophuthatswana and Mabandla of the Ciskei were, respectively, against the idea and unenthusiastic. In May 1973, shortly before Mabandla lost the election for the chief ministership in the Ciskei, he came out strongly in favour of a federation, and his successor, L. L. Sebe, gave the idea his cautious support. Sebe's opinion was that a federation was "one of the weakest forms of government",[5] but two months later he attended the first summit conference of homeland leaders.

Further fertile ground for the federation idea was found in Gazankulu; in July 1971 the Chief Minister Professor H. W. E. Ntsanwisi mentioned the possibility of a federation or commonwealth as the ultimate result of separate development, with White and Black working together and acknowledging a common loyalty to South Africa. Economic issues, he maintained (a year later), would decide whether or not a federation of South African states would be established; the interdependence among the population groups in South Africa made it necessary for White and Black governments to co-operate, and homeland leaders to co-operate together. By May 1973 Ntsanwisi had become so enthusiastic about the federation idea that he was prepared to call a meeting of homeland leaders in order to work out a common strategy on the political problems of South Africa. Matanzima and Buthelezi's propagation of a Black federation, and the support for a federation by Mangope's opponents in the Seoposengwe Party during the second half of 1972, forced Mangope to take a stand on this issue during the Bophuthatswana election campaign of October 1972. Reluctant to commit himself, he declared that it was a policy matter which would have to be decided by the Bophuthatswana Legislative Assembly. He denied[6] a report that he had met Buthelezi and Matanzima in secret with a view to promoting a Black federation; he declared that he was entrusted with the task of serving the Tswana nation and would therefore only do what he considered to be in the best interests of Bophuthatswana and its people. After his election victory Mangope said that the federation had been one of the issues rejected by the electorate, and that it would be a disservice to his people if he too did not reject it in future. The Tswanas, he added, feared domination by the numerically superior Zulu and Xhosa. Pilane's support for a federation was attacked by the BNP's deputy leader, Chief Herman Maseloane, who said that Pilane was being dictated to by his Xhosa wife; to this the SP leader replied that the Chief Minister was sowing the seeds of tribalism and hate by not supporting unity of the Black states.

Some time after the 1972 general election, Mangope changed his mind with regard to the proposed federation. First, however, he propagated a "joint approach". At a meeting during his election campaign, which was apparently not reported in the press, Mangope mentioned the possibility of an economic community and co-operation on issues of common interest, but not the establishment of a single federal government. Again not reported by the press, he said in an interview during the second half of 1972 with a S.A.B.C. reporter while on holiday in Natal that the idea of a federation was not unacceptable, but that "it was easy to talk about federation when we might not be meaning the same thing". It was something that the "leaders" (not only the Bophuthatswana Legislative Assembly) should discuss in detail in order to reach a common understanding on what they meant. A few months later, in January 1973, he called on the Black people of South Africa to work out a programme of unity. Calling a Black "superstate" premature, he said that the homeland governments could take a unified stand in favour of higher wages for their people, who often worked in the same factories as migrant labourers, as well as over the land question, influx control, discrimination, foreign aid for the homelands, the position of the urban Africans and the Bantu Investment Corporation.

Only six months after his statement that the Tswanas had rejected a federation in their general election of October 1972, Mangope declared that he did not oppose a federation: he merely could not decide in favour of joining a federation without consulting the Tswanas in a referendum. They might even decide to enter into a federation with Botswana with which they had geographical, linguistic and "racial" links.[7] Three months later, Mangope was helping to organise the first meeting of homeland leaders for the discussion of, among other things, a federation. Ten days after this meeting, Mangope once again gave preference to "co-operation" instead of a federation.[8] His main fear is that the Tswanas will lose their cultural identity in a federation which is dominated by Nguni groups, and he therefore increasingly favours the idea of strenghening ties with neighbouring Botswana. Mangope's apparently hesitant attitude towards the federation is best understood in the light of a strong opposition to the proposed federation within the BNP of which he was leader until the end of 1974.

Chief Minister Ntsanwisi of Gazankulu proposed a summit of homeland leaders on his return from a visit abroad in May 1973. Soon afterwards, in July 1973, the idea was taken a step further by Chief Minister Mangope of Bophuthatswana, who then began making the arrangements. Mangope, who had previously declared his opposition to a federation, at first omitted the issue from the agenda, but it was put back after Matanzima and Buthelezi had exercised some pressure.

The agenda of the summit reveals some important issues which the homeland leaders regard as common problems. Papers by homeland leaders respectively dealt with transfer of government departments to homelands, a Black bank, the land issue, labour problems, petty apartheid, finance of homeland governments, and the federation idea itself. The summit was attended by Buthelezi (KwaZulu), Matanzima (Transkei), Sebe (Ciskei), Mangope (Bophuthatswana), Ntsanwisi (Gazankulu) and Ramusi (Lebowa), representing Chief Minister Phatudi of Lebowa. Chief Minister Mphephu did not attend, and Chief Executive Councillor Mota of Basotho Qwaqwa was not invited – presumably because of a dispute with the Transkei over land.

On the eve of the conference, only Matanzima and Buthelezi had declared their explicit support for the federation idea; other leaders were lukewarm, whereas Mota and Mphephu were against it at that stage. A joint statement issued after the conference created the impression of unanimity on the federation issue among those who had attended. It stated that a federation was "vital to the unity of Black people", and the conference resolved "in principle" that a federation would be propagated by all homeland leaders, and that achievement of a federal state would be a long-term policy. Referring to other matters, the statement said that financial assistance by the South African government to the homelands was not commensurate with African contribution to the gross national product; that homelands wanted the right to seek overseas aid for development, and that pass laws and influx control measures should be repealed. Matanzima and Buthelezi were delegated by the conference to submit information on an African federation to the next conference. It was thought that the next summit meeting would be in December 1973, but it was held as late as November 1974 at Jan Smuts Airport. The first and second summit meetings brought the homelands no closer to federation, but they succeeded in achieving greater unity of political purpose. The second summit meeting resolved not to seek independent status under separate development, but acknowledged the Transkei's right to proceed towards independence.

Two weeks after the first summit Mangope denied in a radio interview that an agreement existed among homeland leaders on the principle of federation and said that he had told the meeting that he preferred to join Botswana, rather than the other homelands. While casting doubt on the depth of the homeland leaders' concern over and commitment to a federation, Mangope raised another distinct possibility, namely the linking of independent homelands with adjoining independent African states where ethnic relationships existed across the borders, without relinquishing the principle of an eventual federation of states in Southern Africa. Thus, Bophuthatswana is adjacent to Botswana; the Swazi homeland and KwaZulu have a common border with Swaziland; and the Transkei, Ciskei and Basotho Qwaqwa are neighbours of Lesotho.

The Transkei opposition, the DP, rejected a federation because it is based on the prior establishment of ethnic self-governing territories according to the separate development policy which is unacceptable to it. It will only accept a federation if every constituent territory, including the present White South Africa, has a multiracial character.

The propagators of the federation idea gave little indication of any proposed structure, and the entire issue has a somewhat academic character in view of the South African government's refusal to allow such a federation among non-independent homelands, and the homelands' intention not to accept independence unless certain conditions were met.

It was Chief George Matanzima, the Transkei Minister of Justice, who went into most detail on the proposed federation. At the 1973 session of the Legislative Assembly he held out the prospect of African control over the present White South Africa: he proposed the replacement of the South African Parliament by a multiracial assembly where the various racial groups would be represented according to their population numbers. White representatives would derive from the four South African provinces, whereas the Blacks would represent the eight Bantustans as well as the "White" urban areas. Constituent assemblies would remain as regional bodies based on separate development (i.e. racially and ethnically segregated) with control over local affairs only. No other homeland leader either supported or rejected these proposals.

Various federal plans contained in the policies of White South African opposition parties were rejected by some homeland leaders. Perhaps the most forceful speech of rejection was that of Kaiser Matanzima at his party's annual conference in March 1973 where he said that they were "opposed to the United Party federal policy which places the White Parliament in a superior position over the Black states", and that they were "also opposed to the Progressive Party policy, which stands for a qualified franchise. We stand for the principle of one man one vote in all stages of our Government."

The South African government's attitude to the federation is largely negative. It wants to secure the separate political identity of the homelands and prevent the creation of a multiracial parliament based on the South African and homeland governments as constituent parts. After the Transkei and KwaZulu declared their intention of establishing a federation in 1972, the South African attitude was that it would be impossible without South African co-operation. It is significant, however, that ten days after the Umtata summit a leading Afrikaner Nationalist political commentator, Schalk Pienaar, wrote that some form of federation or confederation was bound to follow the present constitutional separation.[9] This immediately raised the possibility that a federation is not ruled completely out of order in government circles, but that the centrifugal forces of ethnic states should first take firmer root in order to create a more favourable climate for a balance of power resting on conflicting interests and common problems. Within this broad objective should be seen the South African vision of a commonwealth of independent states, including White South Africa, but without any formal structure binding them together. The South African government realises that it cannot prevent a federation among independent homelands, but it remains determined not to become a member.[10]

Dialogue

One of the primary reasons for the homeland government leaders' compromise with separate development is that they can use it as a platform for political expression and action. They see an opportunity not only for service to a sizeable portion of their people, but also for negotiation with the South African government. As the number of self-governing homelands increased, dialogue between the respective governments and the South African government loomed larger, and became an irreversible trend in South African political realities.

Declarations of friendship and goodwill by homeland leaders towards Whites generally and the South African government in particular are interspersed with grave warnings on the racial situation and even threats over possible future developments if certain conditions are not met. All homeland leaders believe in the necessity for consultation between them and the South African government, particularly on matters affecting the African only, such as pass laws. Ntsanwisi sees consultation as the alternative to confrontation, whereas the necessity for consultation is dictated by the interdependence of the peoples of South Africa. Matanzima, Buthelezi and Mabandla urge contact across the colour line to promote peace, goodwill and better understanding. Whereas

Buthelezi stated explicitly that he and his government were committed to non-violent change in South Africa, Guzana maintained that the safety and prosperity in South Africa was due, *inter alia*, to the loyalty of the Blacks. Several homeland leaders tried to assuage the fears of Whites. The most notable example was Matanzima who, immediately before the Umtata summit of homeland leaders, assured Whites that they need not worry about African co-operation; the African leaders intended to build a peaceful and healthy South Africa. At the Progressive Party congress of 1973 Buthelezi proposed a Bill of Rights which would safeguard the rights of all minority groups in South Africa, including the Whites. Sebe also affirmed his intention to keep race relations on a friendly basis, and hoped that Whites would return the hand of friendship.

A measure of satisfaction was derived by homeland leaders from their increased political participation on the South African scene, and Mangope declared that the Black viewpoint "has acquired a relevance and significance quite unknown in the past".[11] Buthelezi, who held a similar opinion, would have liked more consultation over the formulation, rather than execution, of policy. The homeland leaders rightly regard themselves as moderates, and adopt the attitude that the South African government must, in its own interests, come to an understanding with them – rather than with more extremist leaders, who will demand more than they do, and with the next generation whose attitudes are unknown. Despite their willingness to compromise with separate development, an increasing impatience among homeland leaders is evident, and they have repeatedly warned that mutual trust among racial groups and the African goodwill were fast disappearing, which could result in racial polarisation and collision.

Fears of Black reprisals and domination, which could follow a shift of power, strengthen White political and economic domination and are reinforced by the threatening remarks of some homeland leaders. Thus, at the summit of homeland leaders at Umtata in November 1973, Buthelezi remarked that the African can bring White South Africa "to her knees" with Black solidarity; and on another occasion he said that a revolution might erupt if the South African government "failed to deliver the goods".[12] Matanzima also raised the possibility of "trouble" if the South African government did not listen to him, a blood-bath if the Blacks got no "satisfaction", and a day of reckoning unless Africans were accepted by Whites as equals.[13] It is interesting that on two occasions Matanzima's remarks were uttered on his return from visits abroad – from Britain in October 1971 and the U.S.A. in August 1972.

A significant warning was sounded by Ntsanwisi when he said that increasing foreign pressure makes Black understanding and friendship impossible in the event of armed intervention in South Africa; the security of the Whites depends on the Blacks. With the threat of terrorism and guerrilla warfare, White survival in South Africa is indeed closely connected with African co-operation, goodwill, loyalty and friendship. Ntsanwisi's words emphasised the unenviable position of White South Africans if their policy left them without Black citizens who could help resist the guerrilla onslaught, but with millions of Black inhabitants belonging to unfriendly independent homelands.

To forestall this possibility, the South African government initiated a policy of dialogue, which it hopes will culminate in co-operation among future autonomous interdependent states. The first round of individual consultations between the Prime Minister and the Minister and Deputy Ministers of Bantu Administration and Development and individual homeland leaders was held on 3, 4 and 5 November 1971. Leaders of the Transkei, Ciskei, Gazankulu, Bophuthatswana, Venda and Lebowa were invited; with Basotho Qwaqwa and KwaZulu not then self-governing territories.

A convention of leaders of all racial groups, proposed by Buthelezi in August 1971, was rejected by the Prime Minister on the grounds that it would not contribute to solving the country's problems. When the (White) United Party and (White) Progressive Party invited several homeland leaders to address their annual congresses in 1973, the Prime Minister threatened to forbid it: however the threat was strongly resented by homeland leaders, and it was given no immediate effect. Following their meeting in Umtata in November 1973, the homeland leaders requested a joint meeting with the Prime Minister, and on 6 March 1974 the Prime Minister, the Minister and Deputy Ministers of Bantu Administration and Development and all the homeland leaders held their first joint meeting. At this eight-hour meeting the following matters were discussed: the government's policy regarding homeland independence, the wage gap, disparity in revenue from African direct and indirect taxation and expenditure in the homelands, the position of the urban Africans, the medium of instruction in African schools outside the homelands, the phasing-out of passes, the land issue, and the transfer of further government departments to the homelands. The discussions were "brutally frank"[14] and it was agreed to hold similar ones in future. Remembering the ignominious end of the Native Representative Council in 1946, there is reason to doubt the outcome of the discussions between the

South African Prime Minister and the Chief Ministers of the homelands: however, the South African government's commitment
to recognise the power base provided by each self-governing homeland, together with international pressure, has introduced a more
hopeful element.

The relationship between homeland leaders and the Afrikaner-
dominated South African government is an ambivalent love-hate
affair. While the Afrikaner is lauded for his straightforwardness
and honesty, he is otherwise disliked by the homeland leaders. Kwa-
Zulu's Executive Councillor for Community Affairs, Barney
Dladla, said of the Afrikaner management of an industry during
the Natal strikes of 1973 that it was impossible to reach an agreement with them because they always think they are boss. While
Dladla's words illustrate dislike of the Afrikaner, Matanzima
voiced expectations based on the Afrikaner's so-called honesty when
he expressed his hope that the Afrikaner would remain in
power in South Africa, adding that he was sure that Africans
would get their freedom from the Afrikaners, even if they had
to suffer at their hands. The immediate effect of these attitudes on
the process of dialogue was the strengthening of the homeland
leaders' determination to enter it as racial equals of the White
participants, and as persons endowed with the status of leaders of
self-governing states. Matanzima reflected this mood when he said
that they no longer respectfully requested the government to do
something; instead "we demand our rights".[15] Attitudes of paternalism among White politicians and officials are much resented in
consequence, as well as all suspected attempts by the South African
Department of Information, Department of Bantu Administration
and Development, the Security Police, the Bureau of State Security,
and Radio Bantu to interfere in homeland politics. At the same time
there is almost unanimous rejection by homeland leaders of the
policies of the Progressive Party and the United Party, because these
policies are designed to maintain White political supremacy in
South Africa (including the homelands) for a certain, undefined
time. Explanations in November 1973 by the leader of the opposition in South Africa, Sir De Villiers Graaff, that the United Party
rejected racial supremacy ("*baasskap*") but that the Whites as the
leading social, cultural and economic community must also take
the lead in achieving political change, brought no change in the
Africans' reactions.

A number of significant changes occurred in South African government policy and public attitudes regarding African affairs between
1970 and 1974. Mounting pressure on South Africa from abroad
and from increasingly powerful African leaders in South Africa

combined to bring about these shifts. They concerned mainly relief in petty apartheid or discriminatory measures (e.g. over the admission of Blacks to hotels and public parks, differing wage levels, job reservation in certain sectors and pass laws), and attempts to bring about settlement of the Rhodesian and South-West Africa issues.

Whereas Africans are supicious of these moves by the Whites, they represent a genuine attempt at extending a hand of friendship across the colour line, weighed down with centuries of racial tension, but in response to the moderation of African participation in the South African political process.

REFERENCES

1. Transkei, *Hansard*, 1964, p. 67.
2. Editorial in *Weekend World*, 8.4.1973.
3. Decision of TNIP conference, Umtata, 22.3.1973.
4. Interview reported in *Drum*, November 1971, p. 10.
5. *Rand Daily Mail*, 10.9.1973.
6. *Weekend World*, 20.8.1972.
7. *Daily Dispatch*, 17.4.1973; *Rand Daily Mail*, 17.4.1973.
8. *Daily Dispatch*, 19.11.1973.
9. *Rapport*, 18.11.1973.
10. Minister P. W. Botha in *World*, 23.9.1970, and Minister M. C. Botha in *The Star*, 14.8.1972; Prime Minister B. J. Vorster in *Rand Daily Mail*, 30.4.1973, and *Rapport*, 27.1.1974.
11. In a speech to the National Development and Management Foundation, Johannesburg, 12.4.1973.
12. *Weekend World*, 11.11.1973; *Rand Daily Mail*, 1.6.1973.
13. *The Star*, 15.8.1972; *Rand Daily Mail*, 1.6.1973.
14. Chief Minister Ntsanwisi's words in his vote of thanks to the Prime Minister, *Rand Daily Mail*, 7.3.1974.
15. *Daily Dispatch*, 14.5.1973.

I 2

TOWARDS AFRICAN UNITY

Several homeland leaders have been in favour of a no-party approach to decision-making, namely Mangope (Bophuthatswana), Mphephu (Venda), Mabandla (Ciskei), and Buthelezi (KwaZulu). The no-party approach opposes the formation of all parties, and consensus must be achieved through the normal channels of communication, interaction of voluntary associations, and deliberations within the governmental framework. It is founded in the opinion that parties might divide the "nation". In this sense, "nation" refers to the inhabitants of the respective ethnic "states". Furthermore the no-party approach is also founded in the knowledge that the material allocative powers of the homeland governments are limited, and that this situation could be exploited by an irresponsible opposition riding the wave of rising expectations. In such circumstances parties are considered to be no more than a luxury and a façade.[1] Mangope, Mabandla and Mphephu thought that political parties were foreign institutions, incompatible with their people's political conceptions, but when confronted with opposing political parties and groups, all three established and led political parties. Only in Gazankulu the no-party ideal has been applied in practice.

Homeland leaders often view parties as instruments of division. For instance in Lebowa, where the formation of political parties was not an issue in the first general election of 1973, the former Chief Minister, Chief Matlala, established a party immediately after he had been defeated in the election of a new Chief Minister, and was promptly blamed by his supporters for dividing the people of Lebowa. Six months later, in March 1974, Matlala's party and that of the new Chief Minister amalgamated.

Even in homelands where opposing parties are found, there is scepticism over the possible positive role of an opposition, and efforts are sometimes made to cast doubt over the motives of the opposition – e.g. in the Transkei.

The existence of an opposition in the Transkei Legislative Assembly is tolerated by the TNIP only unofficially.[2] This attitude of the

TNIP is in contrast to Matanzima's challenge to Poto just before the 1963 general election, that the loser in the contest for Chief Minister should withdraw from other cabinet nominations and form an opposition. The TNIP speakers refused to take seriously a DP motion in the 1967 session of the Assembly that official recognition be accorded to the opposition. The main arguments in favour of the motion were that an official opposition would be a safeguard against poor government and a dictatorship; that the Transkei opposition had already received unofficial recognition when (in 1967) its leader's allowance as member of the Assembly was raised; it acted as opposition in a responsible way; and recognition of the opposition was irrelevant to the policy of the opposition. The TNIP replied, mainly through the then Minister of Education, George Matanzima, that a "witch-hunt" would be necessary to determine whether there were "fit and proper persons" in the opposition, that the DP actually wanted to be represented in the South African Parliament, and that they therefore should stay away from the Transkei Legislative Assembly. "All you are is a pack of impostors, hypocrites and deceivers. How can we recognise such an opposition?" Furthermore the Transkei government could not recognise an opposition containing murderers,* Progressives, Liberals, and communist fellow-travellers. Another TNIP speaker said that recognition of the opposition would imply the acknowledgement of its policy "which is odious to us".[3]

Ruling parties suspect that the diffraction of opposing viewpoints into rival organisations is an expression of alienation to the political system. This strengthens a tendency to equate governing parties with government structures. Feelings of animosity among parties are often deepened by the presence in rival parties of persons from different tribal, ethnic and kinship groups. The institutionalising of rivalry and suspicion in a situation where there are no common values regarding the political system strengthens the conviction of those who feel that parties are divisive and foreign institutions. The political system concept itself is dichotomous and could mean either a particular homeland or the whole of South Africa. The homeland leaders' atempts to achieve African unity in South Africa through the homelands helps understanding of their aversion to division within the homelands.

Together with the no-party approach, and weakening opposition in several homelands, there are several factors which point towards a one-party trend in homelands; "one-party", because parties have

* In 1966 two DP members of the Assembly, J. Nkosiyane and N. Nogcantsi, were convicted by the Supreme Court (upheld by the Appeal Court) for conspiracy to kill the Chief Minister.

been established in the majority of homelands. First, there are the recurring leadership struggles in several homelands which flowed from either a basic distrust among leaders, or from undermining tactics employed by some in their aspirations to the leadership of their party. To this must be added the mistrust among opposing parties. Free and democratic change of leadership or government is unlikely where such attitudes prevail. Secondly, the policy-making techniques in all parties point to a very high degree of centralisation, underlining the high status and power of the leadership. Centralisation of power and a docile acceptance of leadership is further accentuated by the flow of communication within the parties. Essentially, communication is a one-way affair, namely from top to bottom. Members and supporters are informed about party policy, and they rarely take the opportunity to reverse the flow of communication – even in cases of gross dissatisfaction with elected office-bearers' handling of party affairs.

Single-party systems in the respective homelands could promote African unity in South Africa, by facilitating understanding and agreement among the homelands on matters such as amalgamation and federation. There are, however, also factors which inhibit the growth of single-party systems.

First, until 1974 homeland governments had no power to prohibit organisations. When this power was conferred upon them, the South African government made it clear that it would closely supervise the homelands in this regard. Secondly, the low level of participation in homeland elections is an important adverse influence for one-party trends, because the governing party would need more support to prove its legitimacy. The decline in voter participation in the Transkei since 1963 and the poor voting figures for most homelands reflect one or more of the following variables: poor campaign organisation, poor registration of voters, a low level of consciousness among voters of the political process, little interest in homeland politics, the voters' ideological commitments, and the constitutional status and power of homeland governments. Thirdly there is a great measure of consensus among parties (including BPC and Saso) on policy issues, and policy differences are mostly questions of emphasis. This serves to reduce animosity and mistrust. Fourthly, well-developed relations between parties and voluntary associations are necessary for one-party government in order to obtain a steady flow of information on various needs, and to keep open non-political avenues of participation in the policy-making process. The homeland parties have no such relations, and only Saso and BPC have adopted political action through voluntary associations. Finally, the idealistic view of some homeland leaders that political integration will be achieved without the aid of political parties is probably fallacious. Strong primary and secular divisions exist in the African political community: urban-rural, educated-uneducated, Christian-heathen, traditionalists-modernists; whereas there are also divisions according to political values, ethnicity, churches, social status, and economic status. The dispersal of home-land territories into loose blocks of land also create geographical divisions. Organisational bridging of these divisions is required, and although the parties bridge some of these, they themselves sometimes are manifestations of politicised social divisions – e.g. the Fingo-Rarabe and Tembu-Emigrant Tembu divisions in the Ciskei and Transkei respectively. As long as the parties continue to depend on traditional leaders for their grass-roots organisation, ethnicity will remain an important social foundation.

It appears as if homeland-based parties and Saso and BPC are laying a network of political organisation which will knit together the African population. Whereas this is practically possible, little preparatory work has in fact been done. Party leaderships have not fully utilised the organisations at their disposal. Formal organisa-tional work often remained at a low level of efficiency, with frail party frameworks and membership below its realistic potential. Voluntary associations have often not been included in the organisa-tional effort. The ultimate function of the political organisations is that they provide vehicles for continuing political activity. The approximately ten active homeland parties and Saso and BPC together claim to represent almost the entire African population. They participate in the evolving of political ideas and the intro-duction of people to these ideas; and they recruit members and supporters into political activity. They are political brokers who observe, aggregate and interpret diverse interests and needs into coherent policies which they either try to convert into authoritative decisions, or bring to the attention of the South African authorities or the world. They also act as channels of political communication and mobilisation of support for particular and general objectives.

Within the homelands the respective governments perform cer-tain integrative functions through education, creation of a physical infrastructure, encouragement of voluntary associations, and em-phasis on economic participation. Other secondary structures are however also necessary to help integrate diverse interests and recon-cile conflicting social divisions or groups. Parties and associations founded inside the homelands have a potentially important inte-grative role because they may also operate among the Africans out-side the homelands, whereas the jurisdiction of the homeland govern-ments does not extend beyond their boundaries. The relatively few

national and regional voluntary associations which are not homeland-based integrate with difficulty their activities with the homelands' political systems. The Transvaal United African Teachers'
Association and the National African Federated Chamber of
Commerce, for instance, resisted fragmentation of their structures
into ethnic organisations on the grounds that they represent, respectively, teachers and businessmen in both White and African
areas and that there is basically no difference in the needs of teachers and businessmen whether in White or in African areas.
Organisations such as these direct their activities at local and central
government in White and African areas alike, and are not committed to the homeland form of government. Although these organisations bridge the gap, in terms of their membership which include
people in White and African areas, they can not be integrated into
the political system of any particular homeland, or of the White
area. As institutions they remain aloof from the political system,
and relatively uncommitted ideologically, and therefore render
small (if any) contribution to national integration in any homeland.
By implication, flowing from their broadly-based membership,
these organisations help create favourable orientations towards a
broader South Africanism.

The parties in the homelands do not penetrate deeply into local
communities – rural and urban – and are for instance not able to
estimate accurately their support in many areas. They tend to
communicate from the higher to the lower echelons and not *vice versa*.
In this way they indeed help to create a greater awareness of political issues among the public, but they do not involve many people
in the policy-making process and make no conscious attempt to
inculcate favourable orientations towards the political system and
the form of government. They mostly strengthen subject political
orientations[4] – that is, expectations among people respecting the
role of the government as it affects themselves.

The differences among the homeland-based parties and the BPC
and Saso in respect of African social and economic priorities are
small, the main difference being that the latter two organisations
emphasise the primacy of the group or community *vis-à-vis* the
individual, while the former accept the growth of a strong middle
class as necessary for growth and development in economic, social
and political spheres of life. While there is appreciation of the fact
that homeland-based parties correctly repesent the Africans'
needs and aspirations, there is a feeling among urban Africans that
the mostly rural delegates in the homeland assemblies do not fully
understand urban problems. The Transkei's proposal in 1973
that five constituencies be delimited for urban Africans outside the

Transkei, for instance, received the support of Transkeians outside the territory. The large measure in which homeland-based parties are oriented towards the social and economic interests of rural, tribal people necessitates a reorientation in these parties in the interests of national integration. Significantly, in those homelands with large urban townships (Bophuthatswana, Ciskei, and Lebowa) very little was said in respect of urban needs by the candidates and parties who contested the general elections in 1972 and 1973.

Africans in White areas also realise that homeland governments cannot actually do much concerning their situation, apart from making repesentations to the South African government. There is therefore some scepticism among homeland citizens in urban areas in respect of the advisability of fragmenting South Africa into ethnic states which will leave them largely in the cold. The BPC, Saso and the Democratic Party in the Transkei oppose this fragmentation, while all other parties conditionally accept it. At the same time, the leaders of the homeland parties and governments, with the exception of Chief Ministers Mphephu of Venda and Mota of Basotho Qwaqwa, from time to time express their preference for Black unity and Black political participation in South Africa.

Although homeland governments are used as frameworks for political action, there is no attempt among homeland leaders to create exclusively favourable orientations towards the homeland form of government, which might militate against future federal or unitary government within the broader framework of South Africa, possibly including neighbouring states. The very acceptance, however, by homeland leaders of separate homeland governments was a step towards fragmentation. The spheres of interest and ethnic pride respectively created and generated by homeland governments promote political fragmentation and make virtually impossible a future unitary form of government. It is interesting that while accepting the fragmentation implied by homeland governments, the homeland leaders at the same time propagate unity for the future in the form of a federation. However, no existing political organisation in South Africa has successfully related the material needs and political aspirations of Africans in homelands with those in White areas. This remains one of the most serious divisions which any attempt towards African unity has to contend with.

The political integrative effort of BPC and Saso, particularly the latter, is more comprehensive in its conception than anything planned by the homeland parties. Everything undertaken by BPC and Saso is calculated to promote their ideal of Black consciousness, which is in itself an integrative ideology to a certain extent, and to politically activate the entire Black population of South Africa. In this sense, the various programmes and projects of Saso especially are interrelated, such as the leadership seminars for students, the attempts at establishing a Black press, the Black workers' project, the promotion of the expression of Black experences through fine and performing arts, the literacy programme for adults, and the rural community development projects. Although these activities can be regarded as an integrative effort aimed at national integration of all Blacks in South Africa, their actual impact has been less than that of the homeland parties who enjoy an advantage by participating in the manipulation of government, and who, apart from having a more sympathetic press, are not constantly censured by the South African government.

Neither the homeland-based parties nor BPC and Saso are mobilisational organisations in their efforts to achieve African unity and political supremacy in South Africa. Saso and BPC have certain characteristics which approximate mobilisational organisations. There is much greater emotional appeal in the Black consciousness ideology than in the pragmatic approach which has characterised the homeland parties. Whereas the homeland parties do not participate in local development projects and have no particular interest in any aspect of social change, Saso and BPC are development-oriented, and profess their support for changing African social structure by emphasising a co-operative ethic *vis-à-vis* individualism, and a common Black identity *vis-à-vis* ethnicity. These social changes are aimed at countering continued White political supremacy which is maintained through economic superiority enjoyed by the Whites on the basis of individual competition.

The open membership of homeland parties within the framework of ethnic "states" is a manifestation of their silent accepance of the existing social, economic and political framework in South Africa, but its ethnic restriction is not commensurate with their belief that the existing political framework is at best an interim measure. Their membership represent all social divisions in African society, but are predominantly conservtive, and most of the time they do not know the exact extent of their support in any given locality. They are particularly careful of radicals in their ranks. An accommodationist attitude prevails, not only towards South African authorities, but also towards recalcitrant party members – provided they are not a threat to the national leader. In contrast to this pattern, Saso and BPC have a selective membership by admitting only students (Saso) and by excluding all senior government employees and those who co-operate with government-created institutions. A confrontationist attitude prevails among members, and recruitment has been directed at middle-class, educated, influential people, while interest groups (voluntary associations) are purposely drawn into the structure. While being precise as to the ideological basis of their membership, their socio-economic basis of support (essentially middle-class) militates against their professed objective of averting the secularisation of African society by modelling it on a co-operative ethic.

Saso and BPC activities towards workers and peasants have been cast in the mobilisational mould, and were not intended as membership recruitment drives. Thus they have tried to employ social, educational, and economic projects to demonstrate to peasant and worker communities the power of their collective efforts.

The main differences between homeland parties and Saso and BPC are in connection with their ideological convictions, political strategy and where their main support is located. They share certain objectives, such as Black majority rule and African social and economic development, but differ in respect of the way this should be achieved.

Apart from shared objectives, several factors support a possible rapprochement and eventual co-operation among these organisations. In the first place the pragmatism of homeland leaders, together with existing Black consciousness orientations among them, could contribute towards a modus vivendi among the various African political organisations. Secondly, the main support bases of the homeland parties and BPC and Saso are respectively in the homelands and the White areas. Co-operation among them would achieve complementary support for both sides without undue rivalry for support in any area. Thirdly, continued ideological differences depend on continued application of the separate development policy, and differences among them will diminish in direct proportion to the easing of separate development and concomitant discriminatory measures. The prevalence of historical differences, leadership contests, and differing conceptions of the methods and direction of social change will probably be decisive for any attempt at co-operation.

REFERENCES

1. Letter by Buthelezi to *Natal Mercury*, 31.8.1971. Also see Buthelezi's speech at a meeting at Umlazi on 30.4.1972.
2. Kaiser Matanzima in *Rand Daily Mail*, 29.5.1972, and George Matanzima in Transkei, *Hansard*, p. 68.
3. Transkei, *Hansard*, 1967, pp. 66–72.
4. Gabriel A. Almond, and Sidney Verba, *The Civic Culture: Political Attitudes and Democracy in Five Nations*, Princeton University Press, 1963.

WORKS CONSULTED

The following list consists of published and unpublished works consulted and referred to directly and indirectly in this work. Newspaper articles, speeches of politicians, and the numerous laws, proclamations and government notices of the South African and homeland governments are omitted.

BOOKS AND PAMPHLETS

Ashton, Hugh, *The Basuto* (2nd ed.), London, Oxford University Press, 1967.

Bernstein, Hilda, *The World that was Ours*, London, Heinemann, 1967.

Biko, B. S. (ed.), *Black Viewpoint*, Durban, Spro-cas Black Community Programmes, 1972.

Brokensha, Miles and Robert Knowles, *The fourth of July raids*, Cape Town, Simondium Publishers, 1965.

Carter, Gwendolen M., Thomas Karis and Newell M. Stultz, *South Africa's Transkei; the Politics of Domestic Colonialism*, London, Heinemann, 1967.

De Villiers, H. H. W., *Rivonia: Operation Mayibuye*, Johannesburg, Afrikaanse Pers-Boekhandel, 1964.

Downton, James V. and David K. Hart (eds.), *Perspectives on Political Philosophy*. (Vol. III: "Marx through Marcuse"). Hinsdale, Ill., Dryden Press, 1973.

Durand, J. J. F., *Swartman, stad en toekoms*, Cape Town, Tafelberg Uitgewers, 1970.

Feit, Edward, *South Africa: the Dynamics of the African National Congress*, London, Oxford University Press, 1962.

——, *African Opposition in South Africa: the Failure of Passive Resistance*, Stanford, Hoover Institution, 1967.

Forman, Lionel and E. S. Sachs, *The South African Treason Trial*, London, John Calder, 1957.

Gibson, Richard, *African Liberation Movements: Contemporary Struggles against White Minority Rule*, London, Oxford University Press, 1972.

Horrell, Muriel, *Action, Reaction and Counter-action*, Johannesburg, South African Institute of Race Relations, 1971.

Hunter, Monica, *Reaction to Conquest: Effects of Contact with Europeans on the Pondo of South Africa*, London, Oxford University Press, 1936.

Jeppe, W. J. O., "Die ontwikkeling van bestuursinstellings in die Westelike Bantoegebiede (Tswanatuisland)", *Annale*, Vol. 33, Serie B No. 1, University of Stellenbosch, Stellenbosch, 1971.

Kadalie, Clements, *My life and the ICU: the Autobiography of a Black Trade Unionist in South Africa*, ed. Stanley Trapido, London, Cass, 1970.

Khoapa, B. A. (ed.), *Black Review 1972*, Black Community Programmes, Durban, 1973.

Kuper, Leo, *Passive Resistance in South Africa*, London, Cape, 1956.

——, *An African Bourgeoisie: Race, class, and politics in South Africa*, New Haven, Yale University Press, 1965.

KwaZulu Government Diary 1974, Durban, Edupress, 1974.

Langa, Ben (ed.), *Creativity and Black Development*, Durban, Saso Publications, 1973.

Ludi, Gerard and Blaar Grobbelaar, *Die verbasende Bram Fischer*, Cape Town, Nasionale Boekhandel, 1966.

Ludi, Gerard, *Operation Q-018*, Cape Town, Nasionale Boekhandel, 1969.

Manganyi, N. C., *Being Black in the World*, Johannesburg, Spro-cas, 1973.

Mayer, Philip, *Townsmen or Tribesmen; Conservatism and the Process of Urbanization in a South African City*, Cape Town, Oxford University Press, 1961.

Metrowich, F. R., *Communism and Terrorism in Southern Africa*, Pretoria, Africa Institute, 1969.

Morris, Michael, *Terrorism: The First Full Account in Detail of Terrorism and Insurgency in Southern Africa*, Cape Town, Howard Timmins, 1971.

Randall, Peter (ed.), *Anatomy of Apartheid*, Spro-cas occasional publication No. 1, Johannesburg, Spro-cas, 1970.

——, (ed.), *Directions of Change in South African politics*, Spro-cas occasional publication No. 3, Johannesburg, Spro-cas, 1971.

Robertson, Janet, *Liberalism in South Africa, 1948–1963*, Oxford, Clarendon Press, 1971.

Rotberg, Robert I., *Rebellion in Black Africa*, London, Oxford University Press, 1971.

Roux, Edward, *Time Longer than Rope; a History of the Black Man's Struggle for Freedom in South Africa*, Madison, University of Wisconsin Press, 1964.

Saso, *Saso 1972*, leaflet published by Saso, Durban, 1972.

——, *Saso on the Attack: an Introduction to the South African Students' Organisation 1973*, Durban, Saso Publications, 1973.

Schlemmer, Lawrence, *Social Change and Political Policy in South Africa*, Johannesburg, South African Institute of Race Relations, n.d.

Sheddick, V. G. J., *The Southern Sotho*, London, International African Institute, 1953.

Soga, J. H., *The Ama-Xosa: Life and Customs*, Lovedale, Lovedale Press, 1932.

Soref, Harold and Ian Greig, *The Puppeteers*, London, Tandem Books, 1965.

Strydom, Lauritz, *Rivonia: Masker af!*, Johannesburg, Voortrekkerpers, 1964.

Tatz, C. M., *Shadow and Substance in South Africa: a Study in Land and Franchise Policies affecting Africans, 1910–1960*, Pietermaritzburg, University of Natal Press, 1962.

Transkei 1972, Durban, Magrep Investments, 1972.

Turok, Ben, *The Pondo Revolt*, Johannesburg, South African Congress of Democrats, c. 1960.

Van der Merwe, H. W. and D. Welsh (eds.), *Student Perspectives in South Africa*, Cape Town, David Philip, 1972.

Venter, Al J., *The Terror Fighters*, London, Purnell, 1969.

Verloren van Themaat, J. P., *Die deelname van die verskillende dele van die bevolking van die Unie aan sy staatsregtelike instellings*, Pretoria, University of South Africa, 1961.

Vosloo, W. B., D. A. Kotzé and W. J. O. Jeppe (eds.), *Local Government in Southern Africa*, Cape Town, Academica, 1974.

Walshe, Peter, *The Rise of African Nationalism in South Africa; the African National Congress, 1912–1952*, London, Hurst, 1970.

——, *Black Nationalism in South Africa: a Short History*, Johannesburg, Spro-cas, 1973.

Walter, Eugene V., *Terror and Resistance*, London, Oxford University Press, 1969.

Weyl, Nathaniel, *Traitor's end: the Rise and Fall of the Communist Movement in Southern Africa*, Cape Town, Tafelberg Uitgewers, 1970.

ARTICLES

Adam, Heribert, "The rise of black consciousness in South Africa", *Race*, London, XV, 2 (1973), pp. 149–65.

"Bantoes in die tuislande", *Bulletin*, Africa Institute, Pretoria, XIII, 6 (1973), pp. 254–6.

"Bantoe-tuislande: Grondwetlike vordering", *Bulletin*, Africa Institute, Pretoria, XI, 8 (Sept. 1971), pp. 331–40.

"Bophuthatswana: Constitutional advance", *Bantu*, Dept. of Information, Rep. of South Africa, XIX, 9 (Sept. 1972), pp. 2–7.

Breytenbach, W. J., "Eerste verkiesing in Lebowa", *Bulletin*, Africa Institute, Pretoria, XIII, 4 (1973), pp. 146, 151–3.

——, "Eerste verkiesing in Vendaland", *Bulletin*, Africa Institute, Pretoria, XVIII, 7 (July 1973), pp. 273–4, 279–80.

——, "Eerste verkiesing in Bophuthatswana", *Bulletin*, Africa Institute, Pretoria, XII, 9 (October 1972), pp. 387–92.

"Consolidation proposals for Bophuthatswana", *Bantu*, Dept. of Information, Rep. of South Africa, XX, 3 (March 1973), pp. 8–9.

Curry, David, "Blanke S.A.: Ontwaak uit jou droom!", *Deurbraak*, Cape Town, November 1972, pp. 4–6.

Editorial: "Language and communication; the freedom of a people to choose the medium of instruction for their children", *Tuata*, Pretoria, October 1973, pp. 3–4.

Feit, Edward, "Urban revolt in South Africa: A case study", *The Journal of Modern African Studies*, 8, 1 (1970), pp. 55–72.

Frankel, Philip, "Black power in South Africa", *New Nation*, Pretoria, October 1972, pp. 3–7.

Hammond-Tooke, W. D., "Segmentation and fission in Cape Nguni political units", *Africa*, London, XXXV, 2 (April 1965), pp. 143–66.

Hugo, Pierre, "Facts of Bantu Administration", *New Nation*, Pretoria, 4, 8 (March 1971), pp. 11–13.

Kotzé, D. A., "Black nationalism in South Africa", *New Nation*, Pretoria, 4, 8 (March 1971), pp. 7–10, 21.

——, "Thoughts on the rise of political parties in Bantu homelands", *Africanus*, Pretoria, 1, 1 (November 1971), pp. 5–11.

Kotzé, H. J. "Verkiesing in die Transkei", *Bulletin*, Africa Institute, Pretoria, XIII, 9 (1973), pp. 349–52.

"KwaZulu; land of the people of heaven", *Bantu*, Dept. of Information, Rep. of South Africa, XX, 2 (Feb 1973), pp. 2–11.

"Lebowa: Constitutional advance", *Bantu*, Dept. of Information, Rep. of South Africa, XIX, 12 (Dec. 1972), pp. 2–5.

"Lebowa; directives for consolidation", *Bantu*, Dept. of Information, Rep. of South Africa, XX, 7 (July 1973), pp. 2–5.

Le Roux, W., "Ciskeise verkiesing; partypolitiek of stamnasionalismes?", *Bulletin*, Africa Institute, Pretoria, XIII, 3 (1973), pp. 122–5.

Moodley, Strini, "Black consciousness, the black artist and the emerging black culture", *Saso Newsletter*, Durban, May/June 1972, pp. 18–20.

Motsuenyane, S. M., "The activities of the NAFCOC and the role of the Bantu Investment Corporation in economic development of the homelands", *Tuata*, Pretoria, May 1973, pp. 5–6.

Ngidi, B. N. B., "The Interdenominational African Ministers' Association of Southern Africa", *Tuata*, Pretoria, May 1967.

Oosthuizen, G. C., "Black theology in historical perspective", *South African Journal of African Affairs*, Pretoria, 3 (1973), pp. 77–94.

Phago, E. M. J., "A short review of the history of the Teachers' Association in the Transvaal", *Tuata*, Pretoria, December 1966.

Small, Adam, " 'Cry rage': 'n Resensie", *Deurbraak*, Cape Town, 2, 2 (Feb. 1973), pp. 8–9, 22.

——, "Universiteit van Wes-Kaapland: Dramatiese denke nodig", *Duerbraak*, Cape Town, 2, 2 (Feb. 1973), pp. 12–13, 15.

"Suid-Afrika: Demografiese data", *Bulletin*, Africa Institute, Pretoria, XII, 2 (March 1972), pp. 71–6.

"The Ciskei: Constitutional advance", *Bantu*, Dept. of Information, Rep. of South Africa, XIX, 10 (October 1972), pp. 2–7.

"The role of the black teacher in the community", *Saso Newsletter*, Durban, March/April 1972, pp. 16–18.

"The 3rd General Students' Council – an assessment", *Saso Newsletter*, Durban, Sept./October 1972, pp. 13–15.

"The Zulu Territorial Authority", *Bantu*, Dept. of Information, Rep. of South Africa, XVII, 8 (Aug. 1970), pp. 8–15.

OFFICIAL PUBLICATIONS

Bophuthatswana Government, *Debates of the Bophuthatswana Legislative Assembly, First Session, First Assembly, 21 March to 27 April 1972*, 2 vols.

KwaZulu Government, *Verbatim report of a special session of the first KwaZulu Legislative Assembly, 17 January, 1973*, Vol. 2.

——, *Verbatim report of the first session of the first KwaZulu Legislative Assembly, 4–14 May 1973*, Vol. 3.

Transkei government, *Report of the Transkeian Public Service Commission for the period 11 December 1963 to 31 December 1964.*

——, *Annual report of the Transkeian Public Service Commission, 1965, 1966, 1967, 1968, 1969, 1970, 1971*.

——, *Report of the Department of Education for the period 1 January to 31 December 1966*.

Transkei Legislative Assembly, *Proceedings at the meeting of members of the Transkei Legislative Assembly held on 6th, 9th and 11th December 1963 for the purpose of electing office bearrrs, etc.*

——, *Debates of the Transkei Legislative Assembly, Second Session – First Assembly, 5th May 1964–11th June 1964*.

——, *Debates of the Transkei Legislative Assembly, Third and Fourth Sessions – First Assembly, 2nd February 1965, 21st April 1965–22nd June 1965*, 2 vols.

——, *Debates of the Transkei Legislative Assembly, Fifth Session – First Assembly, 20th April 1966–24th June 1966*, 2 vols.

——, *Debates of the Transkei Legislative Assembly, Sixth Session – First Assembly, 19th April 1967–21st June 1967*.

——, *Debates of the Transkei Legislative Assembly, Seventh Session – First Assembly, 24th April 1968–14th June 1968*.

——, *Debates of the Transkei Legislative Assembly, First and Second Sessions – Second Assembly, 19th November 1968–21st November 1968 and 23rd April 1969–19th June 1969*.

——, *Debates of the Transkei Legislative Assembly, Third Session – Second Assembly, 15th April 1970–3rd June 1970*.

——, *Debates of the Transkei Legislative Assembly, Fourth Session – Second Assembly, 14th April 1971–18th June 1971*.

——, *Debates of the Transkei Legislative Assembly, Fifth Session – Second Assembly, 12th April 1972–13th June 1972*.

——, *Debates of the Transkei Legislative Assembly, Sixth Session – Second Assembly, 23rd March 1973–8th May 1973*.

——, *Debates of the Transkei Legislative Assembly, First and Second Sessions – Third Assembly, 19th–21st November 1973–13th March–10th May 1974*.

Transkei Territorial Authority, *Proceedings and reports at the session of 1961*.

——, *Proceedings and reports at the session of 1963*.

Tswana Territorial Authority, *Proceedings and reports at the general session of 1966*.

——, *Proceedings of the second session of the second Tswana Territorial Authority, May 1970*.

——, *Proceedings of the third session of the second Tswana Territorial Authority, March–April 1971*, 3 vols.

United Transkeian Territories General Council, *Proceedings and reports at the session of 1944*.

——, *Proceedings and reports at the session of 1946*.

UNPUBLISHED PAPERS AND PAMPHLETS

Abraham, J. H., "The Proceedings in the Magistrate's Court, Umtata, and the Supreme Court, Grahamstown, against Jackson Nkosiyani and Nicodemus Nogcantsi", roneoed pamphlet, Umtata, 23 September, 1966, 45 pp.

Bezuidenhout, G. P. C., "Die staatkundige ontwikkeling van Lebowa en die betekenis wat dit her vir die blankes van Noord-Transvaal", paper delivered at conference of S.A. Bureau of Racial Affairs, Pietersburg, 16 February 1973.

"Black Theology in a Plural Society", paper delivered at Black Theology Seminar, organised by Saso, 1971. Author unknown.

Breytenbach, W. J., "Swaziland en die Swazi van Suid-Afrika", paper delivered at youth conference of S.A. Bureau of Racial Affairs, Ermelo, 29 March 1973.

De Clercq, J. L. W., "KwaZulu en konsolidasie", University of Zululand, Dept. of Anthropology and Applied Anthropology, May 1973, roneoed pamphlet, 28 pp. with maps.

Kotzé, D. A., "Die stedelike Bantoe", paper delivered at Afrikaanse Studentebond meeting, Port Elizabeth, 11 September 1969.

Schutte, G., "The political function of some religious movements in South Africa", paper read at seminar of Dept. of Social Anthropology, University of the Witwatersrand, 28 July 1972.

"Understanding Saso", introductory paper delivered at Saso's Formation School on Black Consciousness and Community Development, Edendale Lay Ecumenical Centre, 3–8 December 1971.

THESES

De Villiers, C. M., "Die 'African National Congress' en sy aktiwiteite aan die Witwatersrand (1912–1956)", 2 vols., M.A. thesis, University of Pretoria, 1965.

Kotzé, D. A., "Plaaslike Bantoebestuursliggame in die Transkei, Basoetoland en Suid-Rhodesië", M.A. thesis, University of Stellenbosch, March 1964.

——, "Traditionalism in African local government; with special reference to the Transkei and Lesotho", D.Phil. thesis, University of Stellenbosch, December 1968.

Swanepoel, H. J., "Die aandeel van die Bantoe aan stedelike Bantoe-administrasie in Johannesburg met verwysing na die wisselwerking tussen Bantoebelangegroepe en die Afdeling Nieblankesake van Johannesburg", M.A. thesis, University of South Africa, 1974.

DOCUMENTS

Documents consulted are listed geographically. Handwritten, typescript, roneoed, and printed documents and leaflets are included.

South Africa

Memorandum submitted to the Secretary for Bantu Education on 22 March 1968 by the African Teachers' Association of South Africa, as published in *Tuata*, December 1968, pp. 16–17.

Constitution, South African Students' Organisation.

Memorandum from the National African Chamber of Commerce to the Honourable Minister of Bantu Administration and Development, 29 August 1969, roneoed, 8 pp.

The politics of protest for Black students. Roneoed leaflet issued by Saso, *c.* 1970, 2 pp.

Report by the secretary of Asseca for the period 9 February 1968 to 28 February 1970. Roneoed, 9 pp.

Dialectic of higher education for the colonised: The case of non-White universities in South Africa. Roneoed leaflet issued by Saso, *c.* 1970, 9 pp.

Education and liberation. Roneoed leaflet issued by Saso, *c.* 1970, 2 pp.

Urban Xhosa's education council: Aims and objects and committees. Roneoed leaflet issued on Witwatersrand under leadership of P.P.Z. Jini, *c.* 1970, 1 p.

Some African cultural concepts. Roneoed leaflet issued by Saso, *c.* 1971, 7 pp.

Old values, concepts and systems. Roneoed leaflet issued by Saso, *c.* 1971, 9 pp.

Constitution, African Library Association.

Constitution, Masingafi Party, Soweto.

Constitution, Chiawelo Residents' Protection Party, Soweto.

Constitution, Reinland Junior Burial Society.

Constitution, Transvaal United African Teachers' Association.

Constitution, The Association for the Educational and Cultural Advancement of the African People of South Africa.

Constitution, Women's Association of the African Independent Churches.

The definition of Black consciousness, author and date unknown. Photocopy in library of S.A. Institute of Race Relations. Roneoed, 5 pp.

Women's Association of the African Independent Churches: Report covering 1969–71. Roneoed, 5 pp.

A report on recent developments within AICA, as submitted by Revd. Brian J. Brown, adviser to the African Independent Churches' Association (AICA), August 1971. Roneoed, 4 pp.

Motion on Black theology passed by Saso's General Students' Council, 1971, as published in *Saso Newsletter*, August 1971, p. 17.

Constitution, The League of the African Youth.

Principles, The League of the African Youth.

Separate development and Black solidarity. Roneoed leaflet issued by Saso, *c.* 1971, 2 pp.

Black universities in South Africa. Roneoed leaflet issued by Saso, *c.* 1971, 2 pp.

Publications. Roneoed leaflet issued by Saso, *c.* 1971, 3 pp.

"New Farm" project on preventive medicine. Report of Saso local committee, *c.* 1971, 3 pp.

Winterveld community project: A progress report. Roneoed report issued by Saso, *c.* 1971, 14 pp.

The non-republic of South Africa: What it means for the Black man. Roneoed Saso leaflet, *c.* 1971, 4 pp.

Black theology. Roneoed leaflet issued by Saso and written by Vic Mafungo, *c.* 1972, 8 pp.

Black Student's Manifesto. Resolution taken by Saso's General Students' Council, July 1972.

Saso Policy Manifesto.

Alice Declaration: Boycott of Black universities. Declaration issued by a Saso meeting held at Alice, May 1972.

Executive report and reports by local committees presented at Saso's 3rd General Students' Council, Hammanskraal, 2–9 July 1972.

Minutes of Proceedings of Saso's 3rd General Students' Council, Hammanskraal, 2–9 July 1972.

Saso Education Commission, report to Third General Students' Council, Hammanskraal, July 1972.

Saso Planning Commission, report to Third General Students' Council, Hammanskraal, July 1972.

Saso Culture Commission, report to Third General Students' Council, Hammanskraal, July 1972.

Saso Community Development Commission, report to Third General Students' Council, Hammanskraal, July 1972.

Saso International Relations Commission, report to Third General Students' Council, Hammanskraal, July 1972.

Saso Commission on Publications, report to Third General Students' Council, Hammanskraal, July 1972.

Minutes of Democratic Party annual congress, Umtata, 20 February 1971.

Memorandum on Conference, issued by Saso after Third General Students' Council, July 1972.

Alice declaration on Turfloop Crisis. Circular by Saso head office to all Saso local chairmen and Students' Representative Councils, *c.* 1972, 2 pp.

History of the Black press. Roneoed leaflet issued by Saso, *c.* 1972, 3 pp.

Literacy project. Roneoed leaflet issued by Saso, *c.* 1972, 15 pp.

Minutes of an education conference of the Transvaal United African Teachers' Association, Education Committee, 12 February 1972, Pretoria. Published in *Tuata,* August 1972, pp. 8–10.

Minutes of Democratic Party national congress, Umtata, April 1972. Handwritten.

Resolution on Black Bank by conference of National African Federated Chamber of Commerce, Pretoria, November 1971. Published in *African Business,* October 1972.

Black Community Programmes, Year Report 1972. Printed pamphlet.

Constitution, Black People's Convention.

National Union of South African Students, Information Sheet No. 1/1972, entitled: "The South African Students' Organisation", compiled by Paul Pretorius, 12 January 1972. Roneoed, 6 pp.

Enkele waarnemings in verband met Missiologiese Instituut te Umpumulo, Zoeloeland, oor "A relevant theology for Africa", 12–21 September 1972. Typescript notes compiled by Dr. J. du Preez at the conference, 5 pp.

Report by general secretary of Asseca for the period 1 March 1970 to 28 February 1972. Roneoed, 8 pp.

Minutes of Democratic Party national congress, Umtata, 16 September 1972. Handwritten.

Resolution on Black Bank, Buy-at-home campaign, and Scholarship Fund by conference of National African Federated Chamber of Commerce, 1972. Reported in *African Business,* July 1973.

Reports by regional African Chambers of Commerce. Reported in *African Business*, June 1973.

Statement issued by president of the Inyanda African Chamber of Commerce on Bantu Investment Corporaion. Reported in *African Business*, May 1973.

Declaration on Apartheid by group of African ministers of religion of the Dutch Reformed Church, Johannesburg, 16 November 1973. Roneoed, 1 p.

Our point of departure. Printed pamphlet issued by Verligte Action, June 1973, 2 pp.

With further reference to our point of departure. Printed pamphlet issued by Verligte Action, August 1973, 2 pp.

Transkei

Constitution, Transkei Teacher's Association.

Manifesto of Paramount Chief Victor Poto, Transkei general election, 1963. Roneoed, 4 pp.

Manifesto of Chief K. D. Matanzima, Transkei general election, 1963. Roneoed, 3 pp.

Programme of principles of the Transkei National Independence Party. Roenoed, 1 p.

Membership certificate with declaration of loyalty, Transkei National Independence Party.

Constitution, Democratic Party, as amended.

Statutes, Transkei National Independence Party, as amended.

Circular by leader of Transkei National Independence Party to all members of the Legislative Assembly of the party, *c.* 1965. Roneoed, 2 pp.

Know those who offer you an alternative government! Show up the Democratic Party!, leaflet distributed by TNIP, *c.* 1967. Roneoed, 1 p.

Transvaal regional district boundaries of TNIP, circular by secretary-general of Transkei National Independence Party to Witwatersrand region, *c.* 1967. Roneoed, 2 pp.

Democratic Party statement, Transkei general election, 1968. Roneoed, 1 p.

Manifesto of Transkei National Independence Party, Transkei general election, 1968. Printed leaflet, 4 pp. Translation from original Xhosa.

Election manifesto of Transkei People's Freedom Party, Transkei general election, 1968. Roneoed, 2 pp.

To all those who stand for the coming election for the Transkei National Independence Party, circular by leader of Transkei National Independence Party, 12 January 1968. Roneoed, 1 p. Translation from original Xhosa.

To all those who have not yet registered themselves as Transkei voters, circular by secretary-general of Transkei National Independence Party to party supporters, *c.* 1968. Roneoed, 1 p. Translation from original Xhosa.

To all branch secretaries, regional secretaries of the Transkei National Independence Party, Transkei and the Republic of South Africa: Membership fee, circular by leader of Transkei National Independence Party, 14 January 1969. Roneoed, 2 pp. Translation from original Xhosa.

Application form for the establishment of a branch committee for the Transkei National Independence Party. Roneoed, 1 p.

To all regional secretaries of the Transkei National Independence Party, Transkei and Republic of South Africa, circular by secretary-general of TNIP, *c.* 1971. Roneoed, 2 pp. Translation from original Xhosa.

Notice of meeting for the purpose of nominating candidates for the Transkei National Independence Party in Engcobo constituency, 29 August 1972. Roneoed, 1 p. Translation from original Xhosa.

Notice of Witwatersrand regional committee meeting of the Transkei National Independence Party with national executive members, 3 October 1972. Roneoed, 1 p.

Democratic Party statement, Transkei general election 1973. Reported in *Daily Dispatch*, 19 September 1973.

Paramount Chief K. D. Matanzima: Manifesto for the 1973 election. Roneoed translation of original Xhosa leaflet issued by Transkei National Independence Party.

We say no, roneoed pamphlet issued by "Sons of the Transkei", March 1973, 1 p. Translation from original Xhosa.

Manifesto of TNIP candidates, Transkei general election, 1973. Printed leaflet, 1 p. Translation from original Xhosa.

Notice by secretary-general of Transkei National Independence Party to the chiefs and headmen of the constituencies of Mt. Frere, Mt. Ayliff, Qumbu and Tsolo, with names of official party candidates for 1973 general election, 31 August 1973. Roneoed, 1 p. Translation from original Xhosa.

Dismissed Members, statement by secretary-general of Transkei National Independence Party announcing names of dismissed members who decided to oppose party candidates in 1973 general election, 1973. Roneoed, 1 p. Translation from original Xhosa.

Manifesto of P. B. Feke, Democratic Party candidate, Umtata constituency, Transkei general election, 1973. Roneoed, 2 pp. Translation from original Xhosa.

Manifesto of L. A. Finca, independent candidate, Umtata constituency, Transkei general election, 1973. Printed leaflet, 1 p. Translation from original Xhosa.

To all the members of the legislative assembly, Transkei National Independence Party, circular by secretary-general of TNIP exhorting members to hold meetings, *c.* 1973. Roneoed, 1 p. Translation from original Xhosa.

Information circular by leader of Transkei National Independence Party with names of party candidates in 1973 general election, addressed to urban committees. Roneoed, 4 pp. Translation from original Xhosa.

Circular by secretary-general of Transkei National Independence Party to all party supporters exhorting them to vote in 1973 general election, 6 September 1973. Roneoed, 1 p. Translation from original Xhosa.

Bophuthatswana

Lekgotla la Tswelelopele ya Bophuthatswana: Constitution and proceedings of foundation conference, 1–3 July 1971. Printed pamphlet, 28 pp.

Funksies en pligte van 'n verteenwoordiger van 'n regering of 'n streek- of gebiedsowerheid of gebiedsraad en sy rade: Artikels 4 en 5 van die Wet op die Bevordering van Bantoe-selfbestuur, No. 46 van 1959. Roneoed circular issued by Bantu Affairs Commissioner, Johannesburg, 15 September 1971, 6 pp.

Manifesto of Tswana National Party, Bophuthatswana general election, 1972. Printed leaflet, 1 p.

Press statement by the Chief Minister of Bophuthatswana, Chief L. M. Mangope, on 8 September 1972 (concerning African liberation movements). Roneoed, 2 pp.

Manifesto and constitution of Seoposengwe Party, 1972. Printed pamphlet, 14 pp.

Executive committee and manifesto of Bophuthatswana National Party, 1972. Printed pamphlet, 5 pp.

A praise-song for Chief Minister Lucas Manyane Mangope, *c.* 1972. Typescript, 3 pp. Translation from original Tswana.

Election leaflet distributed by A. B. C. Motsepe and N. P. Petlele, candidates in Odi constituency, Bophuthatswana general election, 1972. Printed, 1 p. Original in Tswana.

Handleiding vir kiesbeamptes by die verkiesing van lede van die Bophuthatswana Wetgewende Vergadering, circular by electoral officer of Bophuthatswana, 3 July 1972. Roneoed, 10 pp.

Draft constitution, Bophuthatswana National Party.

Election leaflet distributed by M. N. Tsoke, candidate in Odi constituency, Bophuthatswana general election 1972. Printed in English and Tswana, 1 p.

Personal notes of Chief Minister L. M. Mangope during Bophuthatswana general election campaign, 1972, containing notes for speeches, and criticism of Seoposengwe Party policy, as well as reports of Seoposengwe Party meetings, draft press statements, and schedule of meetings.

KwaZulu

Deed of Trust and Constitution of the Inkatha ka Zulu (Zulu National Congress), 1928.

Comments on land consolidation by the Executive Council of the KwaZulu Legislative Assembly: Friday 21st July 1972. Roneoed, 4 pp.

The Education Manifesto of KwaZulu, 14 February 1973. Issued by Ad hoc Consultative Education Committee under the auspices of the KwaZulu government. Roneoed, 5 pp.

The Implications of the Proposed Consolidation Plan (for KwaZulu). Author unknown, *c.* 1973. Roneoed, 2 pp.

Statement by the Executive Council of the KwaZulu Legislative Assembly on the petition to the Hon. the Minister of Bantu Administration alleged to have been sent by the Paramount Chief, c. 1973. Roneoed, 3pp.

The Big Fraud. Anonymous leaflet distributed by Indians in Pietermaritzburg and Durban on relations with Africans, *c.* 1973. Roneoed, 1 p.

Press release of Executive Council of KwaZulu Legislative Assembly on routine decisions at its meeting of 16 January 1973 (roneoed, 2 pp.), and at its meeting on 26 April 1973 (roneoed, 4 pp.).

Press release by the leader of Umkhonto KaShaka, announcing the establishment of the party, Durban 26 October 1973. Typescript, 3 pp.

Ciskei

Principles of the Bantu Nationalist Conservative Party.
Annual report of the Zwelitsha Library Association, August 1972. Roneoed, 4 pp.
Policy of the Ciskei National Party. Statement issued in 1973. Roneoed, 2 pp.
Manifestoes by the following candidates in the Ciskei general election of 1973:

J. M. Ntshele. Roneoed, 2 pp. Translated from the original Xhosa.

L. L. Sebe, V. T. Nqezo, W. Nkontsho and M. R. Sam. Printed leaflet, 3 pp. Translated from original Xhosa.

S. V. Gantsho, E. N. Mzazi and E. Z. Booi. Printed leaflet, 1 p. Translated from the original Xhosa.

P. T. Guzana. Roneoed, 4 pp.

P. T. Guzana, J. M. Ntshele, L. S. Mtoba and I. L. Sangotsha. Printed leaflet, 1 p.

Multi-racialism – only solution, policy declaration by L. D. Guzana. Printed leaflet, 1 p.

I. L. Sangotsha. Roneoed, 5 pp.

L. L. Sebe. Roneoed, 4 pp.

Policy statement by the Honourable the Chief Minister of the Ciskei (Chief J. Mabandla) in connection with the Ciskei general election of 1973. Printed leaflet, 2 pp.

Statement issued by Chief J. Mabandla, announcing establishment of Ciskei National Party. Reported in *Daily Dispatch* of 25 April 1973.

Constitution, Ciskei National Party. Roneoed, 8 pp.

Principles, Ciskei National Independence Party. Roneoed, 1 p.

Draft constitution, Ciskei National Independence Party. Roneoed, 7 pp.

Lebowa

Circular to chiefs and headmen and those concerned, by Magistrate of Mokerong concerning attempts by certain candidates to involve the magistrate in election campaign, 1973, 19 March 1973. Roneoed, 1 p.

Manifestoes by the following candidates in the Lebowa general election of 1973:

R. J. P. Maponya, L. S. Molaba, E. M. Ramaila and W. M. Chuene. Printed leaflet, 1 p.

I. M. Modjadji. Roneoed, 2 pp.

K. I. Moloko and E. D. Mabotja. Printed leaflet, 1 p. Translation from original Pedi.

P. S. Masekele. Printed leaflet, 1 p. Translation from original Pedi.

H. M. Mmachaka. Advertisement in *Lebowa*, 17 March 1973. Translation from original Pedi.

N. S. Mashiane, S. S. Mothapo, C. L. Mothiba and C. N. Phatudi. Printed leaflet, 1 p.

M. S. Mashao and M. N. Mashao. Printed leaflet, 1 p. Translation from original Pedi.

E. M. Maloma and six others. Printed leaflet, 1 p. Translation from original Pedi.

Ben Malomo and M. M. Matlala. Printed leaflet, 1 p. Translation from original Pedi.

P. Mamarege, S. Chosane, K. Masemola, and B. Matsepe. Printed leaflet, 2 pp. Translation from original Pedi.

K. I. Moloko, M. Maloto, K. I. Malebana and E. D. Mabotja. Printed leaflet, 1 p.

C. M. Ramusi and H. M. Leshabana. Printed leaflet, 1 p. Translation from original Pedi.

Chief M. M. Matlala. Printed leaflet, 1 p. Translation from original Pedi.

C. Ramusi and H. Leshabana. Advertisement in *Lebowa, c.* April 1973.

Manifesto of Lebowa People's Party.

Constitution of Lebowa People's Party.

Venda

Here are your Venda candidates, manifesto issued by candidates supporting the Mphephu faction, Venda general election, 1973. Printed leaflet, 3 pp.

Policy declaration by acknowledged leaders of the Venda people, manifesto issued by Chief Patric Mphephu and chiefs supporting him, Venda general election, 1973. Printed leaflet, 3 pp.

Constitution and Manifesto, Venda Independence People's Party. Printed pamphlet issued in 1973, in Venda and English, 32 pp.

Whither does the Venda Party–V.I.P. want to lead the Venda People? Are the Chiefs and Headmen now being thrown to the wolves? Leaflet issued by Mphephu faction, Venda general election, 1973. Printed, 3 pp.

Venda Politics To-day, statement by J. P. Mutsila, candidate of Venda Independence People's Party, Venda general election, 1973. Roneoed, 1 p.

Gazankulu and Swazi

Constitution, Machangana Urban National Movement.

Constitution, Tsonga Cultural Academy.

Political development amongst the republican Swazis vs. relations with Swaziland, document compiled by D. Lukhele, national organiser of Swazi National Council, c. 1973. Roneoed, 4 pp.

NEWSPAPERS AND PERIODICALS

The following newspapers and periodicals proved particularly useful. Those marked with an asterisk were worked through for the greatest part of the period covered by research, whereas items from the rest were found in press cutting collections. All publications listed are published in South Africa.

* *African Business* (monthly)
  Africa South (monthly)
* *Asseca Journal* (occasional)
* *Daily Dispatch* (daily)
  Daily News (daily)
* *Die Burger* (daily)
* *Die Transvaler* (daily)
  Die Vaderland (daily)
* *Drum* (fortnightly)
  Eastern Province Herald (daily)
  Natal Mercury (daily)
  Natal Witness (daily)
  Pretoria News (daily)
* *Rand Daily Mail* (daily)
* *Rapport* (Sunday weekly)
* *Saso Newsletter* (ten times annually)
  Sunday Times (weekly)
  Sunday Tribune (weekly)
  The Cape Argus (daily)
  The Cape Times (daily)
* *The Star* (daily)
* *The World* (daily)
* *Weekend World* (weekly)

INTERVIEWS

The following formal interviews are listed in chronological order. Incidental and very brief interviews are not included, nor are numerous private conversations on African politics.

Mr. J. H. Abraham, Commissioner-general for the Xhosa-National Unit, Umtata, 15 September 1971, 4 October 1972, 3 November 1972, 26 October 1973.

Mr. G. Mwanda, Secretary-general of the Transkei National Independence Party, Umtata, 16 September 1971, 12 October 1972, 24 November 1972.

Mr. W. J. Tyali, Information Officer, Umtata, 16 September 1971.

Mr. Mdledle, Inspector of Education, Umtata, 17 September 1971.

Mr. J. H. T. Mills, Secretary for the Chief Minister and Finance, Umtata, 21 September 1971.

Mr. J. L. Pieterse, Manager, Transkei Townships Board, Umtata, 4 and 16 October 1972.

Mr. R. P. Wronsley, Deputy Secretary, Dept. of the Chief Minister and Finance, Umtata, 6 October 1972.

Mr. K. M. N. Guzana, leader of the Democratic Party, Umtata, 10 November 1972.

Mr. E. F. Niksch, Secretary for the Interior, Umtata, 11 October 1972.

Chief G. M. Matanzima, Transkeian Minister of Justice, Umtata, 12 October 1972.

Mr. S. P. Nculu, former deputy for the Gcaleka Paramount Chief, Cicira, 12 and 13 October 1972.

Mr. S. Ningiza, teacher and boarding master, Cicira, 12 October 1972.

Mr. R. M. Obose, student at Dutch Reformed Church Theological School, Decoligny, 16 October 1972.

Mr. S. L. Konzapi, student at Dutch Reformed Church Theological School, Decoligny, 16 October 1972.

Mr. L. A. Finca, businessman, and later independent candidate in Transkei election of 1973, Umtata, 17 October 1972.

Mr. L. Mpumlwana, civil servant, and supporter of Bantu Nationalist Conservative Party, Qumbu, 17 and 23 October 1972.

Mr. F. Deyi, Information Officer, Lusikisiki, 19 October 1972.

Mr. S. K. Ndzumo, Member of Transkei Legislative Assembly for Lusikisiki, Lusikisiki, 19 October 1972.

Mr. N. L. Webb, magistrate, Lusikisiki, 19 October 1972.

Mr. A. B. Mkutyukelwa, candidate in 1963 Transkei election, former teacher and member of Emboland Regional Authority, Qumbu, 23 October 1972.

Mr. D. Kleinschmidt, Radio Bantu regional representative, Umtata, 24 October 1972, 19 March 1973, 23 and 25 October 1973.

Revd. H. Kentani, secretary of Students' Christian Movement, Umtata, 24 October 1972, and Butterworth, 13 November 1972.

Chief George Ndabankulu, former teacher and subsequently Transkeian Minister of Education, Flagstaff, 26 October 1972.

Mr. I. Godlwana, businessman, Flagstaff, 26 October 1972.

Revd. E. Mosotoane, lecturer at Anglican Theological Seminary, Umtata, 8 November 1972.

Mr. C. M. C. Ndamse, Member of Transkeian Legislative Assembly for Mt. Ayliff and former Transkeian Minister of Education, Umtata, 8 November 1972, 19 March 1973, 22 October 1973.

Mr. J. de la Harpe, Chief clerk, Dept. of the Chief Minister and Finance, Umtata, 9 November 1972, 22 October 1973.

Mr. S. Moses, representative of *Daily Dispatch*, Umtata, 9 November 1972, 22 October 1973.

Mr. W. Hills, assistant magistrate, Lusikisiki, 15 November 1972. Mr. H. H. T. Bubu, general secretary of Democratic Party, Lusikisiki, 20 November 1972.

Mr. E. B. Dyanti, civil servant, Port St. John's, 2 December 1972.

Mr. Breedt, Information Officer, Mafeking, 30 January 1973.

Mr. N. Maarohanye, civil servant, Mafeking, 31 January 1973.

Mr. De Kock, civil servant, Mafeking, 31 January 1973.

Mr. J. Ackerman, Radio Bantu regional representative, Pretoria, 5 and 12 February 1973.

Mr. Schnettler, secretary of Bophuthatswana civil service commission, Mafeking, 31 January 1973.

Mr. Bredenkamp, social welfare officer, Mafeking, 31 January 1973.

Dr. E. S. Moloto, educational planner, Mafeking, 1 February 1973.

Chief L. M. Mangope, Chief Minister of Bophuthatswana, Mafeking, 1 February 1973.

Chief H. Maseloane, Bophuthatswana Minister of Interior, Mafeking, 1 February 1973.

Mr. S. T. T. Mogotsi, secretary-general of Bophuthatswana National Party, Temba, 6 February 1973.

Chief T. Pilane, leader of Seoposengwe Party, Pilanesberg, 7 February 1973.

Mr. S. S. Modise, urban representative of Bophuthatswana government, Tembisa, 8 February 1973.

Mr. S. J. Lesolang, deputy leader of Seoposengwe Party, Ga-Rankuwa, 13 February 1973.

Mr. Van Zyl, electoral officer for Lebowa, Seshego, 21 February 1973.

Mr. C. L. Mothiba, candidate in Lebowa election of 1973, Seshego, 21 February 1973.

Mr. J. Kruger, training officer, Lebowa civil service, Seshego, 21 February 1973.

Mr. P. Lemmer, Radio Bantu regional representative, Pietersburg, 21 February 1973, 9 April 1973, 4 February 1974.

Mr. P. H. D. Mashabela, lecturer, University of the North, Sovenga, 22 February 1973, 11 April 1973.

Mr. A. O. Makwela, lecturer, University of the North, Sovenga, 22 February 1973, 11 April 1973.

Mr. I. O. H. M. Mapena, lecturer, University of the North, Sovenga, 22 February 1973.

Chief M. A. B. Dumalisile, urban representative of Transkei government, Langa, 5 March 1973.

Mr. A. Duntjwa, urban representative of Ciskei government, Langa, 5 March 1973.

Mr. Ntuli, regional chairman of Transkei National Independence Party in the Western Cape, Langa, 5 March 1973.

Mr. T. D. M. Mosomothane, lecturer, University of Stellenbosch, Stellenbosch, 6 March 1973.

Mr. P. Kesse, branch chairman of Transkei National Independence Party, Stellenbosch, 8 March 1973.

Mr. A. Mpiti, Western Cape secretary of Democratic Party, Cape Town, 9 March 1973.

Mr. E. G. Mputha, lecturer, University of Stellenbosch, Stellenbosch, 6 March 1973.

Mr. A. Small, lecturer, University of the Western Cape, Bellville, 7 March 1973.

Mr. V. Qunta, retired inspector of schools, Langa, 9 March 1973.

Mr. Baba, local government clerk, and member of Western Cape executive of Transkei National Independence Party, Mbekweni, Paarl, 12 March 1973.

Mr. A. Nkanunu, Radio Bantu representative, Umtata, 23 March 1973.

Mr. T. G. Matlhape, urban representative of Bophuthatswana government, Bloemfontein, 2 April 1973.

Mrs. I. Mokoena, founder of Women's League Branch of Transkei National Independence Party, Bloemfontein, 3 April 1973.

Mr. C. Rani, Transkei National Independence Party organiser for central and southern Orange Free State, Bloemfontein, 3 April 1973.

Mr. I. Phala, businessman and leading member of Bophuthatswana National Party, Bloemfontein, 3 April 1973.

Mr. D. Melesi, chairman of Urban Bantu Council and supporter of Bophuthatswana National Party, Bloemfontein, 3 April 1973.

Mr. T. E. Pula, information officer, Bloemfontein, 4 April 1973.

Mr. D. P. Phiri, lecturer, University of the North, Sovenga, 10 April 1973.

Mr. G. Bezuidenhout, Commissioner-general for the North Sotho, Sovenga, 10 April 1973.

Mr. Hurter, assistant electoral officer for Lebowa, Seshego, 11 April 1973.

Mr. S. S. Dubeni, urban representative of the Transkei government, Tembisa, 26 April 1973, 1 May 1973, 16 October 1973.

Mr. S. Dubula, vice-chairman of Witwatersrand regional committee of Transkei National Independence Party, Vereeniging, 11 May 1973, 20 October 1973.

Mr. P. Jini, treasurer of Witwatersrand regional committee of Transkei National Independence Party, 11 May 1973, 16 October 1973.

Mr. J. Langner, South Africa Broadcasting Corporation news representative, Durban, 4 June 1973.

Mr. P. J. J. Roodt, information officer, Pietermaritzburg, 4 June 1973.

Mr. T. Buthelezi, Radio Bantu news reporter, Durban, 5 June 1973.

Mr. S. Ngobese, chairman, Umlazi Town Council, Umlazi, 6 June 1973.

Mr. B. Langa and other staff members, South African Students' Organisation, Durban, 7 June 1973.

Mr. O. Kunene, editor of *Ilanga lase Natal*, Durban, 7 June 1973.

Mr. B. Dladla, KwaZulu Executive Councillor of Community Affairs, Pietermaritzburg, 8 June 1973.

Mr. A. C. Nkabinde, lecturer, University of Zululand, Kwa-Dlangezwa, 11 June 1973.

Mr. J. S. Sibisi, lecturer, University of Zululand, Kwa-Dlangezwa, 11 June 1973.

Mr. J. Nkweba, member of local district executive committee of Transkei National Independence Party, Tembisa, 16 October 1973.

Chief J. Mdingi, first chairman, Witwatersrand regional executive of Transkei National Independence Party, Soweto, 17 October 1973.

Mr. B. P. Feke, Democratic Party candidate, 1973 Transkei election, Umtata, 22 October 1973.

Mr. J. Jonker, information officer, Umtata, 23 October 1973.

Mr. G. L. Kakane, educational planner, Umtata, 25 October 1973.

Mr. M. W. Filtane, civil servant, Umtata, 25 October 1973.

Mr. W. H. Olivier, manager of Transkei Townships Board, Umtata, 25 October 1973.

Mr. D. M. Mphahlele, president of Transvaal United African Teachers' Association, Pretoria, 13 November 1973.

Mr. S. P. Kutumela, leading member of National African Federated Chamber of Commerce, Pretoria, 14 November 1973.

Dr. W. J. Breytenbach, senior research officer, Africa Institute, Pretoria, 6 February 1974.

Mr. A. M. Burns-Ncamashe, Ciskei Minister of Education, Alice, 29 May 1974.

Mr. G. H. S. Mdlalose, Secretary of KwaZulu Legislative Assembly, Nongoma, 7 October 1974.

Prof. H. M. S. Nyembezi, editor, Shuter and Shooter, Pietermaritzburg, 9 October 1974.

Mr. Selby Msimang, trader and former politician, Edendale, 9 October 1974.

Mr. S. M. Zuma and Mr. A. Mayaba, respectively president and secretary of Transkei Chamber of Commerce, Mt. Frere, 14 October 1974.

INDEX

267

African Politics in South Africa is the first comprehensive account of contemporary African participation in the political process in South Africa. It concentrates on the period between 1964 and 1974 when African political aspirations had to seek new avenues of expression, following the banning of the African National Congress, the Pan-African Congress and other organisations. The book traces the creation of new political organisations, their structure, leadership questions and policies. It shows how some of these organisations came (sometimes uneasily) to terms with separate development, the ideology of the incumbent government in South Africa; whereas others rejected everything associated with government policy and its structural concomitants. While shedding some light on the relationship between official government policy and African aspirations, the book also describes Black consciousness as an important reaction to government policy. In the concluding chapters, the important question of the fragmentation of South Africa, resulting from official government policy, receives attention within the framework of initiatives taken by various political leaders in South Africa.

The greater part of the book incorporates material published for the first time. It is based on extensive field research by the author in several urban and rural areas of South Africa, including several of the Bantustans. The purpose of the book is to provide basic information on African politics in South Africa. As such it will have great value as a reference work.

To deepen the perspective on current politics, African political history since 1912 is briefly reviewed, and the legislative framework, delimiting the field of legal political participation by Africans, is described.